Mean

Thank you for being so committed to women like me.

[signature]

aka Britt

HIS Song

How The Sour Notes of My Life Became God's Masterpiece

SARIAH JAMES

WestBow Press books may be ordered through booksellers or by contacting:

WestBow Press
A Division of Thomas Nelson & Zondervan
1663 Liberty Drive
Bloomington, IN 47403
www.westbowpress.com
844-714-3454

ISBN: 978-1-6642-1612-9 (sc)
ISBN: 978-1-6642-1613-6 (hc)
ISBN: 978-1-6642-1611-2 (e)

Library of Congress Control Number: 2020924623

Print information available on the last page.

WestBow Press rev. date: 12/23/2020

A Note from Sariah

Dear Reader,

First of all, I want to congratulate you on having the courage to read this book. If you have been a follower of Jesus for 5 minutes or 50 years, you know that the Christian life comes with suffering. If you've been confused by the things in your life that you've had to endure, trust me, I understand. It doesn't mean that God isn't good, but you might have wondered from time to time, right?

I hope you'll see that the trials of life, in Christ, can be used for amazing purposes if you submit them to Him. For some, that is a deep canyon to cross. I get it. In my experience, trials have produced miraculous things and have drawn me closer to my Savior than I ever imagined.

As you read, keep an open mind. If something I experienced triggers something for you, be honest about it and ask God what He wants you to do with it. We're more alike than we think. I feel as though the only reason I am sane is because I had the tenacity to work through these things by writing them down. If your heart is hurting, talk to someone about it, preferably a professional Christian counselor. God wants you to move forward.

My greatest hope is that you will feel free to share your story with others after you read mine. Don't be afraid to let God show the world what a marvelous creation you are, scars and all.

My Very Best in Him,
Sariah

DEDICATIONS

I dedicate this book to the organization and the church that supported my adoption. Thank you. A special note of gratitude to everyone that helped me there and to my friends, family, and co-laborers in Christ that kept me sane and alive. Thank you for helping me heal and encouraging me to find purpose in all this.

I'd also like to dedicate this to all the birthmothers out there. May you find your peace and purpose in your decision.

To every woman who has felt used, less than, discarded, useless, and damaged - know that you are a gift from God, fearfully and wonderfully made, regardless of what anyone has told you.

One

"At Last, My Love Has Come Along." -Etta James

A handsome face with a warm, bright smile made me pause and take notice. His blue shirt illuminated his steel-blue eyes. He looked friendly and easy-going, but the picture of him on a motorcycle made him look rugged and manly as well. Within minutes, I was emailing a stranger on an online dating site the fateful words, "Nice eyes." We had dinner three days later. When his looks matched his personality, I was sold.

We hardly spent a day apart after that night.

Asher was a competitive bodybuilder who dedicated his life to the gym. The gym for Asher was as much a part of him as his limbs. All of his closest friends were from the gym or the bodybuilding scene, in general. He watched bodybuilding movies and read bodybuilding books. He went to competitions and critiqued everyone. He was meticulous with his workout; no corners could be cut. Form and execution were the mainstays of his workout routine, and he let everyone know it. Asher became who he thought he was through the gym. Nothing could stand in the way of bodybuilding for him.

Along with bodybuilding came other things. When we first started dating, given his size and stature, I surmised that he was using steroids. At the time, I was pretty into the gym myself. That is how we bonded as a couple. I never took them but I never felt the need to either. I knew they were dangerous but not specifically why. They were illegal, and that was wrong. I managed to file that information in the back of my mind and overlook it. Besides, I liked how he looked. I would question him from time to time, but he would assure me that he knew what he was doing. Other people didn't, but he did. That is all he wanted to offer me. Well, that and the Steroid Encyclopedia he stored under the coffee table. He looked everything up before he took it. I was supposed to be reassured by that. He also pledged to me that he never shared needles, and I didn't have anything to worry about there.

I tried to put it out of my mind. After all, we all have things in our life we know we shouldn't have. We all have our sins. That was my justification. I filed it away and said, "Yes" when he asked me to marry him just six short months later. Ten months later, on a sunny summer-like October day in New England, we were married. There wasn't a thing in the world that could come between us. I felt that we were an official team now, but his steroid use was festering between us. When I couldn't justify taking any other kind of drug with the ones he was taking, we started to fight. We had many arguments about his habitual use of steroids. It was a war and I wasn't winning the battles.

What he didn't share with me was his frequent brokering of these illegal substances to his friends and acquaintances. The secret/information slipped out of his friend's mouth one night while the three of us were in the car headed into the city. As soon as the comment hit the air, my feet went numb. Asher tried to gloss over it and rush to another subject. I knew what I heard. He knew what I heard. I felt a cavernous divide grow between us throughout the whole night. The incident replayed again and again. I wanted to know more, but being afraid of what I might learn. It was alarming to feel like he was all of a sudden someone I didn't know. What else didn't he tell me? How much was he selling? Of course, my over-productive mind created this imaginary lucrative business of ill-gotten gains. I dreamt up a web of connections and mafia involvement that would surely be something he couldn't get out of. How much was he making? Did the police know about it? I had so many questions, but they had to wait.

At the first available moment, which was the moment he turned the doorknob to the front door at the end of the night, I pounced. I demanded answers. We were both tired, but I wanted to know why he kept this from me. He was defensive and dismissive. That only stoked my anger. I knew better than to start a fight before bed, but I couldn't help myself. The few drinks I had in me from dinner energized my fight. I pressed on. Things between us got heated. We went to bed without speaking. The next day he told me he would cease all efforts in his dealings. We both knew he was lying but neither of us would admit it.

Months later, and after many attempts, I had a positive pregnancy test. I could hardly contain myself when he came home. I rushed to tell him I was pregnant. I was so elated. Six months seems like a lifetime when you want to have a baby. It is nominal looking back, but we were eager to be parents then. But now that a baby was growing inside of me I was worried. He was nervous. I believed the baby would help Asher would solidify his resolve in quitting the steroid business and focus on things more paternal. I was wrong.

I came home one night after work. Pulling into the driveway, I gathered my things and headed for the mailbox on the side of the road. As I rounded the garbage barrels still in the driveway from the morning's pickup, I noticed something shiny. I looked down. Littered all over the ground in front of the fence were hypodermic needles. He had not only kept his commitment to steroid use, but he was stashing the used syringes into used kitty litter from his cat and throwing them away with the refuse. Clumsy sanitation workers had spilled the bag, and the needles were scattered all over the ground.

In a panic, I dropped my things and started to pick them up. I didn't know what to do with them, but I couldn't leave them there. I got a plastic bag and collected them. I hid the plastic bag full of these atrocities inside another garbage bag. My thoughts raced. Who knew they were there? Did the sanitation workers let the police know? Had any children walking by picked them up? How long had they been there? I felt as though the entire town knew my husband's dirty little secret. I might as well have found out he had a lover; the betrayal felt similar.

I raged within while I waited for him to come home from work. I paced like a tiger in a cage waiting for her next meal. I picked up the phone about ten times, wanting to call and tear through my prey, but I resisted. I wanted to see him face-to-face. I expected him to be sorrowful and ashamed when I stormed to the door as he walked in, announcing his folly. Instead, he appeared removed, unaffected by my discovery. He calmly asked what I did with them and moved on to his office in the basement. I was unable to reorient myself in the conversation. I stared at the door in front of me, unable to understand his reaction. What was my next move on this chessboard? How did I get him to understand how much this whole thing concerned me? Didn't he care? God, do something here!

I felt lost for the next few days. I prayed that God would not include me in the punishing of my husband for failing to care for his pending child and me the way that he should. I just didn't want the DEA kicking down my front door and seizing our assets. I certainly didn't want to spend our life savings trying to hire a lawyer to defend him only to see him go to jail. He was stuck in his vanity. I felt trapped into protecting our image. Sadly, neither one of us was very concerned about his health.

The remainder of my pregnancy was uneventful. We set up a crib, registered with the local baby supply store, and I became obsessed with the nursery. Everything had to be perfect. We learned we were having a baby girl. She had a name, Katie Jane. We went back and forth on names for a while. I like names that are not common, and he prefers traditional names.

One morning he strode into the kitchen with, "What about Katie?" I thought about it for a minute. What about Katie? I had to admit, I liked it.

"Why Katie?"

"After my dad, Karl."

"Why not just name her Karla?"

"No, Katie."

That was it. Katie it was. Jane was a natural choice for a middle name, as it was his mother's name. She had passed away only a few years before.

I procured things for the nursery and rearranged the furniture no less than six times until I was sure it was exactly the way I wanted it. I often sat in Katie's white and yellow glider rocker and wrote to my growing unborn baby in my journal. I read my Bible in her room every morning, and prayed that all was well. It was a haven of good feelings. I couldn't wait to meet her, my little Katie Jane. What would she look like? I hoped she had Asher's blue eyes.

Now that the baby had a name, and the nursery was squared away, I rekindled my hopes that Asher would take on a more responsible, dad-like persona. The gym and his relationship with his motorcycle were just as they always were. I was silent in my resentment over these things. I wanted him to spend more time with me. I wanted to discuss parenthood, specifically how we each envisioned our roles as parents. I didn't want other things to be important in his life anymore. I wanted me, his daughter, and his family to take precedence over the elements of his youth. I was trying to encourage him to think of eternity and his promises to God to take care of his family and be the spiritual leader in his home. Still, these things were not as relevant to him as his Body Mass Index and how big his calves were (which he referred to as his cows).

A Friday night trip to the hospital, two days, and one c-section, and our precious angel arrived. We both thought we'd burst open from the joy. On our day to go home, we bundled her in a sweet white and light pink outfit, placed her gingerly into her car seat, and proudly drove her home. We were now a family of three.

After a couple weeks the nervousness of Katie's newness faded. I was starting to adjust to being a mom. We were figuring out how to be a couple who recently became parents. I longed for his participation and companionship in the weeks of new motherhood. He was lost and confused as to where his place was in my life and the home. He resolved that conflict by spending hours working late and the rest of his time off at the gym. One Saturday afternoon, I hit a breaking point with all of the unexcused absences. I confronted him with the fact that when he announced he was going to the gym, he was gone for three or four hours at a time. My pointed words enraged him.

Angrily he replied, "You can have anything, everything, but you can't have this. I won't let you take the gym from me!"

I sank in my seat on the couch, holding our infant daughter. You can't make statements like that in front of God and not expect consequences.

I was disappointed, but I still pressed on. It was a blessing for us to pray together, and I did read the Bible to us both before bed. At least it was something, but I yearned for him to wake up one morning with a great resolve to lead. That never came. The resentment seeds were planted, and instead of repenting and working towards meeting each other's needs, we watered what we'd sown.

As Katie grew from a sleepy newborn to a giggling baby, Asher started to flourish in his fatherhood. He enjoyed taking care of her and playing with her. It was quite a sight to see my strapping husband with a baby and diaper bag on one arm and a gym bag on the other. He wanted to take her to the gym with him so his friends could see her. To everyone that saw this man with his daughter, the resounding comment was that he "glowed." He assured me that the nursery at the gym was clean and well organized. I knew he wouldn't leave her in there otherwise. He had gotten quite conscientious of things "baby-friendly." He'd often take her to his favorite fast-food chain for lunch afterward or pancakes in the morning at a local restaurant on Saturdays. I enjoyed watching this man engaged in his relationship with his daughter more than anything. I was thrilled that Katie had the kind of dad that I always longed for. My father wasn't at all involved, or very rarely, and open affection in my home wasn't displayed. I often daydreamed of Asher greeting suitors at the door to take his daughter out to a movie and how he'd react or what it would be like for me to watch him dance with his baby girl on her wedding day.

I remember one night explaining to him the value and importance of his relationship with Katie. That her first example of a male relationship would be him. He needed to be the man he wanted to be sitting across from him at the Thanksgiving table. What I said resonated with him. The constant challenge was that Katie was so attached to me. Momma's girl always wanted momma first. I redirected her and steered her towards Daddy as much as I could. Sometimes her Mommy-oriented behaviors hurt his feelings. I pained in that along with him. I wanted to encourage him in his journey with her as much as I could. I wondered if my demanding work schedule had any effect on Katie's need to be with me.

I was rooted in a good sales career. I have to admit, I liked making money. I had never imagined not being in a business career. The transition from maternity leave to full-time in the office was agonizing, and it took several months. I tried to delay it as much as I could by working at home twice a week and abbreviating hours spent in the office. In the end, my employer was insistent that I come back in five days a week. It was made easier only by a dear friend in my church who had agreed to care for my sweet baby in my home. She had two children, and they would play and entertain my daughter. I felt much better about leaving her with someone that I trusted, but I opined for her at my desk most days. I couldn't seem to get back into the groove I once had. I felt pinned between yearning to be a mom and wanting my business career. I felt like my identity was changing against my will. I was unsure and scared of the future for what was one of the first times in my life. I was frustrated by wondering what would happen.

Asher and I talked about me staying home with Katie a lot. We usually ended up arguing about it, but we decided one day that we could entertain a plan of what that would look like. What would I do, though? We still did need me to earn an income. There would have to be a transition period. I thought I found the solution when I signed up for a home-based jewelry business. I vowed to build it into something that would replace monthly earnings. My friend Jessica had signed on with this company months before, and she couldn't stop talking about it. I was infused with new life by her enthusiasm and the possibilities so I gladly took the opportunity to do it for myself. Asher didn't take it seriously, but I did. I told all my friends and begged them to have parties for me. Not too many of them did. I was hurt by their perceived unwillingness to help me meet my objectives, but I wouldn't let it go. I must say, I did pretty well. My performance was consistent, and I started to learn how to engage and be friendly towards women, something I wasn't very good at. I had to learn. I was selling them jewelry!

Thought my jewelry-selling enterprise had an earnest start, my endeavor started to wane after about six months. I became worn down from still working full-time and getting myself up at all hours to care for a baby in addition to doing jewelry parties every weekend. My husband began to see it as a waste of money. I wanted to rally to show him he was wrong, but I was starting to doubt myself also. How could I make this work?

I was plagued by nightmares that Katie would grow to hate me for picking a career over being her mom. In these dreams, she was screaming at me from across my large dark wooden desk. I was standing behind this desk with a library of books lined behind me neatly in built-in shelves in a spacious office. In this scenario, I was defending myself. I had given her everything she wanted. She was going to a good school. Why was she so angry? In these dreams she would shrill at me that I was never there. Over and over again, she would ask me in my dreams, "Where were you?" I was torn.

When my daughter came into the world, things changed. I found myself continually reviewing what my new life would be like as a stay-at-home mom. Could I be the mom who cooks and cleans all day, does playdates, and bakes cookies for the daily post-school homecoming? Did I want to trade my well-tailored suits and heels for track pants and sneakers? I would shudder at the thought of losing my intelligent, self-gratifying persona for a seemingly endless day of toddler songs and mom's clubs with dumb women who couldn't do anything else with their lives, never mind have a conversation with them. I wasn't like them. I didn't want to be them! I was awash in conflicting emotions. However, my heart was winning out. I wanted to be with Katie.

By now, I had shared this dilemma with some women in my Bible study at church. We discussed it at great length, it usually included them berating me for having a career at all. I rebuffed their comments and warnings that my place was in the home, not the office. I thought of the absurdness of their thinking as they railed on. I read Proverbs 31 just as much as they had. They saw a woman devoted to her work in her home and for her family. I saw an ambitious, entrepreneurial woman who had help to care for her family and her house as much as I did. I saw Mrs. Proverbs as an image of me; they saw something else. They offered to pray for me; that I could handle. If someone was going to pray, it might as well be them. I didn't seem to devote as much time to prayer as I had to ruminating over this dilemma. I would pray out of desperation or frustration, but I wasn't focused on getting the right answer. I was bent on feeling better about what I wanted or didn't want. I had moments in my prayer time when I would ask for the right answer, but I never waited around for God's response. I just went about the business of calculating my life using my own intellect.

Asher and I continued to discuss, argue, and seek counseling from our pastor on the subject of me being home with our daughter. In the end, I relented. We just couldn't get on the same page. I didn't want to fight with him about it anymore. I remember sitting in the driver's seat of my car, upset that I was going into work one more time.

I threw my hands up from the steering wheel and yelled, "God, you know what I want to do and why I want to do it. If you want me to be home, you're just going to have to figure out a way. Amen."

I released my future plans to the unknown and focused on what I could. Then I resigned myself to juggling work and home. Whoever invented the term Work/Life Balance needs a slap and a reality check. There is no such thing in my experience. Either both suffer, or one inevitably wins out, leaving the other lacking. With a full-time job, a baby, and a home that was too big for the three of us to deal with, it is no wonder that I had no time for myself or my marriage. I felt guilty for asking for time to see a friend without Katie. It was like I had this idea that I needed to make up for being gone at work all week. I was desperate for refreshing, but I could barely force myself to ask for it. I felt so emotionally barren. Asher only received the leftovers of my energy. I was a removed, tired, angry woman who needed more than a nap. It shouldn't surprise anyone, least of all me, that he returned the favor by withdrawing from me. I got to add lonely to my long negative list of feelings. Clouds started to form over our marriage.

I tried to realign my thinking. I wanted to convince myself that my career life was what I needed and that I just wasn't capable of being a stay-at-home mom. I talked myself into believing that even God knew I wasn't going to be a good mother, and that is why he kept me away from Katie. It broke my heart to think that way, but I had no other answers. I just resolved to live out the life that I was given if that is what God wanted. But I found no peace in admitting defeat.

I didn't surrender my will to God; I just gave up fighting. I grew resentful of the women in the church who focused so heavily on being home. My only way of dealing with them was to avoid them at all costs. In every book they recommended I read, I was doing the wrong thing. This made me bristle with contempt. I tried to do the right thing. God and my husband wouldn't let me. I was doing what I was supposed to, and I was tired of being judged for it. I hung close to women who had successful careers or businesses with families at home. What I discovered, unfortunately, is that they had all but left their families behind in search of their successes and accolades. Most spoke of full-time nannies, children in boarding schools, working 16 hours a day, and their commitment to "quality over quantity" time with their families. I think whoever came up with that idea was the same one who came up with Work/Life Balance. They realized it didn't work so they invented a new marketing tool to make us moms and dads feel less guilt about leaving our children in the lurch to drive the latest luxury car.

Life felt hard all the time even though Asher and I had an exceptional combined income. We argued about money constantly. Shopping had long since been my therapy even before Asher came along. I used shopping as an outlet when I wanted to feel better. My ways of spending to feel better weren't working for him. When he took my credit cards away from me, I selfishly found a way to acquire my own without his knowledge. I used my spending money to make payments on it. I knew it was wrong, but I wanted what I wanted. If marriage and family life was supposed to be such a reward, I found it lacking. I complained to God about it all the time, and lamented my plight in my journal. Nothing seemed to work. I dreamed of leaving it all behind. Maybe I wasn't supposed to be married to Asher. Still, no matter what terrible argument we had, I always came back to the same thing. He was a good father, and I didn't want to take that from Katie. She deserved two parents who were together. I just didn't know how to be happy with it. I wasn't searching for answers though. I pouted and asked God to make it go away.

Asher started having mysterious coughing symptoms at night and only at night. At first, he and I found this mildly annoying. He couldn't sleep, and I couldn't either from the coughing and the snoring. This went on for a few weeks. I probably would have gone to the doctor's office within days of symptoms. He, being a big, strapping man, was going to ride it out. The nights went on and on without change. I washed curtains, cleaned carpets, and vacuumed mattresses, all trying to dispel something in the bedroom that was causing his problem. Nothing worked. I pleaded for him to go to the doctor and find out what was the matter. He very reluctantly agreed, even though he thought I was overreacting.

The next day, he called the doctor's office and made an appointment for that week. He told me that he'd be leaving work early to go to his appointment. I relaxed a little, knowing that an answer was on the horizon. The morning came for his visit. I kissed him as he left for the gym before work and he reminded me that he'd be late coming home that night. I smiled as he closed the front door. Finally, some we would be getting some answers.

That evening, I came bouncing into the kitchen when I heard him come in through the front door.

"What did he say?" I asked.

"I didn't meet with my doctor. I met with his Nurse Practitioner. She said I have a sinus infection."

This made no sense to me. The diagnosis seemed ill-researched. I wondered if he'd given her the proper information. I tried to slow down my thinking, but I felt my brow furrow from lack of understanding. I didn't think the prescription for an antibiotic you give a child for strep throat was going to make any difference. It didn't.

Round two with the Nurse Practitioner made for an equally disappointing trip.

"She says I have asthma," was his report on the second visit to be re-assessed.

So out of nowhere, he has asthma and needs to take every known asthma medication under the sun? I was confirming my under-confidence in the Nurse Practitioner's diagnostic skills when the next sentence came out of his mouth.

"I yelled at her for you, too."

"You yelled at her?"

"I told her you wanted to know why she put me on penicillin, so she asked me if you were a nurse or a doctor. I told her you were an EMT and that you asked your friends who were nurses and doctors, and they wondered the same thing. She told me maybe you should have gone to medical school since you know so much."

I was grateful not to have witnessed this conversation. I probably would have wanted to claw her eyes out! Forgive me for wanting to make sure he was properly cared for. How dare she? I felt a mild comfort within my rage that he at least stuck up for me. This didn't help my assurance level that anyone was doing the right thing at all.

By week three, he was in bed all day. I was angry with him as it was Easter Sunday and he missed church service and dinner with my family, which we were hosting. This did not fit in line with my mental idea of how my Easter was supposed to go. We were to look and dress the part of the perfect Christian family. Asher and I should be pristinely dressed, and baby girl in the very best toddler outfit her mother could buy. Didn't he get it? What did my parents think of my husband being in bed all day? I cooked the picture of an Easter meal, none of which he came to the table for. I huffed as I approached him, lounging on the couch after my family left to grill him about his behavior. He said he felt worse than ever. This melted the ice crystals that had formed on my heart toward him, and I asked him to describe his increased symptoms. He said his breathing had become an exhausting effort for him over the course of the day. He felt like he was drowning in fluid. I couldn't imagine why all the asthma medication was making his breathing worse. I asked him to bend over the kitchen island so I could listen to his lungs with my ears to his back. I heard wet noises. Being an EMT, I knew what that meant but I couldn't imagine he'd have congestive heart failure. Maybe he had pneumonia, but he had no fever and had been on antibiotics recently. I demanded he go back to the doctor tomorrow. I also included my orders for a chest x-ray. I added, "And don't come home without one!"

On Monday, I went to work. I had to work. I had sales to make and clients to call on. Besides, when the going gets tough, I get busy. It is the only way I knew how to stay sane. I did my usual brief prayer, but I didn't actually put much stake in it. I was going to worry instead. Better to try to feel in control by worrying. How do you "Let go and Let God?" I didn't know how to do that anyway. The phone rang at about the time I supposed that Asher would get out of the doctor's office.

Thankfully for him, he didn't have a clue about anything medically-related. This would serve him well. My knowledge would slowly eat away at me. He seemed almost happy when he told me what had happened.

"I saw the doctor this time, and he took a chest x-ray," he announced.

"Thank you, God, I thought they would never do that." I sighed with relief.

"He wants me to see a cardiologist tomorrow, and he put me on these water pills. They should make me feel better, but they make me pee like crazy."

The sudden rush of air out of my mouth made me realize that I had stopped breathing. I immediately informed him that I would be going with him to the cardiologist the next day. I mean, someone needed to take the reins here, right? I felt tightness in my chest, and I lost my train of thought after I hung up the phone. I didn't need to wait until tomorrow. I knew what he had. My 37-year-old husband had Congestive Heart Failure. How could this be? I was hoping to be wrong in my initial assessment when I listened to his lungs. I needed someone to tell me this was a giant mistake, or at least that it would be simple to fix. I barely slept that night. I drifted off thanking God the appointment was in the morning. I didn't think I could take it if I had to wait all day.

I hid my anxiety from Asher. I didn't want to worry him. Besides, I know what he'd say to me, "Pray and wait." He was a much newer Christian than me. He had only been saved just three short years ago. I had several years on him. I had a head full of biblical knowledge and catch verses that weren't helping me now. I envied his simple faith and untrained mind that just embraced that three-word saying, "Pray and wait." I get the pray part, but how do you just wait?

The first order of business at the Cardiologist was a 12-Lead EKG to see what his heart was doing, which he failed with flying colors. When the first blips on the paper made the EKG technician's face contort in dismay. The technician ordered him to remain still and restarted the machine. He hadn't flinched in the first place. She ran about a half a sheet's worth of results and scurried off to see the doctor with it, almost knocking me over as she barreled towards the door with EKG results in-hand. I knew that wasn't going to be part of the good news I was longing to hear.

Next thing I knew, the nurse was ushering us into a tiny exam room with no windows. The doctor and I faced each other as Asher sat on the exam table. I perched on the edge of my seat with our six-month-old baby on my knee. I just needed him to say it. Yes, say it out loud, Doc.

He was a middle-aged man, balding, with glasses that were fashionably outdated and fuzzy brown hair that stuck out away from his head. He was slight in build with a warm face but deliberate speech. After a quick introduction, he sprang up from his stool, ran through some routine procedures of listening to Asher's breathing, and checking his pulses and sat back down. I focused intently on the doctor as he prepared himself to deliver the news.

He started describing, in medical language, the nature of Asher's condition. I interrupted him.

"It sounds like you are telling me that Asher has Congestive Heart Failure." I am not sure if I wanted him to be impressed by my medical prowess or I couldn't stand the suspense any longer.

The next thing he said was, "Are you a nurse or a doctor?"

I stifled a laugh and instead meekly explained that I was an EMT in a prior career. This made him flap his arms with excitement as he leaped off of his stool at me to show me Asher's EKG results. I told him I didn't know how to read cardiac algorithms, but he was all too happy to point out to me what I was looking at. He pointed to the abnormalities in his results.

"See this?" he asked as he pointed to a portion of the squiggly line on the page. "He has a left-branch bundle block."

The term I had heard before, but I didn't know what it meant. He explained that the heart is like a pie. As the words came forth, he put his pointer fingers over his head and made a large circle in the air, from top to bottom. He further explained how the electrical current in the heart runs right down the middle of the pie, from top to bottom with every beat. With that, he pressed his pointer fingers together lengthwise and made a vertical line down the middle of his imaginary pie. Lastly, he explained, the current then reaches the bottom of the pie and splits in two to make the trip around the circumference on either side. He finished his air diagram for me by making his fingers arch in reverse to make his pie go from bottom to top. He pointed out the problem with Asher's pie by saying on Asher's left side, it couldn't finish the trip down the pie, so it tried to find an alternate route back to the outside of the circle to complete its journey. It's kind of like if you knew there was traffic on the highway and needed to take back roads to get to your destination. What this meant was Asher's left side of his heart weakened because of this problem. He also explained that an enlarged heart usually doesn't show up on a chest x-ray, but because his was so big, it did. This was not good news, either. We had a problem.

Asher finally piped up, "So what do we do?"

The doctor ran down a list of what would come next. He cautioned him on what not to eat and made it clear that he needed to cease all supplements that he may be taking to enhance his physique. He lowered the boom in his final instructions to Asher. No gym until further notice. I have never seen my husband so deflated and lost. The doctor might as well have cut off his arms.

Asher tried to look optimistic, but his eyes brimmed with the tears he was struggling to choke back. I bounced our daughter, Katie, on my knee to keep her quiet. She was a perfect angel. I was doing it out of fear that she would fuss and to quiet my rising anxiety all at the same time. Nausea rose to my throat. I wrestled with my lungs to slow down. I wanted to bust right out of that tiny exam room that seemed to close in on me by the second. Please, somebody, wake me up! I am having a bad dream! Lord? Where are you?

We left with many prescriptions in-hand and information on the battery of tests that would commence in the coming days. We walked, dumbstruck and dazed, out of the office and into the elevator. I didn't know what to say. I was powerless to make him feel better. I needed someone to make me feel better. As the doors closed on the office hallway, I felt like my life was closing on me.

"What is really wrong with me, Bug?"

The softness of his voice startled me out of the pause of silence during the drive to the pharmacy. Bug was Asher's nickname for me. It started as Love Bug, then Buggie, then just Bug. He called me Bug more than he ever called me by my name. I assured him that he got the news straight and honestly. The part the doctor left off, and what I knew in my heart already, was that the sand in the hourglass of his life was running. I was wondering how long it had left before it ran out.

The number of pills he had to take was mind-boggling. He put down all the little white pharmacy bags on the kitchen island. We both surveyed them sitting there like some foreign objects we were trying to identify. He sighed heavily and took out the ones he needed to take right now. I watched him move around the kitchen like I was staring at a movie screen.

With the new revelation of my husband's illness not yet a reality in my mind, I found myself feeling like I was drowning. I felt upended and so overwhelmed with emotion that I didn't know where to start. My need to organize absolutely everything in my life, including thoughts, helped me orient myself. It also helped Asher, too. When he would be overcome with anxiety, I would point him to the next appointment with the doctor that would reveal more. We needn't get wound up until we had all the facts, right? I said that for his sake every bit as much as mine. I wanted someone to tell me there was a fix for this, but somehow I knew that wouldn't be true.

His first round of tests consisted of a lot of blood work and a stress test. He would need to report to the hospital first thing in the morning and walk on a treadmill for an undesignated amount of time to see what kind of exertion his heart could handle. That didn't seem too crazy to me, so he went by himself. He wasn't particularly anxious about it. We were both hoping that they would notice something significant, but in the end, the results only confirmed what we already knew. At this point, there was nothing that stood out as far as a definite cause. His doctor was hoping to find a reason, so he would know how to design a course of treatment for it. Next up was an echo-cardiogram. The "echo" was also something that didn't seem too strenuous. He was pretty excited to go, I think, in part, because he would get to see a better picture of his heart.

I was looking forward to them being able to see something that might be repaired with surgery. That didn't happen either. The echo confirmed only one thing. He had a left branch bundle block, and we already knew that. The last thing to do was Cardiac Catheterization. This he was not very excited about. The "Cath" was something his doctor was going to have to do with day surgery, and that meant cutting him in his groin area to insert a little snake-like camera into his femoral artery. I am not too sure I would be excited about it, either. This procedure would let his doctor see Asher's heart from the inside, to get clues into why his heart was in the condition it was in. If the problem was a heart defect of some kind, then it might be repaired with surgery. The cath was done painfully early in the morning, so I dropped him off at the hospital. We both agreed that since I needed to take care of the baby, staying at the hospital was probably not in the best interest of anyone involved. I was sad to drop him off. I hated the images in my mind of him sitting in a waiting room by himself. I went home and anxiously awaited his phone call.

I started focusing on prayer at this point, but my words were merely, "Please let this be over." I was hoping he would be okay and that God would get us through this. There didn't seem to be anything more on my mind at this point than for his doctor to find a cause and determine how to make it go away. I know Asher was hoping the same thing.

This search for answers bridged some of the valleys that had grown between us temporarily. We had a joint mission, and it worked as far as making things a little more tender between us. We'd need to draw on that a lot. Coming into this crisis, so broken from within our marriage, was going to be hard. I never understood how much working daily on a marriage, together, would matter until now. Asher getting better was the end game, and we were committed to working on the strategy. The intimacy forging from this crisis was the most I'd felt between us since Katie was born. It felt like hope.

He called and groggily some time later and said he'd be able to come home in an hour. I packed up Katie in her car seat and headed out the door. The gloomy morning had turned sunny and warm. I took that as a sign. While waiting for them to bring him down from day surgery in a wheelchair, as is the custom at most hospitals, I stopped by the hospital coffee shop for a coffee and to get a treat for Asher. I didn't do much in the way of sweet gestures for him anymore, and I felt compelled to see if they had his favorite cookies. They did. I chirped my order with a smile to the counter girl and waited for her to fetch my order. I felt refreshed by my own generosity. I heard an older woman talking to my baby from behind me. The woman smiled and cooed at her and asked her what her name was.

I smiled and replied,"Katie."

The woman grimaced, and with that looked down at Katie again and said, "You need to tell your mommy to get you a new name. You can't have a nickname with that name."

My smile stretched downward into a frown. I spun myself and my 6-month old around to face the counter. My thoughts were racing but I was unable to think of something quick and cutting to say that would put this nag in her place. I paid for the cookies and coffee and turned to my right to see Asher sitting in a wheelchair looking for me. I felt terrible that he was waiting for me alone. I was trying to do something nice for him. I handed him the cookies, and he said he wasn't hungry. Without so much as a 'thank you' for my efforts, I escorted him and the gentleman who was pushing him to the car. We loaded a slow-moving Asher into the car, and I snapped Katie's seat into place in the back, and we were off toward home.

While driving, he explained that he wasn't asleep but sort of "out of it." The doctor had a little complication with him bleeding but nothing too bad. He was sore and uncomfortable, but it wasn't unmanageable. We'd have to see the doctor in a week for the results. Hopefully, it would say something that we were so desperate to hear - "Here's what we can do for this."

When we got home, I poured everyone out of the car and helped them get settled. Asher slept for most of the afternoon and took some pain reliever to help with his discomfort. I wondered what to do. I didn't want to wait a whole week for an answer.

Asher went to work the next day, and so did I. Work had become a nice little escape for both of us from this daunting drama. At least I could have a conversation with someone about anything other than medications, tests, how they were feeling, and worrying about something catastrophic happening. Asher could feel normal by just being him at work, fixing computers, and entertaining his coworkers. He liked to be the funny man on the job. I know he always kept me laughing. Who else has Godzilla, Mothra, or Ho Chi Min as profile pictures on their webpage? We both craved normalcy.

A week later, we sat eagerly in his cardiologist's microscopic exam room, once again waiting for answers. Katie had stayed at home that day with a babysitter, so it was just Asher and me. I was grateful as I didn't want to be distracted from the conversation. The tide of anxiety rose while waiting for the doctor to come in. I felt my hands go clammy as I sat at the end of my chair, gripping the edge of the seat cushion for stability. Asher sat quietly on the exam table as he usually did. The tightness of the space contrasted greatly with his large, muscular body. I wondered if he felt claustrophobic in these situations. As I sat, I tried to decide whether or not to cross my legs. I didn't want to take up any more space than I had to. I also hated the fact that the exam room had no windows. To be able to simply watch a tree blowing in the breeze would have helped my nerves. All I had available for distractions were labels on the medical equipment. I read every last syllable I could find.

The door popped open, and there he was, the cardiologist. He quickly examined Asher's pulses in his hands and feet. He took a listen to his breathing and then plopped down in the chair in front of us. I was holding my breath. He prattled on about nonsense things, trying to preface what he needed to say. Then it came. There was nothing to note in the catheterization that related his condition to anything congenital or defect. No surgery would repair what was wrong. There was nothing to fix.

The tide of anxiety began to spill into a pool of disappointment. The only thing we could do from here was pray the medication would make an improvement. We spent a lot of time worrying, thinking of the future, and the "what ifs" but not much in the way of prayer. Was it that we felt we had no right to ask? Was it that we thought God ineffective at doing anything about it? The Great Physician rendered obsolete? We put a lot more faith in medicine and doctors than we did God. What a sad state of affairs for a Christian couple. It appeared we had no faith in God to do anything to help Asher.

Two

"I SEE A BAD MOON ARISING." CREEDENCE CLEARWATER REVIVAL

It was Tuesday morning. I was sitting at my desk, filtering through emails at work. I had just moved on to jotting down notes next to names and numbers of people who had left voicemails the day before when the phone rang. It was Asher.

"I want to go home." This was an inside joke. He would say this all the time. We'd chuckle and get on with the point of the conversation. I started to laugh when he interrupted me.

"No, I really want to go home. I don't feel good."

He had seen the cardiologist just the day before. One of the medications Asher took had to be increased gradually as one of its side effects was decreased blood pressure. Since he didn't have high blood pressure to start with, it would take time to ramp him up to the optimum dose. I inhaled on hearing this, reminding him that the doctor told him he would likely not feel well the next day when the medications needed to increase. He pressed his point.

"Is it normal that I woke up in the middle of the night with my heart pounding out of my chest?"

No, it certainly wasn't. I asked him if he'd had a bad dream or if something had startled him awake. He replied, "No, and it happened again this morning. I had to sit down three times just to walk from the subway to my office."

He worked about two blocks from the subway station. It was no more than a quarter of a mile, if even that much. My palms started to sweat. He went on to say that he was dizzy when he walked. I asked if he was still feeling this way, and he said he was slightly woozy but no more pounding heart. I told him to call his cardiologist.

"I am just going to his office," he stated.

Asher would not voluntarily stop by any doctor's office unless he had to. He was taking this seriously, so I was scared. I told him to call an ambulance, but he refused. He was going to take the train back to his car and drive to the doctor's office. When I couldn't talk him out of it, we hung up. I sat dazed, staring at the telephone back on its receiver and became entranced by the red lights blinking on the console. I was so distracted that I didn't notice one of the office assistants standing in the doorway of my cubicle.

Interestingly enough, she used to be a nurse before she injured herself and had to seek another career. I respected her greatly, but sort of thought she'd sold herself short in getting a dull old office job. I never asked why, because it was none of my business. When I first met her, she shared with me the pain of having a sick husband who had some sort of coughing disorder that made him cough until he passed out. The doctors couldn't figure out the problem. I told her my husband's story and she sympathized. We shared a common angst. I felt very close to her in this pain. The aloneness you can experience in a situation like a sick spouse is excruciating. I was also glad that, having her RN, she understood all terminology and medical "blah blah" without me having to describe everything in layman's terms. It was a relief for someone to understand what was wrong with Asher. Usually, when someone asked me to explain, I'd receive a glazed look staring back at me in return for my efforts to explain our situation. She fully comprehended, and we discussed it routinely over cigarette breaks. My past smoking habits had come back from the dead and turned into a part-time career with Asher's condition.

I spoke to her the day before about one of my clients, and I knew she wanted to ask me something about what I needed done for that client. She handled all of my Massachusetts business affairs as far as logistics and billing were concerned. The rustle of papers in her hand startled me into realizing she was standing next to me. The look on my face as I turned to address her made her forget what she needed.

"What's wrong?" she asked.

"Asher called upset and told me that he doesn't feel good. He's on his way to see his cardiologist." I gave her the details about what was going on. Her next question snapped me out of my fog.

"What are you still doing here?"

I refocused and said, "You're right. I am leaving."

I folded up my laptop in my hands, found its case, and hit the Out Of Office button on my phone. I had my cell phone anyway. Everyone called me on it if they didn't get me at my desk. Business calls were the least of my concerns at the moment. I didn't even stop at my boss's office on my way out. I am sure that she told him.

I don't remember the walk to the car. I barely recall the 50-minute drive to the medical building where I was meeting Asher. I was stiff from the tension. I called my mom and told her what was happening. She said she'd pray for me and asked me to hang up and focus on my driving. Why I was so grateful for the prayers of others but had few of my own is something I still think about looking back. Why didn't I pray? Why was I not pleading to God for answers? I prayed every morning and every night. I read my Bible daily. I attended church twice a week. I had a regular Bible study. Why is it that I went to God for everything else, but not this?

I pulled into the nearest parking space that I could find in the always-crammed lot. I spied Asher's parked car. That was a reassurance. I pressed the elevator button for the slowest elevator on the planet and clenched my teeth until it opened. As I entered the waiting area for the doctor, Asher was sitting there, staring at the floor in front of him. I was relieved that they had not dismissed him on arrival to go to some ER and wait idly for an overworked doctor to misdiagnose something. I asked him how he was feeling, and all I got was, "Okay." He was quieted from fright.

Up to this point, the symptoms, albeit bothersome, were not alarming. The tests and procedures were an inconvenience, but they didn't reveal anything startling. It was easy to gloss over the situation and resign to spending a lot of money on co-payments for medications. It didn't change our lives all that much except for Asher's routine at the gym. Even then, he had always assumed he would go back to his regular schedule of weight-training at some point. Not feeling worse sharpened his belief. In any case, we both had seen this as a temporary problem. It would end up being a blip on the radar that we would someday talk and laugh about getting through. It wouldn't be anything that would stand in the way of our future.

Those thoughts were disappearing fast. I was beside myself. What now? I think this was the crossroads that helped me get my head around what was happening. My husband had a bona fide life-threatening illness. This was not a drill. I think he was starting to feel it, too.

The nurse called his name, and after the initial vital signs, the EKG technician set him up on the table for a reading. I didn't even want to look at the paper loaded into the machine. My mind was racing. I was sure Asher had a heart attack. The doctor promptly came in and sidled up to me with the EKG results in hand. He stretched it out in front of my face and tapped at the sawtooth lines that ran across the page.

"He is having an Atrial Flutter," he stated.

What does that mean? In my three brief years as an Emergency Medical Technician, I didn't remember ever hearing that term. What it meant was that Asher's heart was quivering in the right atria instead of beating. That, coupled with his Left Branch Bundle Block, was a bad combination. He wasn't getting nearly enough oxygen to his brain, and neither was his heart.

The doctor immediately scheduled surgery at Boston Medical Center the next morning. He pleaded in vain to let Asher admit him overnight at the hospital before his surgery, but he flatly refused. The thought of sending him home with me in this condition was very unsettling, but none of us could talk him out of it. We left with strict orders to report to the day surgery unit at the hospital at 5:30 AM and to call an ambulance if anything changed at home. Asher promised. I hoped that he would let me know if there was a need to go to the hospital before morning.

As soon as I got home with Asher and sent the babysitter home with her children, I started making phone calls. I called friends still in the medical field and pleaded for answers and more information. Offers came from all directions to get appointments with this world-renowned cardiologist and that one. There was no time for a second opinion. Surgery was bright and early the next day.

I felt my stomach roll over from anxiety. I didn't fully understand everything, and I tried to explain it all to my boss when I called him to say I would not be in the next day. I reassured Asher and told him how lucky he was and drove home the need to tell me everything. All of a sudden, I felt like he wasn't telling me the whole story. I wondered if there were pains or any changes he wasn't telling me before. My urgent sense of his mortality sent me reeling. I couldn't make out what Asher was feeling other than sheer terror. I was afraid to ask for fear that I would have to confirm my own.

The night got very long, and the house was quiet while we internally pondered the day's events. I felt like something hit me in the head. I was too stunned to know how to react. After clearing up the kitchen from dinner that no one ate, I loaded my sweet little baby daughter into her bath. She sat on the floor of the tub, splashing the water and making motorboat noises with her mouth, happy and completely unaware that anything was amiss. This was the first time I broke down and cried. My heart broke for Katie. I thought about the idea that she would never know her father, that something would happen and he would die. I wiped my tears and reckoned it as something that could very well happen. Then I whispered to her, "I never wanted this for you."

I was in agony at the thought of this impacting her life. She didn't deserve this.

I didn't sleep much; neither did Asher. Morning came quickly, and the world's most annoying alarm clock went off too early. It was time to get moving. I was so relieved to hear him stir with the noise. I showered and patched myself together with a baseball hat, minimal makeup, and a running suit. I got a sleepy, limp baby up, changed her little bottom, and quickly fed her. We had to go. The Diersch family piled in the car, and we started to head north for the 30-minute ride to Boston. As I recall, neither one of us said anything. I think Katie fell back to sleep. We pulled into the hospital lot and silently filed out. The city is so quiet at that time of the morning. The air was crisp. It was Fall. The wind tingled the ends of my fingers and nose. Once the baby was fastened into her stroller and bundled up, we headed into the hospital. We found our destination quickly and settled in uniform chairs lined up in a desolate waiting room. Asher would need to be prepped first, and then he would have his surgery.

A petite, slender woman walked in and quietly sat in the waiting room next to us. I admired her full, bouncy dark hair. Her makeup was perfect, and everything she had on was neatly pressed and coordinated. She sat herself down without a word. We looked at her and offered a weak smile which she reciprocated. I wondered why she was there by herself, just sitting. I tried to focus on the news displayed on the television in the corner of the room in front of me, but my mind couldn't grasp anything that was being said. My ears were trained on the door at the back of the room where someone would come out to call Asher in. The silence suddenly broke when the woman sitting next to us asked Asher why we were there. He started to explain and then looked at me as if to say, "How does this go again?" I took over with the medical jargon and details. She asked for the name of Asher's surgeon, and I told her.

She perked up, "Oh, good! He's the number one electrophysiologist in the country. That is who is doing my dad's pacemaker right now."

What a relief. Bozo The Clown could have been doing Asher's surgery for all I knew. I didn't have any time to review or research anything on him. My fear and anxiety were alleviated to find that God had put Asher in the hands of the best without my asking. We both exhaled and looked at each other at the same time. Asher was more at ease as well.

The woman didn't say anything for the rest of the time she was there. I am not much on conversation when I am tense, so I fixed my attention on Katie while getting her a snack, keeping her occupied and quiet. Asher was called in, and the door slammed the door shut behind him. It was the loudest door I ever heard close. He was only a few yards from me on the other side of that door, but it felt like he disappeared into another realm, a medical abyss in which I couldn't find him.

I quietly packed up Katie and her things. We left the waiting room and came out to the elevator banks to go downstairs to the garage. I tried to feel something, but nothing would register. I made my way to the car and loaded Katie in the backseat and the baby paraphernalia in the trunk. I got behind the wheel and sat for a minute. I didn't want to leave. It was the first time I bowed my head and genuinely asking for God's help and protection in all this.

Katie and I made our way home and waited for the phone call that would tell me the surgery went well and to ask me to come take Asher home. Time slows down when you are waiting for those calls. This was the second one I had to wait for in less than a month. The stress bound me like duct tape; I was unable to move around my own house for fear that I might miss the call. It's funny how babies seem to know instinctively when something is not right with their parents. Katie was unsettled and fussy all day. I chalked it up to waking her so early. I spent most of my day trying to stay quiet yet being interrupted by a cranky baby.

The phone call I was waiting finally came in. The nurse on the other end of the phone ran down the findings and the results. The problem was fixed. What happened was the electrical impulse in Asher's right atria was misfiring. It wasn't completing the path in the right way that it needed to make the atria contract correctly. The surgeon went into the heart through a small incision, found the impulse that was acting up, and burnt that piece of the heart with a laser to get the impulse to correct itself. That didn't sound very pleasant at all! The nurse reported Asher was doing well and that I could pick him up that evening. He could come home. Thank you, God, for taking care of him.

As the discharge time got closer, I loaded baby and baby things into the car again and started for the city. I arrived to find Asher in a hospital bed in a semi-private room with a homeless man who was admitted to the hospital for chronic alcoholism-related issues. As Asher was in the process of having an IV removed and getting himself dressed, I half-listened to the scratchy voice behind the exam curtain explain things to the doctor who was attending to him. I was wondering as he talked about the wasting of this man's life. The doctor cited all the years and the opportunities that alcoholism had stolen. I wondered whether he once have a wife? Kids? A job? A home? It seemed so senseless. Did the homeless man think so, too? Life felt too precious to me to waste at that moment, and I wanted to pull back the curtain and tell him so.

Asher interrupted my train of thought to announce that he was ready. He looked impatient to get out of there, so we left. I was happy to see him. He was glad to be going home, but he seemed irritated. As it turns out, he was not completely under anesthesia when he had his procedure. He felt what they had gone into his heart to do, and that did not sit well with him. He would be happy never to have another surgery.

He sat quietly in the seat next to me for the ride home. He was dazed and a little overwhelmed by this whole experience. I couldn't blame him. He stayed home the next day, and so did I. I wanted to keep an eye on him. He fixed himself up in the spare bedroom with the television and a blanket on the futon. Little did I know he would be a fixture there for the foreseeable future.

The following week we met up at the cardiologist's office again. The results of the previous procedure would be reviewed and discussed. As his doctor got to his routine examination of vital signs and precursory questions, I happened to notice Asher's file flapped open right in front of my nose on the side table next to me. I glanced at it. It was the electrophysiologist's notes on the condition of Asher's heart. I looked away but curiosity overcame me. I turned back to read it. He used words to describe the heart's condition, such as gross, severe, and moderate-to-severe. My heart leapt into my mouth. I could feel my teeth tingling from the adrenaline rush. I sat silently, trying to avoid the rush of tears. I knew his cardiologist had read what I did. He and I both knew the real details, and I understood the prognosis. It hit me like a brick in the face. I never told Asher what I read. His doctor never brought it up either. It was our accidental secret. It's an awful feeling to hide the truth. However, it was the best thing for the patient, which is now how I saw Asher, rather than as my husband.

The surgery was a success. With that behind us, it was time for Asher to have another echocardiogram to see what effects the medications were having on the improvement of his heart. As far as I knew, he hadn't gotten worse. At least, he hadn't told anyone about any glaring symptoms that would alert us to any problems. I worried constantly about him hiding symptoms. I knew how badly he wanted to recover. I wondered if it was so much so that he would ignore anything that meant he was worsening.

The echocardiogram was not a big deal to him. He went by himself, and Katie and I carried on our normal routine. Weeks came and went. We sat once again in front of the cardiologist. It was later on in the day, and it had become dreary and rainy, accentuated by the cold weather which had now returned to the region. It is hard to be cheery and energetic in that kind of weather. We were both anxious to get this appointment out of the way so I could go home and get out of the damp weather with the baby. He had planned a guys' night out; he was venturing into the city to see a movie with his friends from work.

The doctor came in, and once more, did his introductory vital signs and "How are you feeling?" routine. I sat nearby, trying to unwrap wet clothing from myself and the baby. His cardiologist uncharacteristically didn't address me as he usually did, with a big smile and intense stare waiting for my reply. Instead, he gingerly sat down in his chair and held in his hand that familiar beige office file folder he usually referred to before speaking to Asher. He didn't open it this time before he began talking. He already reviewed everything. He was simply going to recite the speech he had likely prepared before we came in. The results were worse than I expected. He wasn't improving. The medication combination was designed to create a significant improvement at first and then taper off over time. Asher never had that steep incline.

His recovery was barely enough to label as minimal. The tests were done; the medications had their opportunity to work. There was nothing left to figure out, and he was out of things to try.

Asher's face sank and his shoulders drooped. He wanted so badly to know that there was an end to this trial, but now the hope was gone. I pained for him but could not find words nor actions to comfort him. Silently, I stared at the floor and held Katie tighter. I couldn't save him and neither could his doctor. We left somberly and headed to the car. I put the keys in the ignition and backed out, trying to think of what to say. It was getting dark early, as was normal for that time of year. I started driving him toward the subway.

"Just go with your friends to the movies. Let's forget about what we heard for tonight and just enjoy it," I said.

Surprisingly, he perked up and said, "I'd planned to."

When I pulled into the station, he kissed me quickly, bounded out of the car, and headed for the train platform. I was stunned by his sudden change of attitude. I drove home happy he was not devastated, but I felt like I needed him. I needed someone. I needed comfort. The news broke me. I wanted to fall apart, but I had to take care of Katie. I didn't want to show her any sign of anything wrong, but she felt it. It was so hard to comfort her that night and get her to bed. I was desperate to be relieved of my mom duties so I could attempt to wade through the avalanche of emotion that surrounded my thinking. I didn't sleep. Asher got a ride home after the movie from a friend and promptly went to bed as soon as he arrived. He was asleep in minutes as his condition and the medications always made him so worn out. He snored away while I spent my nighttime hours thinking of worst-case scenarios, wondering which one would come to fruition.

I reported the news to my mom over the phone the next morning rather matter-of-factly. I get like that when I am overwhelmed. By nature, I am not an emotional person. I am not the kind of girl who typically cries at sad movies or gets misty over sentimental cards and sincere compliments. In fact, I tend to get annoyed with those displays. On the other hand, my husband was a very emotional man. He reacted to things quickly. He cried more often than I did. There were many situations arose where he got emotional and then felt miffed at my lack of in-kind response. He used to say, when things got tense, I would go "all-business" on people. It isn't that I don't get emotional. I just manage to organize emotions into little compartments and stuff them into the corners of my mind. The resulting "all business" attitude is just me trying to protect myself from losing control. I confess it doesn't serve me well, and it didn't work at all when communicating with a man who is not afraid to show his feelings.

My mom seemed to take the news as best as I expected. She sounded confused that there was nothing else to do. There was no other answer for her. "Weren't there other medications to try?"

"No."

"Heart transplant?"

"Not, bad enough."

"Nothing else?"

"Nothing suggested."

I approached him about getting a second opinion, but Asher didn't take an interest in discussing the idea. He didn't want to be poked and prodded anymore. I understood why he would feel that way. If the second opinion was different, then I'd want a third to counter the different opinions. All that takes time and money, and neither one of us wanted to spend it either to verify what we'd already accepted nor to give us false hope.

As I conveyed the findings to our other family and friends, I generally got the same response. Nothing else to do? Nope. Not a thing. People offered to pray and also said they had been praying. That made me feel a little bit better. I felt comforted by the fact that someone cared even though I felt so emotionally spent all the time. I desperately craved relief.

By now, we had whole churches praying for us. I believe those prayers may have been the only thing that got us through some days. It is incredible what can be enacted when people pray corporately. Too many underestimate it. I was genuinely bowled over when people told me that their churches and Bible studies dedicated time to pray for us every week. There is nothing like the love and caring of your church family to make you feel like you can go one more day.

Despite being sustained by the prayers of others, I was desperate to talk to someone who could relate to what I was going through. My mother reminded me of a friend whose wife had been in a tragic accident. The accident cost the life of his mother-in-law and sent his wife to hospitals and rehabilitation centers for the better part of three years. I remembered talking to him in those early days of the accident. I had nothing to offer him in terms of comfort, and any attempts I made at bringing the love of God into the conversation were met with fierce opposition. His wife had been a devout Catholic, and, as far as he was concerned, her devotion to God hadn't done anything for her. Thinking back on the memories of those conversations, I wondered if he'd be willing to talk to me. Would he be emotionally capable of sharing a little of himself and the struggles he has with dealing with a sick wife? I reluctantly picked up the phone, not knowing what the response would be.

He answered, surprised to hear from me. We exchanged pleasantries, and I launched right into my news. He told me how sorry he was, and his voice became melodic and quiet. He asked a lot of questions, and I relayed information.

Then he asked me the one question almost no one ever asked me when I spoke of my husband's plight, "B, how are you doing?"

Those words were a breath of life. I didn't realize how much I wanted someone to ask me that. I instantly broke down into tears. The truth was I was barely hanging on. With a full-time career, a baby, a house to take care of, and now this, I felt like Atlas. I got up and put the world on my shoulders every day and headed out the door. No one cared to ask how I was doing, so I never told them.

We spoke for a long time in that initial conversation. We mostly talked about me - how I was coping with everything and what I was doing for myself. He encouraged me to acknowledge my feelings and to say what I wanted to say. He told me there wasn't anything I thought that he hadn't probably thought during his situation. He emphasized that it was okay to talk about it. I needed to hear that. After I had a good cry, feeling like I'd kept him long enough, I thanked him and hung up the phone. He called me regularly after that to check on me. I needed someone to do that. He was insightful. I am not one who reaches out for emotional support. I sensed that because he is the same way, he knew he needed to call when he didn't hear from me for a while.

As the initial shock and numbness of the situation began to pass, I was surprised to find anger was becoming my primary feeling. I felt it stir up in me like a hurricane at times. The intensity of those feelings scared me. I puzzled over the origin of why I felt this way. I was resentful of having to work full-time. So much of my time was devoted to a job that I found boring and non-stimulating. The commute was laboring. There were many days I was stuck in traffic, wanting to be home with my family.

I was grateful Asher got to pick Katie up from daycare now. He spent one-on-one time with her before I arrived home. They would play before he would feed her dinner. He loved spending time with her. Sometimes, he would take her to a fast food restaurant for dinner. He enjoyed hamburgers and French fries and would eat them at every opportunity. I didn't relish the fact that either one of them was regularly consuming this garbage, but it was something they shared.

I would have intrusive, random, morbid thoughts of Asher dying in the car while driving or at home with her, and Katie would be all alone. I thought of these things when I wasn't with them. That paranoia was always in the back of my mind when he was alone with her. I'd later learn that it was a thought that plagued him as well. I wished I could be home with them both. I pressed the issue with Asher again, this time a little more fervently. We began to circle that argument regularly.

With emotions brewing between us, God saw it fitting for us to be in a Bible study on the Biblical principle of the roles of husband and wife. God needed us to hear His design for our marriage, whether we realized we needed it or not. The Bible studies were separate, tandem studies offered by our church on Sunday mornings before the service. I wanted to attend because I thought Asher would get something out of it. He was all for attending because he thought it would make me change. Neither one of us went for us.

As I read the first chapter of my Bible study book, I barely refrained from sending it sailing across the living room. Thankfully, the author said the concept initially made her angry at first; otherwise, I wouldn't have bothered to read on. The concept was respect for my husband, or rather that ugly word, submission. The idea of being "submissive in all things" was like fingernails on a chalkboard. It was an out-of-date concept made to keep women under a man's rule. *You have got to be kidding me.* I was all for submission as long as I agreed with what I was submitting to. Asher and I married later in life than most, so we were already well-accustomed to our own ways of doing things when we met. This Bible study was going to be a struggle to get through, but I had to do stay with it so he wouldn't quit.

Of what the men discussed in their study, I have little knowledge. I know that God had a purpose for him hearing whatever he heard, although he didn't discuss much of it at all. I wondered what exactly he took in beside the fact that one man had decided to throw out his family TV on a conviction that television was an evil in his home. I spent a lot of time reassuring him that dispensing with his prized giant screen beauty in the family room didn't have to happen to be a real Christian.

One of the biggest hurdles was letting go of my finances. Part of the submission process in this bible study was submitting financial control to my husband. I felt as though that silly notion of blindly trusting someone with my well-being had burned me in the past, and now, I was the wiser. Turns out, others in my bible study had similar misgivings about financial submission.

Years before, I thought it would be a good idea to let Asher handle the finances because I was pretty bad at managing them. Asher appeared to have more restraint and skill in this area, so I had joyfully handed the bill-paying over, feeling freed that I didn't have to deal with it any longer. This didn't work out as well as I'd hoped. We came up with the idea of putting everything on a charge card to keep as much cash in the bank as possible and pay off the cards at the end of the month. That plan didn't happen. He had only made minimum payments, and the balances grew. He did this entirely without my knowledge. Asher was too embarrassed by the financial misstep to inform me.

In addition to our poor money management skills, we decided to buy a house. It was an unnecessary purchase because we had a perfectly good condominium with two bedrooms. Nevertheless, we endeavored to seek a house. Wasn't that what people do after getting married? We looked at many houses, and Asher fell in love with one in particular. When we looked at it, the house seemed to have everything Asher wanted and little of what I wanted. The house was too large for us with way too much property for two working people to maintain. My dislike for the house was exacerbated because Asher bid on it without my knowledge. He called me at my office and informed me over a morning phone conversation that he'd bid on the house. I was furious. By the time the actual state of our finances came to light, I was pregnant with our daughter, and we were a year into mortgage payments on Asher's dream house. We bit off more than we could chew; rather, as far as I was concerned, Asher was the one who got us into this mess.

Therefore, the idea of submitting any more control to him was something I wouldn't even consider as an option. Rather than try to learn from those who had come through adversity in this area and could now see the beauty in it, I decided to commiserate with the others who were unsettled with this topic.

We both agreed that one major blessing from the Bible study was prayer. We decided to incorporate prayer time together in the evenings before bed. We thought it would be best to pray earnestly and as one unit for the things we needed help with. It was something I grew to treasure and recommend to anyone. Sharing my faith with my husband was something I will always hold as a great and valuable bond. Even when we had nothing else, at least we had Jesus together. It would draw us back from the brink of marital disaster, time and time again. Reading a chapter of the Bible together helped us settle in and fix our minds on the things of God before prayer and bedtime. On the nights we would fight, it was even more instrumental in us "not letting the sun go down on our anger."

Marriage is hard, let no one fool you, but a marriage that is afflicted with a serious illness creates a constant stressful undertone that highlights even the simplest of relationship flaws. We were sinking under the weight of it all, but we forgot to hold each other up. No issue in a married person's life should ever be dealt with alone, separate from their spouse. I learned that all too painfully.

I also began journaling my thoughts and emotions about my marriage and my husband's illness. The journal entries quickly turned into letters to God. Sometimes I was pleading for relief, sometimes I was complaining about my situation. I had moments of gratitude at the end of every entry, and it helped to recount them and thank God. I needed to see there were good things at work intertwined amongst this pain. I called them rainbows in the storm. I love that rainbows are very often gleaming brightly against a grey, cloudy backdrop. It is a reminder to me that God can make anything beautiful. As my journaling progressed, some of my anxieties softened. I believed only one friend and God could understand the magnitude of the feelings I was experiencing. I didn't think I had anyone else with whom I could speak. A great journaler and friend advised me to write at least three full pages. He told me it would help get through the clutter of the mind first, so the real things that I needed to write about would come through at the end. He was right. My most honest conversations with God on those pages were in the last one or two paragraphs. When I felt ungrateful or overwhelmed, I would read back. It was funny to laugh at some of the entries. I was, at times, so desperate over things that became so trivial to me later. It is incredible how that works. We get so caught up in the minutia of the moment's troubles that we lose sight of how fixable it is to God. Nothing is too difficult for God. Many things seem so impossible to us that sometimes we forget we can go to Him for help with anything.

There is one more important thing I took out of the Bible study - don't discuss the problems in your marriage with your friends and family. Take the struggles to each other and take them to God, not someone else. I am glad not only to have spared my friends the details, but also the conflict that would have occurred between Asher and myself when and if he had found out what I had discussed with people outside of our relationship. Little else can cause division so quickly.

Things did improve between the two of us during that Bible study. Our attitudes towards each other and our situation got better, but as the study ended, so did our efforts to enhance communication between us. The burden of our finances and the undercurrent of Asher's illness took over again, and we were back to disagreeing on almost everything. He would demand, and I would dig my heels in. Neither action produced great results for either side.

We spent more than a few sessions in front of our head pastor for counseling. It was Asher's idea to do individual counseling but he was more or less using the sessions to complain about my behaviors, so the pastor and his wife asked to meet with us both. They were instrumental in taking the heat out of situations, but since the sessions were not designed to be more than a one-time thing, we didn't get much out of it long term. Outside of counseling, Asher and I would get to arguing about the same things - my career, money, and my lack of submitting to his way of doing things. Then we'd wind up in my pastor's office yet another time. I thought I was right; he thought I was wrong. Our pastor had become the referee instead of wise counsel for us. It didn't help much.

My sales career was taking a turn for the worse. No matter what I did, I couldn't seem to turn it around. I wasn't losing clients, but they weren't buying. I blamed it on a lot of things as most people do. Looking back, I believe God was speaking to us in it. Asher would get angry with me and tell me that I wasn't trying on purpose. He would get fired up by the notion that I was sabotaging my career for the sake of making a point. Nothing could have been further from the truth. As my income decreased and bills increased, Asher became very resentful towards me. When I pressed the idea of me leaving my job, we wound up in front of the pastor again. Our pastor sided with me this time. He agreed that it was vital for me to be home. Culturally, being a housewife was something that was well-accepted within my church, even to the point of causing a divide between the women who worked outside the home and the ones who didn't.

We met with my pastor and his wife one last time on the issue of one income. They pleaded with Asher, and he got increasingly frustrated and angry as the conversation continued. We left without resolving much. My pastor looked disappointed that we were unable to make an impact on Asher's position.

The truth finally came out on the ride home from that meeting. Asher was scared. He was afraid of what would happen to Katie and me financially if he were to pass away. The thought that I would lose everything and be helpless to care for our daughter kept him up at night. He also thought about what might happen if his health further deteriorated. He thought about the lack of health insurance and income. He was concerned about me being faced with finding a job and putting Katie back in daycare. I got it. I yielded to his feelings and told him I wouldn't bring it up again.

I resigned myself once again to the fact that I'd be a working mother and tried to accept it. It wasn't easy.

I didn't share this revelation with anyone. I simply gave up the conversation and planning to be a stay-at-home mom. This was confusing to the women who had often counseled me on my Biblical responsibilities to my family and my home. They thought we had made so much progress with my thinking. When I announced I was in the running for a management position with another company at the Sunday morning Bible study, I was met with silence. One brave friend commented that I wasn't doing the right thing. Resentment burned inside of me. They didn't understand. After all, I was obeying my husband's wishes and doing what I needed to do. My anger increased and finally got the best of me. I stopped going to Bible study. That angry, resentful mindset was going to plague me for months to come.

Asher didn't talk much about how he felt about being sick; at least, he didn't talk to me. I wish he had. I always worried about the effects his medical condition was having on him. My fears began to materialize as he retreated more and more into solitude. The spare bedroom which housed the only television upstairs in our home became his refuge from everything, including Katie and myself. When he wasn't at work, he was laying on the futon in silence, watching television. It seemed he had little interest in anything else. He spent whole days watching Magnum PI and MASH reruns. He had entire weekends devoted to the television on a regular basis.

At first, I let him have the time. He started napping a lot. His medications were taking their toll on his energy, and he wasn't able to do much in the way of exercise at the gym. As the weeks dragged on, I became more concerned. He didn't engage in life anymore. The only way to converse with him or spend time was to invade his space in the tiny spare bedroom he now called his "cave." I started to think depression was closing in on him, dark and heavy. I didn't know how to pull him out of it. I tried to encourage him to call his friends or to do things with Katie and me, but he always had a cynical excuse as to why he couldn't see his friends. He complained he was always too tired to leave the house to do something as a family other than going to church.

At times I forget he was even home because he spent so much time tucked away in that room. My care and concern turned into resentment as I struggled with weekends full of being alone with my baby girl and the lack of my husband's participation in our lives. I spent less and less time out of the house alone because I was worried about him. My fears of morbidity returned, and I obsessed with the idea that something tragic would happen if I left Katie and Asher home alone. As it was, when I did go, he'd take what he needed to entertain her into that little room to keep her occupied. All he wanted to do was tune out the world in favor of watching pretend private investigators and Vietnam-era soldiers. The days of wanting to take Katie out for pancakes or to the gym were long gone at this point. As for me, I was tired. I was tired of feeling alone, tired of taking care of the baby by myself, tired of work, and tired of taking care of the house by myself. I was just plain tired.

This solitary confinement exercise reached its boiling point for me one Saturday morning. I stormed into his little cave and started yelling at him about how selfish he was for holing himself up in that room to mope about his life.

My anger spilled out as I yelled, "Do you forget that there are two other people who are affected by your condition? You're not alone in this, you know!" I wound down on exhale, paused, unsure of where to go from there, and trailed off with "Why don't you stop feeling sorry for yourself and get some help?"

He responded by getting angry at my verbal assault on his isolated haven. After we both calmed down, he agreed to at least talk to his doctor about his depression. "I don't want to talk about it. I feel like I lost my life, and I don't know how to be happy anymore," he responded in a desperate, quiet voice.

Those words pierced my heart. If he didn't have hope, we both had nothing. I went with him to the doctor on his next visit to make sure he would talk to him about his depressed feelings. Much to my disappointment, the doctor didn't recommend anything other than finding a counselor. I knew Asher wouldn't do that and he didn't. Things changed very little in terms of his mental outlook from there on out. He stagnated in the spare room, and I continued to build a wall around myself to separate from the pain.

I talked to God a lot during this time. I was begging for relief. The feeling of being alone in my marriage was crushing me. I didn't know how to feel better, and I didn't feel like I had anyone I could talk to about how separated I felt from my husband. We had become more like roommates than a couple. We shared responsibilities and rejoiced in our daughter, but that was the only source of joy we had between us. I couldn't understand why God would want me to live in such a desolate situation. Looking back, I wanted to blame God and told Him to fix it; rather, I should have asked Him to show me the lesson He had molded for me out of these difficult times. I prayed, cried, and shopped. Shopping and zoning out in front of the computer were my escapes. If I wasn't parked in front of the computer talking to friends and surfing the internet, I was shopping online and hiding purchases from Asher. I felt guilty about my shopping addiction and hiding it from Asher, but it provided me with thrills and excitement to get boxes of goodies at my office, safe from the sight of my husband. I'd effectively replaced my relationship with my husband with a relationship based on material goods, false happiness, secrets, and lies.

My shopping obsession grew into a monster before I even knew what was happening. I had been hiding the payments to my charge accounts in allowance money that I was able to take out of our account every week. The balances had been getting higher, and the minimum payments now exceeded my allowance. I had to confess to Asher my transgression. To my surprise, he didn't yell or get angry. I asked for his forgiveness and handed him my credit cards. We hugged, and I thought that was the end of it.

However, letting go of my shopping habit was difficult. I was, at times, soured and full of self-pity that my manic shopping sprees had ended. Rather than take it to God, I increased my smoking habit. Smoking had become a guilty pleasure and stress reliever, but my husband hated cigarette smoke. He scolded me whenever he smelled it. I couldn't seem to find the right combination of mints, car sprays, and body splashes to mask the scent. I thought I would be able to quit for good when I found out I was pregnant with Katie, but since I wasn't looking to find my solace or peace in God, I simply turned to other things besides cigarettes during the pregnancy. Now, without the malls and online shopping, I soon found myself wooed by Marlboro. Over time, Asher seemed to ignore my smoking. I was happy he wasn't harping on me to quit smoking anymore. After all, I didn't smoke with the baby in the car. When I wasn't home, my daily cigarette intake took off at rocket speed.

Three

"You don't bring me flowers any more." -Neil Diamond and Barbra Streisand

The decline of our relationship was dizzying. The more depressed Asher became, the more he retreated to his spare bedroom for solitude, and the more I withdrew from him and grew bitter. I never considered myself this kind of person. I don't like to think about being capable of it, especially in the context of how the Bible describes bitterness:

«Look after each other so that none of you fails to receive the grace of God. Watch out that no poisonous root of bitterness grows up to trouble you, corrupting many." Hebrews 12:15 NLT

I didn't understand how the seeds of bitterness get planted and how quickly they grow if you don't pluck them out by their little roots when they sprout. Instead, I nursed and cared for mine. I was lonely. I wanted my husband back. I felt scorned by him. Not only was his attention to our family lacking, but our physical relationship had become non-existent and had been replaced by withdrawal and silence. I felt justified by how I felt. When I should have been begging God to give me a right heart and His eyes to see my husband as He sees him, I wanted to simmer in how he had wronged me. The poisonous fruit took hold of us, and we ate of it freely, expecting the other person to suffer.

Once this attitude became anchored in my heart, compassion went running out the front door screaming. My love as his wife was replaced by employing myself as his nurse and medical advocate. I no longer cared to be a loving and gentle spouse. I wasn't caring for him emotionally. I didn't feel cared for, so I withheld my affection. If I didn't put myself out there to be rejected, then he couldn't hurt me again. My fierce advocacy for him with doctors and nurses was automatic. I thought he would appreciate it, but what he wanted was someone to love him through this. I was too afraid to show him how I really felt about all of this, how broken I truly was because I thought it would make him more depressed. I didn't want him to worry about me emotionally. I hid it from him and took on the unemotional persona of his representative to the medical world. Once again, I was all business, and he felt alone in facing his fears.

Both of us suffered our own consequences, unable to understand how to resolve this distance between us. On some days, it would felt like a presence had moved into our home - anger personified. It was so real to me that I would talk to it. I would demand that it leave my family alone and get out of my house. I prayed to God for this demon to leave, and it would. However, we kept inviting it back in. I couldn't see how the way we were treating each other gave the demon of anger a seat at the head of our family table. It isn't that we exchanged heated words or unkind acts. We just ignored each other. Every day was spent avoiding anything that would start an argument. We thought that the avoidance of conflict would make for peace; instead, its results were decidedly opposite. In avoiding arguments, we simply stayed away from each other. The Cold War, as Asher put it, was alive and well in our home.

"Love keeps no record of wrongs." paraphrase of 1 Corinthians 13:5 NIV.

The silent treatment allowed another transgression to infiltrate our marriage - scorekeeping. This was very painful for me. During the times when the silent tension would build between us to the breaking point, we would argue passionately. During the first couple of times this happened, our arguments would go from the issue at hand to Asher recounting every negative behavior I had done since our last argument, usually spanning months. I was wounded by the recount and scarred by the apparent unforgiveness. I told him how cruel he was to keep these lists of infractions just so he could hurt me when he felt like it.

What I wouldn't admit to myself was that while he was keeping a record of behavioral infractions, I was keeping a record of emotional ones. I didn't see how I was doing the same thing because I rationalized with myself, describing how it was different, and therefore, right. When I felt injured, I poured fertilizer on the roots of my bitterness. I could easily forgive the constant lack of picking up after himself and dismissing himself from trash duty. In my mind, what was inexcusable was his lack of love and kindness towards me. On the rare occasions that he made an effort to help, I didn't thank him. Rather, I scoffed at his expectations of appreciation. I asked him why he should receive accolades for doing things he should normally be doing. Was I supposed to have a parade and throw a party every time he emptied the dishwasher for me? No one said anything to me about the whole house I would clean on Saturday or the endless onslaught of laundry I processed daily. The roots of my bitterness were getting healthier and deeper by the day.

As bitterness continued to grow, I became less able to see how to resolve it. I never imagined I would consider divorce an option. We talked about it, but it but neither one of us was serious about following through. It was just that we didn't know how to heal what had come between us. When we did talk about divorce, the conversation usually ended with it being a silly consideration. We would then go back to the pastor's office for another one of those fix-us-up sessions. We were desperate for a light bulb to go off in our heads about how to make all this go away. Interestingly enough, neither Asher's spiraling depression nor my reaction of withdrawal ever came up in any of those conversations with our pastor. We just focused on how we'd been quick to hurt each other. Like any doctor would do, our pastor would address the reported symptoms and send us on our way. We never gave him anything he could use to get to the heart of the illness in our relationship.

If we could have seen, if we would have, just for a moment, paused and asked each other what it was underneath it all, we would have uncovered that we were both terrified of Asher's condition. We feared what that meant for the future. The promise of "'til death do us part" had become something that might not happen as we convalesced in some old-age home together in our 90's. The realization, the possibility that his demise would come sooner rather than later, was something we refused to discuss. However, it was weighing on us more than anything.

Asher confided in me one day that he had a recurring nightmare that he was rocking Katie in his arms in her nursery rocking chair. They would both fall asleep, but he would never wake up again. He finally told me out of desperation because he was afraid it would one day be a reality. The recount alarmed me, but I reassured him that it was just a dream.

As we discussed his nightmare, I found myself reflecting on my constant daydreams. The most persistent one detailed how I would come home to a husband on the floor and a crying toddler alone in her house. We should have recognized his chronic dream as something for us to focus on with our pastor because it described our greatest fear. It never happened. He continued having the dream, and I continued feeling panicked every time I pondered the possibility.

A ray of hope came one day during a routine visit with Asher's cardiologist. It was supposed to be a regular check-in visit. It felt like a long time since I'd gone to the visits with Asher, so I wanted to catch up on his condition. The doctor launched into a conversation about an internal defibrillator/pacemaker that would be a possibility in preventing Asher from dying in the event he had a heart attack. Asher was not jazzed by the idea of another surgery. He seemed frightened by the concept of a mechanism under his skin that would shock his heart as needed. He stated that if he had chest pain or if he felt something that he would just go to the hospital. The doctor was quick to rebuff him and let him know the condition of his heart would not allow the time to get help if he needed it.

I remember exactly what the doctor said. "Asher, your heart would not withstand a cardiac event like this. There would be no warning; it would be 'lights out.'"

The statement took my breath away and left Asher speechless. Asher ended the conversation with, "I'll think about it."

I stared at him in disbelief. He'll think about it? What exactly was there to think about? I thought about it for two seconds and had made my decision. He needed to have this thing. Taking our chances was not an option with a baby depending on her daddy to be around, not to mention my sanity.

It took me three days to convince him to agree to the procedure. Three days of my begging him to think of his family and our little girl who needed him. He didn't want to go through the whole process of surgery again, I understood. The atrial ablation surgery to fix the last issue was not pleasant. He didn't want to revisit the experience. To me, he had no choice.

He didn't want to walk around with a device in his chest and wonder if and when it would go off. I could see his point. Who wants to sign up for a voluntary shocking. But if anything were to happen, it would save his life. I asked him to please look at the big picture. A jolting moment of discomfort and he gets to be around for his family versus instant death should his heart take a turn for the worse. Reluctantly and ultimately, he agreed. I made plans to call the doctor the very next morning and report the good news.

As soon as the doctor's office was open the next day, I was dialing the number. I chirped to the receptionist that I needed to speak to the doctor. I stated my name and told her that he would be expecting my call. He, of course, didn't know that I'd be calling that day, but he was awaiting an answer so I knew he'd come to the phone. The doctor's voice resounded after several minutes of waiting. Anxiously, I told him that I had spoken to Asher, and he agreed to have the procedure done.

"We can't do it," he replied.

I felt like I'd been punched in the stomach. My cheeks flushed. Blood raced to my burning ears. What did he just say? "What do you mean we can't do it? Why?" I huffed into the phone through my adrenaline rush.

"The insurance company declined the coverage on it," he sympathetically reported.

I was confused. Why would they refuse to cover something that could save the life of a young man? I asked for the reasoning. He stated Asher didn't meet the criteria. What criteria? Wasn't he a doctor? Didn't he know the criteria? Couldn't he fit Asher into the insurance company's criteria? I pressed him with questions. I really needed him to justify their decision because I certainly couldn't accept why this company would want to sign my husband's death warrant so easily. The doctor listed the criteria. The items on the list that disqualified him were 1) his age, which actually worked against him, and 2) he had not had a cardiac event related to his underlying condition. I was reeling. The insurance company practically required my husband to have a heart attack. If he had a heart attack, he wouldn't survive it, yet he needed to have one in order to consider the procedure? This information was inconceivable. The doctor said there was nothing that could be done and ended the conversation. I was crushed. I felt like our only hope had been stripped from us. Some random employee at an insurance company looked down the list that Asher's doctor had supplied on a form, firmly stamped "DENIED" right across the paper, and faxed it back. Just like that.

With no remorse, the insurance company said my husband wasn't worthy of paying to save. I wanted retribution. I wanted a hearing. I wanted someone to see the value of this man's life and agree that it was worth the price of saving. There was no audience for me to plead my case. No one wanted to hear me. How could they be so callous? How could this be so final? These questions swam around and around in my head for days on end. I was frustrated by the finality of it all.

After over a week of being distracted, Asher asked me to let it go. He told me we needed to accept it as the way it was. I am a fighter; I don't ever want to give up until I win. I was ready to take on Big Insurance, go to the media, and do whatever I needed to do. He didn't want to talk about it anymore. Didn't he care about his own life? Even more frustrating, neither my husband nor his doctor geared up to fight with me. I had to lay my sword down and accept it. I pleaded with God to help, but the answer I wanted didn't come. God, why is this happening? I felt rejected by God and left alone to see what would happen from here on out. I didn't understand.

We decided to move on. I asked Asher if there was anything he'd really like to do. This question startled him into paying attention to me. He asked why I would ask that. I responded that I wondered if he had something on his list of things to do in life that he would like to scratch off. He took it to mean that I thought he was worse off than he thought he was. He was correct, but I insisted it was just a question. This thought process of me and his doctor hiding something from him about his condition persisted and ate away at him. I kept up my charade, unwilling to tell him that I feared the worst. I kept recalling what the electrophysiologist's report stated in his medical file. I made a pact with myself that I would never share that information with him, and I was bent on keeping it to myself. But I was feeling the weight of it in a very real sense now. Time and time again, he would insist that there was information I was not divulging. I wouldn't change my story for anything. I was convinced he would get worse or give up if he knew. It was worth keeping to myself, but it cost us both dearly with the stress and anxiety we endured daily.

I began to feel the pressure of my silence again. I reached out to my friend, the one who had a sick wife, for comfort. He was pleased to hear from me and my desire to have an actual, honest conversation instead of the short quips I had for him during his occasional check-in calls.

"Sariah, you can tell me anything. There is nothing you can say or think that I probably haven't said or thought of saying." He tried to comfort me to get me to talk.

I started in. It was like a shaken soda bottle ready to explode when the cap gets loosened. I poured out. I told him about the loneliness, desperation, and sorrow over Asher's depression. I spilled out the hopelessness, the rejection from his insurance company, and the seemingly endless anxiety over if and when my husband would die. I was overcome with emotion as I sat on my cell phone in the privacy of my car in the evening traffic. I was practically yelling at him over the phone. He listened patiently and quietly. The height of the tirade peaked with angst as I blurted out, "I didn't sign up for this!"

He quickly interrupted me with, "Yes, you did!"

My mania stopped instantly. His words came quickly as I honed in on his voice.

"Sariah, this is the problem. Everyone takes their vows never expecting to have to cash in on 'in sickness and in health, for richer or poorer...' you are being asked to live up to what you promised is all."

Wham! The truth hit me right between the eyes. Faster than a bullet, it hit my consciousness and my soul. He was right. I was being asked to live up to what I had promised Asher and God. I never knew how hard the other side of those promises would be. Doesn't everyone expect that life will be better in marriage? The realness of my life settled in. Even if there were no relief in this saga, it was my job to honor my commitment, regardless of how it felt.

Feelings dominated a lot of my thinking and prayers. Now that I had to accept my life was the way that it was and I still needed to live in it, my prayer time and journaling were consumed with how I felt. Spiritual immaturity caused a lot of problems in this arena. I always felt entitled to feel happy and to be treated the way that I wanted. If I didn't feel that way, it was my natural inclination to retaliate and make my opposition feel worse.

A lot of my downfall and problems with communication, namely with Asher, came from the ugly things that would spew from my mouth. If I made him feel bad, and he wanted to let me know, then I was going to justify my actions by telling him how he was the villain. I often used my unhappiness with the intimate aspects of our relationship. I would lob my responses at him when he would criticize my inability to be more emotional and sensitive to his depression. His depression, in my mind, caused our intimacy issues. I had asked him to get help, but he kept putting it off. To me, he wanted to wallow since he wouldn't seek counseling. If he wanted to do that, and he knew the negative effects it was having on our marriage, then he didn't care, and he didn't care about me. These were the thoughts I had to justify my behaviors. They started to form the foundation for how I felt about his character. The roots of bitterness grew deeper still and multiplied into new ones. I longed for change, but I wasn't willing to look at how to change myself. I just kept focused on Asher and what he did to make me feel this way. Pity parties were often thrown in my mind. I felt so sorry for myself.

Late in the winter, an announcement was made at my church for a women's retreat. I didn't give any thought to going as I always had before because I honestly didn't want to hear any more about The Proverbs 31 woman. As far as I was concerned, she was an unrealistic ideal that women in the church used to puff themselves up and put others down. Everyone got it wrong, and I didn't want to discuss it further. As the announcement came during a brief intermission in the normal church opening routines and business, Asher nudged me and told me I was going. Beautiful, just what I want to do, I thought. I told him I would go, but I was resentful. I was being forced to go on a weekend away, to hear what I didn't want to hear, and it would be encroaching on my precious free time. I signed up, and purposefully avoided any literature that would tell me what it was about. I didn't want to hear anything that would make me want to skip out. I figured if God wanted me to go, He better not tell me what He wanted me to hear. God agreed, and I had no idea what I was in for until I checked into the hotel and strolled into the ballroom area where our retreat was to be held. Sure enough, Proverbs 31:31 was the theme verse.

"Give her the reward that she has earned and let her works bring her praise at the city gate." Proverbs 31:31NIV

After suppressing my gag reflex upon reading our banner and theme verse at the back of the room, I settled in and found some friends to talk to, trying to ease my nerves. The room buzzed with excited moms who rarely parted with their children, let alone husbands. I always felt so out of place around most of them. With the added strain of my sick husband and all-but-dead marriage, I sensed a great chasm between my dear sisters and me. I never shared with them much of anything as I felt I would be judged or validated for just how different I really was from these women. I was about to be proved wrong.

Our "ice breaker" game was something of a Truth or Dare scenario. There were several things written on little pieces of paper that someone might have done in their youth. They ranged from the innocuous to things I thought only I would be guilty of. One would read the paper picked out of the pile in the middle of the table, and anyone who was guilty of such an offense would have to take a marble out of the basket. It was kind of silly and cute. One of the slips was drawn, and the sin on the paper read: Smoked pot in high school. I was shocked and comforted by the fact that nearly everyone, including myself, took a marble. Similar infractions were read with the same results. When the game was over, we all had a good laugh and felt comforted by feeling less odd about being normal. I took note of those whose cups of marbles were as full as mine.

Next, I found my friend Micah. She was someone with whom I always felt at ease. She was honest about things, and I am drawn to those kinds of people. I love people who speak the truth, even when it might make them look bad or be hard to hear. We grabbed a coffee and a corner in the room and were joined by one of my other friends, Lilly. I have always been endeared to Lilly. Somehow the conversation got serious, and we started discussing difficulties in marriage. All three of us had them. We went around discussing, thankfully, in confidence and with the understanding that our sharing should not include the maligning of any husband's character. Micah was further along in the healing stage of some of her difficulties, so I wanted to hear how she overcame it. Of course, with God's help, but she also offered up the benefits of counseling and a couple of good books that had helped her and her husband in their times of marital dryness. I went to bed late and caffeinated. It amazes me that you really can have honest girl time and sharing without the use of excess wine, as was my customary ritual with friends outside the church. I fell asleep feeling comfortable for one of the first times since this whole saga began.

The next morning I rolled out of bed, a little groggy from lack of sleep. Going to bed after two cups of coffee and spiritually stimulating conversation didn't make for a lot of rest. More eager to see what was for breakfast than the content of the day, I readied myself and made my way to the other side of the hotel toward the ballroom. The room was alive with conversations. I sat down with some familiar faces sidled with a few I had never seen before. I was told that one of the women was not a Christian and had been brought by a friend. I instantly decided I should have a better attitude for her sake and tried to be more smiley and interested in the table conversation. Her name was Nellie, and she was very quiet and withdrawn. As much as people tried to engage her, she would reply with one or two-word answers to questions and stare blankly off into the room. I wanted to act just like her, frankly. I wasn't too sure I wanted to hear the speaker either. I finished up my breakfast, got some hotel coffee in a little Styrofoam cup, and sat down at the front of the room so I'd be forced to pay attention. I have trouble with concentration in general and even more so when I don't want to be present. My mind has a wonderful escape hatch to an alternate universe when I want it to and even sometimes when I don't. I arranged my belongings under my chair, being ever so careful to mind my hot coffee and took out my pen and paper so I could take notes I would never read again.

After the opening prayer and songs, an older woman with a slight and slender build walked carefully and demurely to the front of the room. She was a southerner, well-spoken, and purposefully controlled with the volume of her voice. She radiated dignity and refinement. The slow drawl in her speech added to her sweetness. My mind immediately started to write her off as being someone who wrote a book about how scrubbing my floors and making elaborate dinners for my family was honoring to God. I didn't have time to continue that thought because she immediately launched into what I would describe as the best illustrations of how marriage is supposed to mirror the relationship of the Holy Trinity.

I fixed on her face and drank in what she said. She spoke not of one spouse over the other, as society taught, but each in equal importance, having distinct roles. I had never heard that before. She went on to talk about how it relates to a structure, in particular, a temple. She elaborated on women as being pillars in a temple. What did the pillars in a typical ancient temple look like? They were large, exquisitely decorated, and painstakingly carved out of marble. They lined the inside of the building. They were functional, important, and also aesthetically pleasing to behold. Solomon's temple describes some of the most beautiful workmanship of pillars that you can find in the Bible. I thought of their descriptions as she spoke.

Next, she equated men to the roof of the temple. The roof was the top; it was the protector of the building. It had to be built to last because it would take on whatever the elements pressed upon it. Year after year, it needed to be dependable and able to do its work, and it would never be a successful roof if it didn't have the pillars holding it in place. What an amazing picture! I wanted to hear everything she had to say. I wanted to encapsulate it all and take it with me to have more of it later. Her descriptions finally laid to rest my unsettling with the concept of submission and my role in the marriage as the wife. My role was not one of lesser and subservience at all. I had an important job. I had a function that entailed holding up the roof of my relationship. She breathed new life into my thinking.

A lot of what she drove home was being a life-giving source and not a destructive one. We women have a tendency to open our mouths and say what comes to our minds at exactly the right moment when they should remain closed. So much is written in the Bible relating to the tongue being used as a weapon of destruction and women, in particular, being warned about being contemptuous. This would be a theme I would not only hear about in this retreat, but other venues as my tongue was always my greatest resource against my perceived enemies. I could unsheathe that mighty sword unrelentingly and without remorse. Over the years, I started to notice the damaging effects it was having on my relationships and those around me. When I heard verses and conversations about how painful words can be to the listener, it pricked my soul. I knew I was being asked by God to change, but I had much to learn still.

After the women's retreat, I returned home. Without missing a beat, our life and our relationship resumed its old course. A weekend marriage retreat was announced, and we signed up. We couldn't afford it, but we couldn't afford not to. Asher and I were now desperate for answers to what had now become more pain in our relationship than we ever imagined possible. We wanted to move beyond what we had gotten ourselves into, spiritually and emotionally. We wanted this time of barrenness in our lives to end. We didn't give it much discussion. We signed up and asked my mom and dad to watch the baby. Things did feel lighter in the house with the hope that this conference would help. We wanted to learn something new that might help us. So many in our church had gone in years before, and they highly recommended it. Why not give it a try? Everything else we tried seemed to result in further destruction. I wondered if it wasn't too late. We had to be hopeful, but I wasn't in it 100%.

The weekend came, and we headed north to drop off the baby with my parents and then on to the hotel where the conference was to be held. It was only a short distance farther. We had thought about not spending the nights at the hotel to save money, but both of us realized we needed to be immersed in the whole experience. We had a good time. The conference was not for the weak of heart. The couples that spoke during the weekend had some serious and pointed things to say to those of us who attended. They were confident that if we wanted it to work, and even if we didn't want it to work, God did. God was our only hope for this marriage. We grasped hold of that thought. Lots of discussion and note-taking happened. We had a lovely date night that weekend. We were relaxed and happy, and we enjoyed each other. My attitude went from "here we go again" to "maybe this has merit."

There came a time of the weekend where we had to write love letters to each other. We were to take time apart and write them. They were pivotal to the weekend. I took a lot of time apologizing to Asher in mine about my attitude and how I felt about him being sick. It was the first time I shared anything about my true feelings with him. He was very grateful to hear my heart about it. When he replied to my letter, he told me that he was resentful that I had gone from wife to his nurse, and he felt emotionally he was not supported through his very real and fear-laden crisis. He was right; I wasn't supporting him emotionally. I verbalized how I was afraid to show emotion because I feared he'd get more depressed or assume the worst if I did. He encouraged me to be more honest about my emotions in the future.

His turn came to read his letter to me. It was brief, and rather void of any apologies or loveliness that I would have expected. Rather, it seemed as though he had blamed me for the stated of our marriage instead of making a note of anything he could do to improve it. As I sat on the bed in our hotel room, trying to process his letter, I could feel the disappointment and bitterness rising. I left that retreat feeling like it had been worthless. Maybe our marriage really was over.

After another fight about nothing important, and we decided to seek counseling from a couple at our church. They had recently returned from seminary with the intent of counseling families. They had set up shop for their ministry in the church building and were now taking couples under their wings. We wasted no time getting in front of them for help. We enjoyed getting to know them before and had anxiously awaited being able to reconnect with them since they left for their four-year hiatus out in California.

The day arrived for our consultation. We pled our case before them. They sent us home with a questionnaire to fill out and some ground rules. We discussed how counseling would help us, expectations, and how the process would work. It felt serious to me. I was in.

We filled out our answers on the paperwork. As soon as we got it completed, we returned and handed it into the couple who'd be working with us. We briefly reviewed the questionnaire. A date was set to meet for the first time, and we awaited the day. Just before the session, Asher and I had yet another disagreement. This time I fully lost control of my emotions. It was the final cut. I told Asher in a conversation over the phone that I was moving to my parents' house with the baby. I hung up the phone and sat in an empty cubicle in my office. Then I sent an email to the pastor who'd be counseling us, thanking him for his time and his desire to help us, but I stated I was done. No counseling for me; I was leaving. Moments later, he rang my office. I was surprised when the receptionist announced who was on the phone. Then I realized I'd sent a message from my work email, and all my contact information was at the bottom. Of course. When you have signatures on your work email, people know how to contact you at work.

I felt like I'd been called into the principal's office as I picked up the receiver. He spoke with a quiet and comforting tone. He reminded me about the famous quote that was also at the bottom of my email. It cited the need to keep one's enthusiasm, despite the circumstances of life. I was willing to be reminded of that in business, but not in relationships. I never read that quote in the context of my marriage, but he was right. I was encouraged to attend the appointment scheduled for the next night, and I agreed.

Our time came to meet, and we all sat down together. We had met one time before only to go over their findings on our questionnaires but no real discussion. They described Asher and I as "two of the most dynamically different people ever to be married." Well, they were right. We were exceptionally different, but it had served us well in balancing each other. We evened out a lot of our negative tendencies by being together. Asher liked to get excited about ideas; I liked to read the fine print and slow things down. He liked to feel safe; I encouraged him to take chances. I liked to run with scissors around the edge of a cliff; he liked to encourage me to think things through. He was very emotional, and I was not. I called his outbursts "emotional lemmings." I told him, "Just because you want to run yourself off an emotional cliff doesn't mean that I am going with you." It was funny, but it was true. I reminded him to get a hold of himself at times when he would spin out of control.

With all of this information in hand and out in the open, we could meet and talk. We spoke about my meltdown and my desire to leave the marriage only the day before. I told him that I didn't really want to leave. I had just reached a point that was so painful that I couldn't take any more. I wanted Asher to seriously consider healing the negativity between us. I believed the threat was the only way to make him engage in a serious examination of our relationship struggles. I was right; Asher got focused. I scared myself with how close I had come to the idea of divorce. Finally, at long last, we were both willing to work on our marriage.

Our conversations with our counseling couple were fruitful. We both learned that each of us had our downfalls that needed to be worked on. A big part of our conversation centered on our lack of intimacy. This had long been a painful subject in our marriage. I had various moments where I cried myself to sleep over it, tried to make Asher feel guilty about it, and nothing worked. I felt rejected and unattractive to my own husband. I simultaneously resented and reveled in the attention I would get from other men. To me, it meant someone noticed me, but I was also uneasy about men being so flirtatious with a woman who had a wedding ring very prominently displayed on her left hand. We met individually with the counselors on this topic so we could speak guy-to-guy and woman-to-woman without feeling awkward. We didn't know what the other side shared, but we were both together when we heard the diagnosis in this area. Asher's lack of engaging intimately with his wife was a sin, plain and simple. I felt validated to hear this. He read us both the verses that talk about intimate responsibility in a marriage, and we heard from God what He had to say about it. There was no argument in this anymore. God said it, and Asher understood. This was something he had to fix with God. I left it to God and Asher from that point on.

The next time we met was rather informal. We had discussed our progress over the last three weeks, and there certainly was some. Things felt lighter between us. We now had something tangible we could work with in terms of our broken marriage. God could and would heal us if we sought him. Eureka! Our conversations turned from one of despair to one of the hope of redemption.

I recalled the weeks before when I wanted to pitch my cross. Now, I was willing to carry it if it meant it would bring rebirth like the story of the crucifixion. We thanked them for helping us. What had really come up for us in that session out on the porch of our counselors' home that night was lack of forgiveness. We both were willing to work on letting the past be the past, forgive, and rebuild. Asher had informed our counselors that he was going on a guy's weekend to go fishing with a couple of buddies. They were going to hang out in Maine at a cottage his friend, Mike, owned. It was going to be a small group of three, and they were all going through their own trials in life. They planned to spend some time bonding and talking through what was going on in their lives. He was glad it had worked out that he would go away right after this meeting. At the end of the time with our counselors, he said he would use his time away to focus on talking to God about how to forgive me for all the things he was holding on to and let go of the bitterness. I felt tenderness in my heart as I heard him say that. We all hugged and left the cozy glassed-in front porch, hungry for healing in our marriage. They were eager to hear about Asher's weekend when he returned. So was I. This was going to be the new leaf we were going to turn over. I could just feel it.

Asher left the next morning for work. The plan was to go to work and leave for Maine with the guys at the end of the day. We said our goodbyes, and he kissed the baby and headed out with his duffel bag for the weekend. Honestly, I was a little sad. I was happy he was going away to be with his friends, but we had made progress, and I wanted him home with Katie and me. I wanted the new us to start now. He had gone to this cottage with his friends before in years past, so I knew his cell phone connection would be spotty. I probably wouldn't hear from him. I thought it was just as well since he would be dealing with some stuff with our relationship and probably needed his space to process everything he felt. His condition and my paranoia about him forgetting his pills or no one knowing what to do if he developed symptoms always unsettled me when he would go anywhere without me. I sent him out the door with a little note about the list of his pills, dosages, his diagnosis, his heart history, and his doctors' names and numbers. I folded it up and gave it to him to give to one of his friends like a little kid with a permission slip. He promised to give it to whoever he wanted to be in charge of his information. I know it made him feel helpless, but it made me feel better that someone would know something about what was going on with him.

As expected, I didn't hear from him. This made me feel lonely, but Katie and I had a busy weekend together. We had a Princess Birthday Party for her best friend planned for Saturday morning, and I needed to get a princess outfit for her to wear to it. They would be making their own tiaras as favors, so I just needed a dress her. After a trip to the mall and perusing the cheesy selection of costumes, I decided to make my own for her. We arrived home a short time later, and I bounded to the closet to get my sewing machine, eager to make my first costume for my daughter. My mother had always sewn my dresses and Halloween costumes, so it felt very special for me to do this for her. In a blink, it was done. A cotton candy pink perfection of a princess dress for a two and a half-year-old. Katie was overjoyed to have to dress-up to go to her friend's house. We arrived at her friend's party, princess garb and all, and made our acquaintances with the hosts and their friends and families. Katie then went about her business as Princess Baby, as I called her. She was smiling and giggling as she joined the party of little girls. The sun was shining, and the girls were having a great time with all the festivities at the outside affair. The grey morning had given way to a beautiful day with a perfect temperature. I admired their soft, lush grass in the backyard under my bare feet as I sat in a lawn chair, making small talk with parents and grandparents I knew.

My cell phone rang as I enjoyed the warm rays of the sun. It was my mother. She just called to say, "Hi." My mother never calls to say hi out of the blue in the middle of the day. I pressed her.

"What's going on, Ma?"

"Your father had a heart attack yesterday."

She launched into the details and what his next steps were as I held my breath, unable to say anything. My mind was a sudden merry-go-round of information, and I was dazed that this was really happening. She also told me that he was refusing to take his medications, and he was not willing to listen to the doctor. I told her I was on my way to see him as soon as possible. I let Katie enjoy her time a little longer at the party. It didn't seem fair to yank her out of her good time if my dad was home from the hospital. It was painful to sit there and let time go on as I became unnerved about my father's condition. Heart disease ran in his family. Both his younger brother and his mother had not survived their only heart attacks, so I was relieved that he survived his. I was also stunned by the very real fact that he may not survive another one. Not taking his treatment seriously was just not an option if he were to live for any continuous period of time. When I couldn't listen to my head talk to me anymore about the worst possible outcomes, I called out to Katie, and we said our goodbyes. I fastened us both in our seats and made a fast track to my parent's house, over an hour away.

I arrived with Katie, still in her princess costume. I walked around the side of my parents' house to the back deck to see my dad sitting at the head of the outdoor table. I pulled up a chair in front of him and asked him what had happened. He was obviously uncomfortable with my assuming the position of someone in authority during the conversation, but I couldn't stop myself. I had two long, painful years of heart treatments and cardiology terminology with my husband, and I rebuked the idea that my father was just going to ignore what he had to do to take care of himself. "It's no kind of way to live," was his response to having to take medications every day. I reminded him that Asher did it every day, several times a day. He was confused as to why he had to see a different cardiologist than the one he saw in the hospital the night before. I explained to him that the one that he saw in the ER was there because he was likely the surgeon on duty that night, and he was there to determine if my dad needed an immediate procedure. I also pointed out all of the questions he would need to ask the new cardiologist at this appointment on Monday. He bewilderingly refused to accept what had happened to him, but he did agree to go to the doctor's appointment on Monday. Plus, he agreed to take his medications until then. I left some hours later, exhausted from the whirlwind of emotion. My mind reviewed every last detail of my conversation with my mother, the time I spent with my father, and compared and contrasted them with the experiences and feelings I had about Asher's condition over the last two years. The feelings of fright, helplessness, and being overwhelmed were the same.

Katie and I arrived home, and we settled into our evening routine. We had dinner at my parents, so I bathed her quickly and got her settled into bed. She fell fast asleep from all the excitement of birthday parties, dress-up, and our unplanned trip to Nana and Grampy's house. I was relieved to finally have quiet. I wanted to call Asher and tell him what happened but then stopped myself. I didn't want to talk to him about heart stuff while he was on a weekend trip, trying to forget he had heart problems. I decided I would tell him when he got back. I left him a goodnight message and an "I love you," watched a little television, had a good cry, and went to bed. Upon settling into bed, I prayed for Asher's time with God that weekend, about my dad and his situation, and thanking him for my little Katie. I drifted off seconds after the amen.

The morning came, and I was excited to go to church. It was Sunday, and it was a gorgeous yellow-sunny, warm day. Katie and I got dressed and did our normal beautification routine and headed out to for services. I felt refreshed by the weather. It appeared that summer was making her debut in full glory. I had on my favorite summer cardigan with birds and birdcages on it. It was whimsical, light, and fun. I always felt good when I wore it. The service was uplifting, and as I was leaving, I ran into a dear friend of mine with whom I always enjoyed talking. We chatted about how things were going with Asher and me. She had been one of the members of my small group and was there during my explosion of emotion some weeks before.

My cell phone rang; it was Asher. I pressed the Ignore button on the phone because my friend and I were wrapping up our conversation. I couldn't remember if he was coming home that day or on Monday. I finish my conversation and got into the car with Katie. We headed to the carwash as was my ritual on Sundays and called him on the drive. I was dismayed that I didn't get him live, but, rather, I had to leave a message. I asked when he would be home, told him we were looking forward to having him home, and that we were headed into the wash and that I would talk to him later.

Katie squealed and giggled at the spraying water and bubbles all over the car. After the wash, we headed home, had lunch, and nap time. All the windows in my house were open, and I was breathing in the warm, sweet-smelling air. I hadn't realized I was tired, but somehow I fell asleep on my loveseat next to my bay window. It was a lazy Sunday afternoon on a perfectly created day.

Four

"Even perfect days can end in rain." -Francesca Battistelli

I was startled awake by the sound of my daughter crying as she woke from her nap. My excess grogginess and inability to snap to attention told me that we had been sleeping for a long time. I scanned the room for the clock. We had slept for three and a half hours! Trying to rally, I shook my head to straighten my stagger as I made my way down the hallway to Katie's room. I plucked her from her bed and carried her out to the living room.

I settled on the love seat again, and as I set her down on her feet, I noticed she had a piece of lollipop in her hair from the treat I gave her after church. My sleepy brain searched for information on removing sticky lollipops from hair. I knew peanut butter works to get gum out, but did it do the same for lollipops?

As I fingered the sticky lock of hair trying to see what I could gently pry free, I heard a car pull into the driveway. I leaned over to get a full view from my bay window. It was just a police cruiser. Our house was the last house on this street in the town, so turning around in our driveway was a usual occurrence. The police routinely patrolled my rural street in search of speeders. I turned my attention back to the sticky situation my daughter was in. Then I heard the car door to the cruiser shut. The officer was making his way down my walkway toward my door. I was still unfazed as I let go of Katie's hair and headed to greet him. A pair of officers had shown up unexpectedly at night the week before asking if we had dialed 911, thinking they were in the next town. I had assumed this visit would be a repeat of last week and opened the door with a smile and greeted the officer.

"Are you Sariah Diersch?" the officer asked in a purposeful voice.

"Yes, I am," my tone reflected inquisitiveness.

"May I come in?" he asked, leaning in to let me know it really wasn't an option.

"Of course," I replied.

My heart pounded, and sweat dewed my upper lip as I led him out of the doorway and into the house. Standing between my living room and my kitchen island, I turned to face him. All I could think was, "What did I do? I was in church all morning!" He faced me and paused for what felt like a decade. As he moved his hand over his gun, I thought I was about to be arrested. Was he really going to arrest me in my own home in front of my toddler? His voice lowered as he locked his body like a statue with his full attention toward me. He zeroed in on my face. I felt weak from panic. What was going on?

"I have some news. It's bad; it's really bad." I strained to hear his quiet tone over the confused voices in my mind.

My mind went to Asher, possibly on his way home from Maine. Had he been in a serious accident? The thought formed in my mind but I didn't have a chance to ask any questions because a split second later, the officer delivered his third sentence, "Your husband passed away this afternoon."

I don't have the resources to describe how hearing those words affected me and be able to bring some justice to the emotions behind them. I felt like an avalanche of snow had just covered my body. My mind sounded like an ocean wave as I rocked and tried to digest the information. "I need to sit down."

I found the couch and plunked down. I tried to speak. I had questions, but I was so overcome all I could do was wail and sob. I lost fifteen minutes of reality to absolute grief. I don't know who was there, what was said, or where Katie was. I vaguely remember her standing in the middle of the living room, staring at the two of us, having no idea how much her life had just changed since that morning.

My mind broke off its chaos for a moment, and I stopped crying. I had to call someone. It occurred to me that I needed someone there. I announced to the officer that I needed to make a phone call and walked over to my kitchen island to get to my cell phone. I was desperate to reach out to someone but who? My mind was racing again and I couldn't focus. I fumbled with the phone, but I couldn't focus on a single name or face of anyone in my contact list. Who did I need to talk to?

I instinctively dialed my parents' number. My dad picked up. I relayed the information to him between sobs. He announced that he would be right over. He didn't even say goodbye before he hung up. I was relieved that he was on the way, but it would take him an hour to get to me. My mother was much farther away, visiting a friend, so I wasn't sure when she'd arrive. I frantically thought about someone else to call. I needed someone, anyone, to be there with me. I didn't want to be alone. Who was nearby? Who was home? My brain could not complete a thought pattern no matter how hard I tried to focus. I was frustrated by my own inability to think clearly. I dialed my supervisor from work. She lived right down the street, but she didn't answer. I looked at the clock and realized it was time for evening services at my church, so no one from church would be home. I called my pastor's home anyway and left a message knowing he would call back as soon as he was able. I had to sit tight and wait for my dad to come.

I looked at the poor officer standing motionless in front of my kitchen island. I somberly announced that the only person I could get a hold of was an hour away. He asked if there was anyone else at all that I could reach out to, but there wasn't any that I could think of. He contacted his dispatch from the portable radio on his shoulder. He informed the dispatcher that he was staying with me until someone else arrived. I was so grateful for his generosity. The idea of sitting by myself and drowning in my grief was one of the most dreadful and agonizing things I could think of doing.

We looked at each other silently for a brief moment, and then I spoke. "Thank you for being here. I really need someone here." I am sure he could hear the desperation in my voice amongst the steady stream of tears.

"This is one of the hardest things there is to do in this job. I've only had to tell a young wife this once before in my sixteen years on the force."

Hearing this made me humanize him. I didn't think of how difficult this must be for him to interrupt a woman and her sweet little toddler on a beautiful Sunday afternoon to bring information that would shatter their lives forever. The weight of it must have been incredible during the two-mile drive from the police station to my home. I now had the presence of mind to take him in. He was less than average height, very dark hair, and deep brown eyes. He had a kind face. He didn't look like he'd been out of the academy for more than a few years, let alone sixteen. He informed me that he had a wife and two children of his own and that he only lived a couple of miles from me. The information was comforting, even if it seemed a bit random and out of place. He wanted to let me know that he was a real person, too, not just a uniform.

"Didn't someone call you?" he asked.

I looked at my cell phone call list and checked for a voicemail, but there was nothing. I also went to my home phone, but no calls had come in while I was sleeping and no indication of a message there either.

"No, nothing," I said as strained through tears to see the numbers on my phone. "I've been home all afternoon, too."

I don't know what made me say what came out of my mouth next but it amazed me. In all of this turmoil, my thoughts turned to God, His presence in my suffering, and His presence in this officer. "Would you want to call me?" I looked at him with my eyebrows raised.

"No," was all he said.

"Me neither," I said. "No one was supposed to call me. You are a God appointment. You were supposed to be here." I held confidence in my voice.

"I can't imagine getting this news over the phone here by yourself," he added. "I am glad I can be here with you."

"You know, people wonder why I believe what I believe as a Christian," I blurted out the words, not really knowing where this was going. "I feel so comforted by the fact that my husband is now in Heaven, despite the pain of him being gone. I know God is with me in this as well, He is with me now, and this proves it." I kept going. "My church family is meeting right now, but as soon as service is over, there will be a whole bunch of people here. It is so great to have a wonderful church to share your life with, especially at times like this." I didn't know what to say next, so I just looked at his face and awaited a reply. He seemed honestly encouraged by my words. I was not hopelessly lost in despair, even with the news. I think that shocked him a bit. I told him about my church in town and asked him if he knew where it was.

"West Street, right?" he asked.

I confirmed the address. "It's a great church. The pastor is terrific. Not preachy, but he knows his stuff, and he loves to teach people the Bible."

Something said my work was done there. The officer turned his mind and attention to my little girl. She had been standing in front of us, fixing her eyes on the policeman's uniform. I suddenly realized that Katie had been there amongst all this without a peep. Even in her toddler mind, she must have felt the gravity of the situation.

He smiled down at her brightly and said, "Hi there!" Katie smiled a little, but she was confused. I walked around him and picked her up so she could get a better look at him and know that he was "okay." I instructed her to say hi, and the three of us talked about the police and how they help people. I told her that this friendly police officer was here to help us and that if she ever needed help she should find someone who had clothes on just like him.

He let me know that the department was aware of my husband's death, and since I lived in a more remote area of the town on a big, secluded plot of land, they would be spending extra time patrolling the neighborhood. He instructed me to call if there was any reason that I wanted them there. That was such a blessing to hear. I really didn't like being home alone with Katie, even just overnight. It was too quiet. I knew he'd refuse, but I offered him a drink or to sit down. As I thought, he politely declined. He spent a whole hour on his feet waiting for a friend or family member of mine to arrive. I felt indebted to him for that.

As I walked Katie toward the living room to sit down, I saw my dad pull up in his truck in front of the house. I sighed with relief to see someone whom I loved finally come to my rescue. The truck lurched as he quickly came to a stop. Not bothering to walk around my post and rail fence to the walkway, he hopped over it and ran to my door, which by now I had come to and opened for him. He practically ran into me and grabbed me into a big bear hug when he reached the top of the stairs. He was softly crying and telling me how sorry he was. We embraced for a moment, and he gathered himself together emotionally and broke away toward the inside of the house. I followed him in, and the police officer who had so dutifully stayed with me once again expressed his condolences and left. My dad asked me what happened, but I only had scattered details at that time. I was still awaiting some kind of word from one of his friends he was on his weekend with. What I knew is that he had been found by some passersby on the road. He was face down, and his friend's dog was with him. He had been out walking Mike's dog. I knew what that meant. He had a heart attack.

My heart skipped a beat as I thought of his two friends, Mike and Rick. I imagined what it must have been like to have this all take place, especially on their weekend away. This weekend was meant to help each other through some difficult times, not add to them. I wondered if they didn't want to call or if they were afraid to tell me what had happened. I really wanted to hear from them, to tell them it was okay, and that I was so sorry they had to go through this. I ached for their pain, too. As much as I needed comfort, I wanted to comfort them all the more. I wished I had a number to reach them, but I didn't even know what town they were in so I couldn't call information. I just had to wait until one of them called me.

My brother showed up minutes after my dad. I was surprised and wondered how fast he must have been driving to arrive in that short of time living a half-hour north of my parents' house. I was just glad he was okay, given that realization. He came in and headed straight for me to hug me. He didn't say anything; he just cried into my shoulder. He didn't have to. I knew what he would have wanted to say. My mother arrived sometime later. I was so happy to see her face and so was my daughter. Katie has always had a special bond with her Nana. I am sure Katie was in need of comfort and a feeling of security, too. My mom scooped Katie up and greeted her with hugs and kisses through her mist of tears. My poor baby was getting lost in the shuffle of people and the outpouring of emotion.

It is my dad's nature to want to be useful in times of great stress. He offered to make phone calls and asked for contact information. I forced my mind to concentrate, and I rattled off some names of family members he could call. I included some of Asher's family members except my father-in-law. I didn't know what to do about him. He was very close to Asher. However, he was in his eighties and had already lost his wife some years ago. I didn't know how to break it to him in a way that would soften the blow. I fretted about it and searched for the best way to get the news to him.

While I was pondering over my father-in-law, the phone rang. It was my pastor. He asked what happened related to the brief but emotional message I left for him. He prayed right then and there and said he'd be right over. Within minutes, two carloads of pastors, elders, and women from my church were pulling into my driveway.

I walked out to them as the sound of car doors broke the silence. I tried to say something, but as I opened my mouth to speak, I let out a wail and fell to my knees in a pile of grief. My church family enveloped me and began praying. I found such solace in their pleas to God. I was soothed by their touch as they laid hands on me collapsed on the pavement. It felt hot, and I was uncomfortable, but I couldn't move. The hurting in my soul paralyzed my movement, and I knelt there until they finished. I didn't realize my dad was watching all of this from the end of the walkway. Since he is not a Christian, I was encouraged a little that he had gotten to see fervent prayer in action. My pastors raised me to my feet, and we went inside.

The issue of notifying my father-in-law was still pressing on my conscience. I didn't want him to try and drive himself over to my house after getting the news because I knew he would be in a state of shock and denial. I expressed my anxieties to my pastors. They promptly offered to go tell him and bring him to my home. I was so relieved to not be the one to tell him and that he was going to be brought to me.

My father had resumed making calls, and when he was done with his list of people, he asked me what else he could do. I gave him a couple more assignments knowing full well that he needed to feel like he was accomplishing something for his own sanity. I didn't need the things done that I assigned to him, but it was something I could do for him that would let him feel like he was helping.

The women who arrived busied themselves immediately. They bustled around my house like a coordinated team. In my kitchen, they quickly pieced together snacks and coffee to put out for guests. Others brought out tissues, entertained Katie, and tidied the house. People tried to talk to me, but I couldn't focus on a conversation without an overflow of tears. I zoned in and out of what was going on around me. I wanted to find a solitary place, but no one would leave my side. I was both annoyed and grateful at the same time. People from church came and went. As the news circulated following the service, people called and asked what they could do. Others brought food. No one had an appetite, but it's what you do when someone dies, I guess.

I saw my father-in-law arrive amid the sea of faces and bustling bodies. One of his sons drove him over and the pastors followed in their vehicle. I was worried that he would be mad at me for not bringing the news myself, but he understood. He sat, silent and dazed, as my brother-in-law nervously spouted random things to the guests around him, unable to settle into the news himself. Coffee was poured, and I welcomed a cup. I needed the caffeine stimulation. I was already wearing down from all the crying and emotions blowing around like leaves in my head. I knew it would be a very long night.

Finally, the phone rang with the news I was so desperate to hear. It was from Mike, Asher's friend. I could tell from his disorganized opening remarks that he didn't know where to start. He launched into a chronological monologue of the events of that day. He told me how he and Rick were going golfing, and despite their efforts to convince Asher, he wouldn't go. Instead, he opted to take some time alone and play with Mike's dog. The plan was to call from the golf course to tell Asher when they'd be done so he could meet them in town for lunch. They became concerned after a few calls to both Asher's cell phone and the cottage phone went unanswered. They went back to the cottage to find Asher. Upon their arrival at the house, they found it empty. No Asher and no dog. Figuring he'd taken the dog to the lake, they headed for the shoreline several feet from the back porch, down a path to the dock. They were sure he'd be there, but he wasn't.

They walked along the lake until they ran into some neighbors and asked if they had seen a man with a dog recently and described Asher's attire. My heartbeat was audible in my ears as he continued on with the story. I wanted to tell him to stop, but I needed to hear what had happened more than I needed to stop the anxiety of learning Asher's demise. The neighbors gingerly asked them not to be alarmed but that the local police had found a body on the road up the hill that fit Asher's description. With that news, they ran up the hill to the road. There they found a crew of police and staff surrounding a scene.

They approached and urged the group of officers to tell them what had happened and if they knew who the person was. They refused. It was now an investigation, and the two friends had become intruders. They were questioned about their relationship to what was now visibly their deceased friend. It was a blessing to me to learn that the dog had never left Asher's side and was found lying next to him, protecting Asher's body. After a long wait, many questions, and identification being exchanged, they were allowed to move in to see him.

On the other end of the phone, Mike broke down. I knew this was extremely difficult for him to relay all this to me. Listening to the events being described let me know how painful this was for them. I tried to comfort him through my tears, but I couldn't. We were both suffering as we let the information settle.

I had one last question, "Was he facing toward or away from the house, Mike?"

He seemed jarred by the question. "Away," he answered.

"Then he never saw it coming," I said.

I knew Asher would have tried to go back to the house if he wasn't feeling well. It would be a natural reaction to go back and take it easy. He never had an opportunity to realize that anything was amiss. It struck me that he had probably called me within minutes before his passing. His voicemail was cheery from earlier that day, so he left me no indication that he thought anything was wrong even then. I hated the thought of him dying alone, though. I could hardly stand the thought of his body lying strewn on the side of the road waiting for someone to notice. I felt he deserved more dignity than that. Mike told me he and Rick would be at my house the next afternoon to bring his things. That ended our conversation. Now I had the details. Did I really want them? Yes, but it compounded my grief.

Nothing about the day truly set in. It felt dreamlike. It was as if someone pushed me into a rabbit hole like *Alice in Alice in Wonderland* and now I had to find my way back to the real world. I was having trouble grasping ahold of any information I was receiving. I am sure it was my mind's way of protecting me. I felt more confused by the hour, unable to grasp the finality of what had happened.

As the evening progressed, I thought of Asher's extensive network of friends. Asher was a very popular guy. I'm certain the word "gregarious" was developed especially for him because it was the best word to describe how he related to others. He loved to be around people. He would often lament how time, age, and life changes prevented his friends and him from getting together as often as they used to. He took it personally, as he was sensitive beyond what people knew of him. I would pang with empathy when he felt that way because I knew what his friends meant to him. He took each relationship to heart.

I thought of this as I realized I needed to start letting people know. Where did I even start? I thought of who would know the most people in certain groups of friends and who would be willing to make calls for me. I started with a childhood friend of his who would know the guys he grew up with. Each call to a designated friend seemed more and more strange. I didn't want to utter the words. I asked them to make phone calls for me; no one refused. Everyone said the same thing: "Call me if you need anything." I'd grow to hate that phrase. With the responsibility of phone calls designated to friends, I sat down to relax.

I had been standing all day, pacing, standing, pacing, standing. I couldn't be still. My back and feet were starting to remind me that my body wasn't immune to exhaustion. I sat. The house quieted as visitors dispersed for the night. My brother went home; mom and dad remained. My father fielded calls for me as they came in. I overheard one conversation as my dad asked who was asking for Asher. He had informed the person on the other end of the phone that Asher had passed. Then my dad ask the caller if they wanted to speak to me. I took the phone immediately. It was the best man from our wedding and one of Asher's closest friends, Jack.

I crumbled when I heard his voice. He was confused. He had called because he had heard something happened to Asher, but he didn't know what it was. I was devastated that he had to hear to the truth from my father. I wished I would have thought to tell him, but the damage was already done. He asked questions, and I answered as best he could. He seemed unable to get his mind around the information as well. He asked if he could please come over. He needed to make sense of this. I agreed, knowing it would be a solace to have him here. My father made his goodbyes known and headed back home. It was just mom and me, waiting for Jack. The tension was enormous. I had no idea how I was going to greet him or console him when anyone was helpless to do the same for me. It was too much to take in.

Jack came in without knocking and made his way to the kitchen. By now, my mother and I had started making what was the only alcoholic beverage in the house into drinks - vodka and lemonade. I made him a drink without a word. I knew he'd want one. I started reliving the events of the day as the alcohol settled in, dulling my emotions. I was exhausted, but I couldn't wind down. I was grateful for the company so I could stay awake. I didn't want to face the day that was coming in just a few short hours.

We drank and shared stories about Asher. Unexpectedly, Jack started sobbing. We both shared tears and hugs, and he decided he would head home. I urged him to stay at my house as we had several drinks by then. He politely refused, but I got out a pillow and a blanket and set up a bed on the couch. When he staggered getting off of the kitchen chair, he reluctantly agreed to stay. Mom had already been sleeping, and now I needed to make my way to my dark, lonely bedroom. I used to love having the bed to myself when Asher was away, but the realization that I would always have the bed to myself was more than I could bear. I laid down without undressing and tossed the comforter over myself. Exhausted and intoxicated, I started to cry. I buried my head into my pillow so no one would hear me. I don't know if it was the vodka or the emotion, but I vomited into a blanket on the floor and suddenly fell asleep.

The next morning came too quickly, as one could imagine. I awoke to the sound of Katie stirring in her bed, asking for me. There were the sounds of my mother shuffling toward her bedroom door, urging her to be quiet so Mommy could sleep but alas, too late.

The haze of last night's booze and the emotional hangover made the ugliness of awaking on my first full day of widowhood even worse than I thought. I rousted, threw on a bathrobe, and slowly breached my bedroom doorway. My mother apologized for waking me, but it really wasn't her or Katie. I probably would have awoken to the sound of a pin drop from the simmering anxiety. Coffee was promptly made, and I downed the last of the lemonade for hydration, sans vodka. Poor Jack, who was a confirmed bachelor and not used to young children waking him at 6:00 AM, pleaded with a very excited Katie to let Uncle Jack sleep but to no avail. He jutted straight up, folded his blanket, and said goodbye.

"Call me if you need anything."

I think it is what people say when they don't know what to say. I couldn't even tell anyone what I needed. I needed my husband, but no one I could call was going to do that for me, not even God.

I nodded to Jack and let him walk himself out.

It was Monday, the beginning of the work week, but not for Asher or me. I was hit with the notion that I needed to call my boss and Asher's office to tell them what had happened. The very idea made me nauseous. I grabbed the receiver and started dialing my supervisor's number. I was hoping she wouldn't pick up, but she answered. I started crying the second I had to say anything. I cleared my throat and told her quickly that Asher had passed, and I wouldn't be in for the rest of the week. She asked a few questions about what needed done at the office and asked me not to worry about work. She would see to my team and any outstanding business. We exchanged call-ending pleasantries and wound down the conversation.

"Call me if you need anything."

I answered that I would, of course, knowing full well that I wouldn't. The next call was to my husband's office. I didn't know what would happen or how to find the right person in a gigantic Boston-area hospital. I was struggling to remember the names of his coworkers and supervisors when I dialed the main number. After several attempts to reach someone, I finally managed to speak to his department director. She already knew what had happened, which was both a relief and a mystery. I never asked how she could have possibly known.

"Call us if you need anything."

With the difficulties of job-related phone calls over, I now lacked purpose in my morning. I turned my thoughts to the emptiness of the house. I instinctively started picking up, not so much for the sake of the mess but to occupy my mind. The phone rang, and I was told that my in-laws would be over to come to get me and take me to the funeral home for the arrangements. *There is nothing I want to do less than make arrangements for my husband's funeral*, I thought. I signaled with "okay," acknowledging the plans for later. I went back to my sorting and shuffling of paper goods and plastic-wrapped goodies that kind people left for visitors to snack on.

Calls, flowers, food, and balloons filed in my door by the armload that day. I was overwhelmed by the response and outpouring of condolences and well-wishes. Trays of lasagna and presents for Katie covered my kitchen island. I just watched people come in and out all day. One of the most beautiful things about that day was the women from church. A team of them descended on my home mid-morning and started cleaning and doing laundry. They didn't ask what to do, they just got busy without a word. Others just came by to cry, pray, and sit with me. Still more entertained Katie; that is, when they could pry her free of my mother. I was unable to do anything. I didn't even shower. I didn't care. I just had to get through the day. I threw on something clean to wear, not caring if it even matched, and pulled my hair into a ponytail on top of my head. Someone else got Katie dressed, fed, and washed.

In the next few weeks, there would be days on end that all I could do was exist, but someone was always there to tend to me, my daughter, and my home. I was like a ghost floating from room to room, unable to do anything but breathe and cry. How grateful I was to my church women for their service to my family. Most of all, I was thankful for the Christ-like love that was poured out on us. My non-believing friends and family marveled and commented at how amazing the people from my church were. I was so glad that they got to see John 13:34-35 in action:

"A new command I give you: Love one another. As I have loved you, so you must love one another. By this, all men will know that you are my disciples, if you love one another." John 13:34-35 NIV

Will my church family ever know what a substantial impact they had on the non-believers around me? I don't know, but many a conversation about my church and God followed those weeks. I was so grateful for their faithfulness in demonstrating Christ's love for us through their actions. Despite my sorrows, I still spoke honestly about God, answered questions, and talked about my own hope in Christ. It seemed to be the only thing that lightened my mood. I got to share pieces of my spiritual life with both believers and non-believers. My circumstances, while desperate and uncertain, still had hope in God. I clung to that realization with every God conversation I had with people who asked.

I was surprised that morning to get a call from the State of Maine Coroner's Office. It was all very official, a stark contrast against all the other calls of sympathy and love that day. They wanted to know if I'd be asking for an autopsy.

"Given the history of his condition, I know what he died from, so I don't need an autopsy," I informed the faceless voice on the other end of the phone. I described the nature of Asher's condition.

"We'll need to speak to his cardiologist," he ordered in reply.

I gave him all of his doctor's information and said that I was sure that he'd be willing to speak to him. Somewhere in the conversation, he spoke of sending Asher's body to the state's capital for the procedure. He said to expect it to take over a week. I had no intention of waiting that long to see him and say goodbye. I needed to see Asher looking like he did the day he left for his long weekend. It was strange to think that was only a few days ago.

Later that afternoon, I got a call from his cardiologist. My tension was alleviated to both hear his voice and to know that he had been informed of Asher's death. He was sympathetic and told me that the coroner was satisfied with the information he received and would be releasing his body to the funeral home. I sighed with relief. The State could always demand an autopsy if they wanted to, and there would have been nothing I could do about it. It is often done in cases where young people die unexpectedly. We knew Asher's death was going to happen sooner rather than later, but for the State, a thirty-nine-year-old man dying of a heart attack wasn't ordinary. I saw the merit in their hesitation to release his body.

"We knew this could happen," the doctor said with sadness in his voice.

I started to cry, but I responded with an affirmative moan. "I know," I mustered from my throat.

"I wish I had filed an appeal for his defibrillator," he whispered after a pause.

That sentence slapped me across the face as I inhaled. What did he say? The room spun as I tried to take in that sentence. Why wouldn't he have filed an appeal? Isn't that automatic? It's a piece of paperwork that you fax into the insurance company for crying out loud! It takes minutes! No appeal? I wanted to scream.

"It might have made a difference," he continued.

"We don't know that," I replied. I couldn't believe my own response. The response was correct, but in my mind, Asher was denied the chance to live simply because his doctor didn't do a little paperwork that he could have done. I ended the call abruptly and sat at my dining room table in astonishment. Lunching visitors chewed quietly and stared blankly at me. I didn't even know what to say to them. I couldn't believe what I'd heard.

My in-laws arrived later that afternoon as planned. I looked like a wreck. I hadn't showered, my eyes were puffy from crying, and I hadn't even brushed my teeth. I didn't care. They loaded me into the car, and we were off to the funeral home.

I sat in the grossly-outdated room of a law office that was connected to the funeral home. We sat around a table as questions were asked, and people responded without my input. I sat silently, crying, unable to respond to anything. I had to strain to produce a voice to my choices; otherwise, they were made on my behalf. The man asked to spell Asher's middle name, Alan. His family responded with an incorrect spelling, but I never bothered to correct them. I didn't feel part of the process, and I really didn't want to be either. All I wanted was for it to be over as quickly as possible.

After the agonizing questions were answered and the staggering total was delivered to us as their compensation for preparing my husband's last days above ground, we left. I was returned to my house still buzzing with people. I found an empty seat at my dining room table.

I had the information I wanted - when, where, and at what time I would see Asher's face for the last time. I couldn't wait, and I couldn't wait for it to be over, all at the same time. It was too awful to imagine.

I was directed to pick out his clothes so they could be taken to the dry cleaners the next morning before our visit to my pastor's office. We had an appointment for funeral service arrangements. It was a bit ironic because I had always picked out Asher's clothes when it came to special occasions. He loved to have me put his things together and meet my approval on dress requirements. I put him in my favorite combination of shirt and tie, along with his favorite sport coat. He'd always looked so handsome in that. My heart weighed heavily as I put them into a shopping bag, kissing each piece of clothing.

The meeting with my pastor was a combination of comfort and sorrow. In this aspect of the arrangements, I wanted my say. I wanted the funeral the way I wanted it, and I let everyone there know who was in charge. No one confronted me. I knew his family had a church that they had belonged to for generations. There was no way I was going to let the funeral be held there. Asher's funeral would be held in OUR church. It was the church in which he was saved and baptized. It was the church where our daughter was dedicated to the Lord and the church we attended with people we had grown to love so much. This church was where his final service would be. The church meant the world to him, and he needed to be there for this final rite of passage.

The pastor shared Asher's story of faith with his family during this meeting. I was so grateful and privileged to hear him share it as we sat in his study. More seeds planted in the minds and hearts of non-believers through the death of a child of God. I couldn't think of anything more beautiful than that. After that long conversation in my dear, beloved pastor's office, we returned home once again.

I began to notice a pang in my heart each time I left the house. I hated being separated from Katie. I started to feel these desperate longings to be close to her, to guard her. I needed her presence. Katie was all that I had left of Asher. I yearned for my sweet angel, his beloved daughter. *Oh, my baby girl, will you ever know how so very much your father loved you?* The thought of her growing up not knowing that was a crushing blow to my spirit. Whenever I arrived back home, I scooped her up in my arms, kissed her, and soaked in her smell as I nuzzled into her neck. I pressed her to me as I rocked her back and forth, standing in the hallway near the door. She was the only person who could comfort me.

The days were blurry as I awaited the first round of services; the wake. Seventy-two hours can be the most prolonged hours of your life if you are waiting for something you are dreading. I continued to aimlessly wander my house. People kept coming to offer help and condolences. I was growing weary of guests. I relished the small windows of time where no one was there but me, Katie, and my mom, who wouldn't dare leave me by myself; however, those moments were few and far between. I needed quiet. A dear and trusted church friend who had lost a son to cancer told me from her own experience to let people know when I was done visiting and just to leave the house if I had to. Still, I couldn't muster the courage to tell people to go away. There were times when I so badly wanted to stand on my dining room table and scream at the top of my lungs "Get out! Just get out of here!" I would instead have pockets of time where my mind faded out of what was going on around me. I'd sit and watch people go about my house chatting and eating as if I were an apparition instead of being there.

Sure enough, even though time had slowed to a crawl, the day of the wake arrived. I had to get dressed, fix my hair, and do my makeup. I had done those things every morning for most of my life, but today it seemed such a daunting task. I wanted to look nice but not too nice. After all, I was going to bury my husband. I would see him, but he wasn't going to see me so what difference did it make anyway?

I chose a suit I wore routinely - black pinstripe with a white blouse and gray snakeskin pumps. Those were my favorite shoes. At least I could wear something I enjoyed, and the heels gave me height, so I was satisfied with my choices. I dressed as if for my own funeral, purposefully and painstakingly. Katie's favorite babysitter was coming to watch her. I couldn't fathom taking our daughter to her father's funeral. How do you explain to a toddler that her still, cold father couldn't get up and greet her?

My family arrived in their Sunday dress and milled around the house waiting for me as Katie greeted everyone, unable to understand why all these people had been coming to visit every day. Smiles were cracked as she beamed up at them, chattering in her best toddler speak and waiting for replies from them. She had a way of lightening the mood. Once I was ready, we were off. I was supposed to arrive early so I could have some private time before the mourners arrived. How precious little that time turned out to be.

I thought I'd be fine. Intellectually, I knew Asher was with the Lord and not in his body. It was just his earthly covering. I kept telling myself that as we parked and I walked the long drive to the door of the funeral home. My in-laws arrived before us, so it was just my family and me walking in. I crossed the threshold of the entryway and became unable to move. The realization that Asher was just a hallway away from me froze me in my steps.

The funeral director told me to relax and take a seat for a minute before proceeding. I felt like I was going to faint. My vision tunneled, and I couldn't hear anymore. I sat as directed in response to my failing senses, bewildered by how I felt. After a few minutes, I stood once more and started walking, one foot in front of the other. I got to the room where Asher's open casket was displayed. I turned my head away and sat in the first available chair I could find. I was awash in emotion and anxiety. I didn't know it would be this hard.

Determined to see him, I rose to my feet again, flanked by my parents holding my arms. Their support proved useful because once I saw my husband in full-view, I nearly dropped to the floor from the tsunami of emotion that washed over of me. I wailed as I struggled to take another step toward him. I felt the wave of sobbing in my chest but I was unable to hear myself. My mind raced as I struggled to control my rapid, shallow breath. Still, I didn't want to stop moving. My parents gripped my arms tightly as I pressed on. I finally made it to Asher and knelt beside his lifeless body. At last, we were face-to-face.

He looked the same, like he was sleeping. I wanted him to speak so badly. I wanted to yell at him to get up. My pitiful sobs became agonizing moans of pain. My lips quivered. I was unable to say a word to him. I just looked at him, and stroked his hair. The his lifelessness was startling.

Gaining my composure after a few minutes that seemed like an hour, I rose to my feet and greeted my in-laws. My heart pained in my chest for my father-in-law. I believed he was the only person who was going through more pain than I was. Losing a child, to me, is the most unbelievably brutal thing one can experience. It is a wrenching that you cannot put into words. I could hardly look at his worn, grief-stricken face. His anguish radiated from him. I wanted to be able to comfort him, but I couldn't while facing my own pain. God, alone, would have to be the only comfort him in that moment.

I made my way to the end of the family procession line to my spot. Why I wasn't first, next to my husband, I do not know. No one offered it to me, and I didn't have the strength to ask for it either. I simply found my spot at the end of the line and sat until everyone started arriving.

I pondered what the turnout would be for a few moments until I heard the front door to the funeral home open. So it began. I wouldn't sit or stop crying for over three solid hours. The ribbon of people in line winding around the funeral home and out the door was a sight to behold. It seemed to go on forever. Asher's friends, family, my friends, family, neighbors, Katie's daycare teachers and helpers, church members, past and present co-workers, people I knew, people I didn't know, all there to pay their last respects. Asher was truly a loved man, and I felt very cared for by the visitors.

It was over before I knew it. Miraculously, even with four-inch stiletto heels, my feet felt fine. After the service, a few close friends of the family and mine made their way to a local tavern. I was warmly greeted by the jovial atmosphere inside. It was a respite from the oppression of the last few days, and I was glad for the positive atmosphere. Even in the most barrenness of deserts, sometimes you find an oasis. I enjoyed my late evening. It was only a couple of hours of smiling faces and laughter but it refreshed my soul. In between conversations, I quietly pondered what the next day would bring.

The next morning I arose for one more public appearance as Asher Diersch's widow. There is a celebrity-like air around you in a situation like that. You don't want the attention, but it still gathers around you anyway. I had chosen to give a eulogy at the service. How I was going to accomplish it without breaking down, I didn't know. I didn't write anything down. I wanted God to tell me what to say to these people. I wanted God to speak to them. It might be my last opportunity to tell them who God was to Asher and me and to gain some good through this tragedy.

My church was packed wall-to-wall with people. I stared at the floor as I made my way down the center aisle to my seat at the front. I knew any eye contact would result in an immediate loss of my composure and a meltdown. I lined myself up in the pew alongside my family members and lowered onto my spot on the bench. I had moments of panic, thinking about having to get up the altar stairs with no railings. Would I be able to do that? Would I be able to utter a word anyway?

The funeral service began, and I fixed my attention on the pastors. The associate pastor who had been counseling us at the end of our marriage spoke first. The one thing that stood out for me was the one thing I really needed to hear after all Asher and I had been through. He looked right at my face and said, "Sariah, you need to know that he died loving you."

It burned into my ears. I clung to that statement. With the things that had been said and not said in the last two years, I felt like the most hated person in my house. I believed Asher thought of me as a burden he had to endure. I felt like I had failed him too many times to count and hurt him even more with my lack of sensitivity to his emotional needs. I needed to believe that the words the pastor spoke were true. I needed to believe that the times Asher shared alone with this man, his love for me was what came out of the conversation.

The next speaker was Asher's prayer partner. I had asked him to speak of Asher's spiritual life. He would know it best, and I wanted Asher's friends to hear about the kind of Christian man that he was and what was important to him about God. John delivered a beautiful rendition of Asher's love for God. I was so glad that Asher's friends got to hear the message that Asher would have wanted to give to them himself.

Next, one of his brothers spoke briefly, and then it was my turn. I was brought up to the pulpit by family members, and I was relieved to have help with the stairs. I turned my body and rested it against the pulpit for support. I stared out at the crowd. My thoughts turned to Job, and I began to speak of him.

"No one has suffered more loss in the history of any one man than Job," I began. "He lost his family, his home, his livelihood, everything in one day."

Then I read:

"Naked I came from my mother's womb, and naked I will depart. The Lord gave and the Lord has taken away; may the name of the Lord be praised and in all this, Job did not sin by charging God with wrongdoing" Job 1:21-22 NIV.

I said, "So don't be angry with God. It was Asher's desire to go home to God."

I went on to tell them what they may not have known about my husband. As his wife, I saw a different side of him than his guy friends would have seen. I wanted them to understand the things about him that he would have wanted them to know like how much he valued and loved them. Once I concluded and sat back in my seat, the head pastor delivered his message of hope in Jesus Christ and the Gospel. I was satisfied, believing God would have wanted the service to be just as it was, focused on the love that He has for His people and how He comforts in times of trouble. I wanted everyone to see that I didn't blame or resent God for what had happened. I wanted them to see how I found comfort in Him despite knowing this painful time was part of His deliberate plan.

Five

"Red rain coming down on me." -Peter Gabriel

I spent two weeks pacing my house and looking homeless in wrinkled, thrown-on clothes I picked up from my bedroom floor. I totally lacked any beauty regimen other than showering. At this point, I felt it was time to get back into some sort of routine.

I had started Katie back on her routine the week before. It occurred to me that having her out of it too long was not having a good effect on her. Not to mention, I was not interacting with her in my usual form. Serving pudding for breakfast because I couldn't deal with the repercussions of irrational toddler requests was not helping either one of us. Her social interactions included staring at me or being entertained by the television. I figured it was in her best interest to get back to daycare with her friends and back to having fun and real social interaction.

A week after returning Katie to daycare, I realized my depressed emotional state was scaring me. I wanted to get out of it. I called my boss and told her I'd be back that following Thursday.

"Are you sure?" She implored.

"Yes, I need to come back to work, I'm going crazy," I said.

I'm positive she heard anguish in my voice but she wanted to make sure I had enough time to grieve. "You can take all the time you need, you know," she stated.

I refused the additional time and looked forward to getting out of my house again. My father had triple bypass surgery on the Wednesday before I returned to work. Initially, he had been scheduled for a balloon stint the previous week, but the surgeon decided he needed something more evasive upon beginning the procedure. I called my supervisor to let her know that I'd be late on Thursday so I could see my dad in the hospital. Naturally, she agreed.

I numbed as I walked into the hospital to find his room. I didn't know what to expect when I saw him. He was such a rugged, do-it-all kind of guy. The idea of my dad in a fragile state in the ICU sent my anxiety through the roof.

My emotions were nearing panic as I felt my hands begin to shake and my knees grow weak as I rode the elevator to the correct floor. It was all I could do to breathe normally. I stepped out and rang an intercom for the nurses to let me into the locked unit. I found his room, inhaled, paused, and peered in. He was awake and had just been served a light breakfast. He was quiet and weakened. I found him struggling to open a cardboard milk container for his cereal. I helped him fix his breakfast and tried not to ask too many questions while I choked back my emotions. The visit was brief, but it calmed me because I could see for myself that he was feeling okay. I asked him to rest and went off to my office across the Charles River. I retrieved my car from the adjacent parking garage, sat down, and cried. The ocean of anguish was overcoming me. I needed to collect myself and return to my work. I needed anything to just feel normal for a couple of hours.

I arrived at my office and was greeted excessively by my coworkers and office mates. I didn't like the attention. I didn't want to be reminded of Asher, his death, or to talk about how I was doing. I tried to go incognito - blend in and find respite in some normalcy. I was briefed by my supervisor on the status of business and client reports so I knew where to start. I was ready to dig in and put things out of my mind for a few hours, but I was hampered by the cloud of emotion I felt hanging over my head. I kept trying to ignore it, but it hung there despite my efforts.

The day ended too quickly. I was glad to get Katie and spend time with her. The longing I felt in my heart when I wasn't with her was almost unbearable. I needed to see that she was all right. I had moments in my prayer time where I would beg God through tears to let me keep her. "Please don't take her, too," I would plead. The paranoia of losing her made my mind swirl irrationally at times. Coming on the heels of losing Asher, I didn't know what to expect from God in terms of gifts and mercy. Nothing felt sacred. After all, He could take whatever He wanted. He could take whatever was His, and I suddenly had the stark realization that everything was His. In my mind, it became a matter of convincing Him to let me keep certain things, namely my daughter. I was gaining a great sense of God's omnipotent power and sovereignty, but I was losing the feeling of his great love and kindness by the day.

I made it through my first two days back at work. I felt a little relief in getting dressed for the office, and I had a sense of purpose back in my day beyond the thought *Simply get through today.*

The weekend came, and I was slated to attend an engagement party for a dear friend of mine that Saturday night. My mom, albeit her husband in the hospital, wanted to take Katie for the night. "Do you really think you are up for this?" I wanted to make sure she wasn't taking on more than she could handle. I think she wanted the company in her quiet house and to be close to her only grandchild in her own time of grief. We agreed to meet at the hospital when we both went to visit my dad. From there she would take Katie back home with her.

My worries started building up my anxiety again. I wasn't keen on being alone in an empty house for the first time. I wasn't sure how I would manage my first social gathering this early on either but needed to celebrate something nice. A gathering for a close friend getting married, surrounded by people I knew and loved for an event that was not about my dead husband or me, was more than welcome.

A call early that Saturday morning came from my mother. My father's lung had collapsed during the night. The doctors needed to put a chest tube in to drain the fluid and release the pressure it was putting on his heart. I could feel my heartbeat quicken as I heard her speak these words to me. My jaw slacked, and I could feel a tingling in my ears as I struggled to focus and ask questions. Trying to regulate my breathing, I paused and asked if it was really a good idea for me to bring Katie to the hospital. She tried to reassure me, and I almost canceled last minute. There was a moment where I acknowledged this could be the beginning of the end for my father, and I wanted him to see Katie and me. I needed to see him one last time.

I dismally collected the two of us and our belongings, settled us in the car, and set out for Boston. When I arrived at the hospital, I saw that my father had been moved to another room since I last saw him. This floor was busy, noisy, and cluttered. I was annoyed by the chaos. I found his semi-private room and looked over at him, sitting silently in the chair next to his bed with IVs and apparatus extending from his body. I was shocked at the sight of him. He was too weak to talk, and it was clear to me that he was both heavily medicated and tired. I asked if he was in pain, and he nodded in the affirmative. My mother walked my chatty, excited toddler out of the room so we could have some time alone, but I was the only one talking. I could hardly stand to look at him in this condition, so I fixed my eyes on the floor as I leaned back on the edge of his bed. Despite a sense of alarm and dysphoria, I tried to organize my thoughts and talk about cheerful things. He started to nod off, and in the next moments, my mother returned with Katie. I told him we would go; he looked like he wanted to sleep. We all kissed him goodbye and filed out of the room as the nurses came in to attend to him.

As I was transferring Katie's things from my car to my mom's, I begged her to tell me if she was not up for babysitting. She kept repeating that she was fine to take Katie. I buckled Katie into her car seat, and watched them drive away, sick to my stomach over my visit with my dad. The daydreams of losing my father amongst the pain of mourning my husband were unpalatable as I headed back home. I was drowning in dread.

I arrived at a friend's house to drop something off, already dressed for my night out at the engagement party. She was the wife of one of Asher's closest friends. My blanched look prompted her to ask what was going on. We sat at her kitchen table and she asked if I wanted a glass of wine. We talked and had another. Her husband came home from work and joined us. I gave up on the idea of the engagement party to stay and talk, cry, and comfort each other.

Later that evening, after the wine wore off, I headed home to my dark, lonely house. There was no one there but me. I checked for messages, but there were none. I knew my mom would still be awake so I called to see how the night went with Katie. Mom said there was nothing to report. Katie was sleeping.

Unable to figure out what to do with myself, I readied for bed. Sitting in the middle of the bed, I read my Bible as I did nightly and started praying the routine prayers I usually recited to God. Then something changed and

I started talking to Him. I poured out my heart and everything on my mind. Tears rained on my hands in my lap as I went on, begging him to spare my father.

Next, my thoughts turned to Asher and how our relationship was left in the last few months before his passing. "Does he know, Father, how sorry I am?" I pleaded, "Does he know?" I was desperate for Asher's understanding and forgiveness. I also needed God's forgiveness. I needed to know that Asher knew and understood the "Hows and Whys" and that his resentment had been put to rest. I needed to not feel like a criminal in my marriage any more. I needed to be set free of the guilt I had in my heart for failing so miserably as Asher's wife. I exhausted myself in the conversation and said, "Amen."

My father rallied the next day and was able to go home a couple of short days following. I was grateful to God sparing my father. A little break in the trauma was felt by everyone now that the worse part of my father's surgery was over. The only problem was I had no one to focus on. No one and nothing was in crisis except me. All around me, life was going on as it always had. The novelty of returning to work was wearing off, and Katie and I were trying to acclimate to our new life as a family of two. Asher had always picked Katie up from daycare because his work days ended earlier than mine. Her routine with her dad was now replaced with me running in the front door of the center in the last seconds before it closed to retrieve her. There were plenty of times when I was a few minutes late. Katie was at daycare from the minute it opened until the time it closed every day. I felt so guilty. I wondered how she felt about it. I wished there was more help but I lived an hour away from the closest family. I felt so alone. No one could help me with her unless it was absolutely necessary to make the drive. I thought we would grow used to the new schedule and be okay with it in time. I pressed on in the weeks ahead no matter how oppressive it started to feel. I figured this was how single moms did it and that I should stop whining about my new life.

Saturdays were no better. They consisted of the piles of laundry I had no time for during the week, a gambit of errand running, grocery shopping, and Katie's mid-day nap. In no time at all, we would find ourselves at the dinner table and winding down the day. Sundays were church and the possibility of a visit to my parents or a play date. That was the only fun we got to have. I loved going to church on Sunday as I always had but even that had changed. I sensed the singularity of walking in, just Katie and me, and finding a seat by myself. I watched the happy faces of couples coming in, greeting one another, and finding their usual spot in a pew. I pretended to look occupied so no one would ask how I was doing.

I hated that phrase. "How are you doing?" How would anyone expect me to be doing? How would they be doing in a situation like mine? Did they really want to know how lonely I felt, how remorseful I was about our marriage's condition when he died? Did they care to hear how tired I felt all the time? I told them what they wanted to hear anyway, "I'm doing okay." Next would come to my favorite closing remark, "Call me if you need anything." Just once I wanted to say to some poor unsuspecting person, "If I didn't call you for anything before, why would I call you now?" I would think about that sometimes and chuckle. It would be mean, and I know that people say those phrases because they don't know what to say or how to help. The fact of the matter is they are the least helpful things someone can say next to "I know how you feel." I wanted to tell people, "You can't possibly know how it feels, no matter how hard you try," but, of course, I never did.

I would sit in my pew after everyone sat down and remember the arm that used to come around me as we fixed our posture and got comfortable before the service would start. Now, I tried not to sit too close to anyone. I focused on setting my things under my legs and reading the church bulletin before the music would start. I rarely initiated or engaged in a conversation. I hated the empathetic looks I got when people would say hi or look over at me sitting there, alone. Some would pretend they weren't really looking at me; others would extend a nod and a sympathetic smile. Either way, it conveyed the same message - a reminder that this was my reality and they were glad it wasn't theirs.

After services, I would dash as fast as I could out of the sanctuary and the lobby to retrieve Katie from the children's church in the next building. I didn't like being inundated with well-wishers, gossips, and the like, all barraging me with questions. It seemed to be a contest of who could get to me first, to grab my arm and pat it, and ask my favorite question again. The phrase "I'm praying for you" offered little comfort. I wondered if they really were or if they just wanted to make me feel better. I would wriggle free as soon as I was caught so I could get on with my precious Sunday hours. I needed those Sunday afternoons before the grueling week started all over again.

Sunday nights, on the other hand, were miserable. I knew the work week was coming. I could do nothing to stop the onslaught of stress and activity that would be mine as soon as the alarm clock rang early Monday morning. I felt my anxiety rise with each passing hour until my bedtime. My cigarette smoking became my friend in the lonely hours at night before bed. I would open my back door and stand in the doorway, dangling my foot off the step and looking up at the stars as I puffed away. Asher wasn't there to tell me not to smoke, but I still detested the smell of cigarette smoke in the house, so I never lit up unabashedly in my home. I'd exhale with each drag and watch the smoke disappear into the night time air, wafting to nowhere and nothingness. I thought smoking helped curb my anxiety when, in reality, it probably added to it. I was too anxiety-ridden to eat a lot of the time; otherwise, I would have preferred ice cream to Marlboro Lights. On rare occasions, I would call a friend as I hung my head and foot out the back, but I preferred to hide, both physically and emotionally. Solitude was both my enemy and my friend. The loneliness never asked how I was doing; it already knew.

Desperate for answers or comfort, my prayer time took on a new attitude. My prayers had become conversational. I needed to verbalize. I poured out my regrets over my treatment of Asher to God. I begged God to tell Asher I was sorry. Somewhere along the way, someone had talked to me about Asher having the full knowledge of God now that he was with Him. That brought me so much healing in terms of my angst. To know that Asher looked at me with a full understanding of what I did and why was comforting. He knew everything that I felt in that time and with total forgiveness in his heart, just like Jesus. I clung to those beliefs in the times I shame threatened to overwhelm me.

I prayed and called out to God about my finances. Without another income, how would I make ends meet? I started the process of finding out about Asher's life insurance policies, annuities, and 401Ks. I barely knew where to start. I had been putting it off, but I needed to address those issues. I dutifully made calls in the coming weeks, found the paperwork, and cried out to the only one who could help - God.

I felt vulnerable at night, alone with my sweet little baby in a big dark house on a secluded lot of land. I prayed for an army of angels to surround and protect my home. I would lay in bed with my eyes closed after I finished praying and imagine glowing men in white with wings and swords drawn, standing at attention in my yard to guard against evil. It brought me peace so I could fall asleep. The rest of my solace came from my home security system and every motion-detecting floodlight on from dusk until dawn.

The Lord was quick to answer prayers and bring many blessings in terms of finances. My days were a flurry of phone calls, receiving packages of paperwork, and resigning myself to spend time every night after Katie went to bed filling out information and sending necessary documents to companies where Asher had holdings and insurances. Unbeknownst to me, there were a lot of other available funds, and letters came in the mail without me notifying them. There was a lot to do, but I had to do it. I was grateful to see that there was a means to take care of money. I needed to pay bills and pay off debts that I could no longer afford without his income. Letters with monetary figures came to my mailbox, and checks started arriving. I compiled a list of what I could financially expect to receive. From that list, I planned what I could pay off and what I needed to supplement the monthly household finances. Everything seemed very manageable. I thanked the Lord both in prayer and tithing. I decided if God provided it to me, it was only fitting that I respond in kind. The more I gave, the more I received. Letters and checks from various companies came in. I even received a letter from one of Asher's former jobs notifying me that I was entitled to his pension through them. I just needed to fill out the forms. I was astounded; I didn't know that was possible.

The principal sum of my financial relief was Asher's life insurance through his current employer. I estimated it to be a normal and customary payout for employer-provided life insurance; two times the annual salary. I was sent my packet from the human resources department and got to filling in this question and checking off that box, compiling official documents, and getting those in the mail for them to process. This sum would pay off all debt we had acquired and pay off my car loan. With those bills out of the way, I could make the monthly bills and mortgage work on my own. I also learned I was entitled to Social Security benefits for Katie. I was pleasantly surprised by what was available to me. It was three times what I was expecting. It gave me great peace of mind knowing I would receive this benefit until she was sixteen. As soon as everything was off in the mail, I just had to wait for replies. I was a little concerned, though, about how Asher's diagnosis would affect any insurance claim I made, namely the life insurance. I tried to put it out of my mind, which was easy considering the heinous daily schedule I kept.

A letter arrived from Asher's life insurance company some weeks later. I retrieved it out of the mailbox as I returned home with Katie one night. It was very thin. My chest tightened. I stared at the envelope as I walked down my driveway to the front door with Katie following close behind me. Had they denied the claim? Could they really do that? I started to tremble. My throat dried as I opened the front door and put our belongings down on the kitchen island. I decided I couldn't open the envelope right then and there. I needed to wait until Katie went to bed in case I had an emotional breakdown. I placed it on the countertop and left it there as I made dinner. I tended to Katie and fixed my attention on the nightly routine. However, as I puttered around my kitchen, I would glance over at the envelope. I tried to refrain from worrying about the awful things it would say if it were a denial letter; at this point, I was convinced it was. I didn't eat dinner that night. I couldn't wait until Katie's bedtime so I could get to the horrifying news about my finances.

With Katie in bed and the house picked up, I went to the kitchen and stood over the envelope sitting on the countertop. I smoothed my hands over my hips and took the envelope to the back door. I suddenly had the urge to smoke. I opened the door and lit up. After a couple of puffs, I decided to get to the business of reading the letter I was convinced would have the worst news I would ever receive regarding my financial future.

I slid my fingertip inside the corner of the envelope and pried the paper open. I removed the tri-fold piece of paper and flipped it open. I didn't get a chance to read it as my eyes were drawn to a figure in the middle of the page in bold print. It wasn't twice Asher's annual salary. It was twice the amount I expected! I started to shake and cry in unbelief at what I was seeing. The letter stated more information would be coming but this amount was my settlement. Once the adrenaline stopped rushing, I called my mother to tell her. I needed to tell someone to make it real. I hung up and swallowed hard. Still drawn to the letter, I reread it. Thank you, Lord Jesus. Thank you.

With my finances in order and debts paid off, I could relax a little bit. I didn't worry about the future so much in terms of keeping a roof over my little girl's head and meeting my monetary obligations. I profusely thanked God nightly for His generosity toward me and my daughter in this way. I thanked Him for His protection over us. I was called to a passage that brought me such great comfort and peace:

"Father to the fatherless, defender of widows- this is God, whose dwelling is holy." Psalm 68:5 NLT

I would find myself meditating on it, thanking God and reminding myself that this is who He is. I felt safe and protected by this verse. I praised God for holding Katie so tightly in the loving grip of His hand. I would find myself drifting off to sleep thinking of this verse, reassured that he was with me in my circumstances.

Like me, my toddler's resiliency started to wane. She complained and cried daily that she didn't like "school" and didn't want to go. I was powerless to do anything to relieve this. I would sometimes sigh over another tantrum she'd throw as I was putting her shoes on, signaling to her that we were about to take on yet another workday, and say, "You know, Katie. I don't want to go either, but I have to." Eventually, she'd calm herself, and we'd head out the door.

The racing, the stress, and the constant rigor of life of single motherhood combined with responsible businesswoman and supervisor was all mounting on my fragile emotional state. The continuous pressure started to have its effects on my sleep. Unable to wind down from the day, I'd stay up later and later just trying to relax, but I was tense all the time. I was continually strategizing on how to make the most of every second of the day, but I never seemed to have enough time for me at the end of it. I was slated to do something at every turn. My hours of sleep dwindled until I was existing on an average of three hours a night. I made up for my lack of rest with more cigarettes and a ridiculous amount of coffee. It seemed like I always had one or the other in my hand. When I could have neither, I suffered anxiety pangs. I was tired and overwhelmed every waking hour. I took myself to the doctor when I started oversleeping a lot. I was having trouble wanting to get out of bed. She promptly prescribed me anti-depressants with the understanding that it was temporary. She stated I needed counseling and an exercise routine if I was going to really be on the mend.

Emotional things improved slightly with the admission that I was exhibiting signs of depression. I was taking the medication as prescribed, but it was only having a minimal effect on my mood and no impact on my sleep. I went back to the doctor with my findings a month later, and she upped my dose of anti-depressants and recommended a sleep aid. I flatly rejected the idea of drugging myself to sleep. I worried that if anything happened in the middle of the night, I would be unaware or too out of it to do anything. I needed to hear Katie call for me. I tried to make the best of it and hoped the increased dose of happy pills would have some effect on my sleeping. It didn't. As the nighttime anxiety increased and I was unable to cope, I started to self-medicate with a glass of wine before bed.

I was warned by another woman, a widow who was older than me, not to drink by myself. She told me about making alcohol her nighttime companion after her children went to sleep. She urged me to not take the path she had taken because it gave her much trouble in the end. I dismissed her words of advice, hocking it up to only being her story, not mine. I have to admit, the nighttime glass soothed my nerves. Wanting to feel even better, I started to have two glasses.

In no time at all, I was having two drinks of whatever was in the liquor cabinet. No wine? No problem. Visitors frequented my house and usually brought alcohol with them and left it in my refrigerator. I didn't have to work hard to find anything in which to partake. When my supply dwindled, I went out for it on Friday nights and stocked up on my wine for the week. I had collected wine before so I started fooling myself that I had started collecting again, as a hobby. I rationalized that reinstating hobbies was an important coping skill for my mental health to battle depression. I was really making sure I had what I needed for those lonely nights in a too-quiet house with me being up too late. I believed the alcohol would make me sleep. It didn't. Instead, it made my nights of scant slumber more restless, and I was even more tired during the day from having alcohol in my system from the night before.

I looked online for websites or a way to communicate with other young widows, but I found no encouragement there. I searched bookshelves for books on being a young widow, but alas, there was nothing to be had on the subject. I did find some general books on widowhood, but they were geared towards older women and the trials they face having never managed finances or a full-time job, let alone ever lived a single life on their own as I had already. They had raised their children. Their stories were not mine. Nevertheless, I picked up one from the bookstore. I was going crazy with the loneliness and feelings of abandonment by my husband and my network of people. The book ended up being really helpful.

The first chapter addressed the fact that I was not going crazy. I found this was a relief. The second chapter told me I was angry. It said there was nothing more dangerous than a widow who doesn't know she is mad about what happened to her. Was I angry? I didn't feel angry. Was I supposed to be angry? That statement had an impact on me and I thought about it constantly. If I were angry, what was I angry about? If I really didn't feel angry, why was I dangerous? I pondered and asked God if I was angry. I wanted to know if I was, considering the harrowing words I read in chapter 2. I decided to put pen to paper and find out whether or not I was angry. I was surprised by what I found.

I realized I did have underlying anger towards Asher. It had been narcissistic of him to spend so much money and to damage his body for the sake of looking a certain way. He once shared with me about his pain of being the tall, skinny teenager who got beat on and ridiculed by his older brothers. I started to realize how going to the gym and becoming the size that he eventually became gave him a very false sense of confidence. When I would ask him to stop doing the steroids and pushing his body so hard, I was literally stripping him of his artificial dignity. The steroids, over time, would wear on his body and damage his heart, completely unbeknownst to him, until it was too late to do anything about it. Without knowing it, he volunteered me to be in this situation and leave his daughter fatherless.

I admitted my anger, but it felt so ugly. I didn't want to feel this way. I wrote letters to Asher, telling him how mad I was and why. I talked to God about it in my prayers. I acknowledged that I was frustrated by Asher's lack of empathy for what could happen and that he was so blasé about how steroids could impact his health. However, even admitting my anger, allowing myself to be mad, and making it known to God and Asher wasn't enough. I couldn't find any answers in it. There was no cosmic breaking of the clouds with the voice of my dead husband saying, "I'm sorry," to me. The anger brought me no peace. I determined it better to just accept and forgive. There was no vindication in fighting about it with a dead guy and a God who did nothing to cause this to happen.

At this point, I felt as though I was wandering through life, unable to be understood or to find people who would understand. I did have a friend who suffered the loss of a husband at a similar age. I clung to this about her. We talked periodically, but time and distance kept us apart and unable to engage much. It at least helped to know that someone was out there who thought of me and in the midst of thinking of their own suffering. I desperately needed to know that I had allies. I was the unfortunate, involuntary member of a club that no one ever wanted to belong to.

There were days where I almost felt okay. There were more days where the pain and emotion would wash over me like a tidal wave. No matter what, I still needed to function and try to carry on. I wanted to wear a sign that said "Widow" so everyone would know why I was the way I was all the time. I felt like I wore my pain like a big overcoat that was too warm for the season. My mourning was stuffy, hot and heavy. I felt different and uncomfortable. No matter what, I couldn't relax and feel good. I had a hard time not bringing how I felt up to people with whom I socialized. I didn't want their sympathy, I felt like I needed to explain my behavior. I had an expanding hole in my heart, and nothing seemed to fill it. I had been thanking God for His provision and protection, but I had not asked Him to come into my life to help with the longing and loneliness.

The idea of God filling this gap in my life didn't seem plausible. Could God take the place of a relationship like that of marriage? Could I see that being fulfilling? I couldn't get my mind around the idea, no matter how hard I tried to picture it. I didn't ask because I didn't believe that He could. Maybe I didn't know that He would want to. Perhaps I didn't really know what it was like to feel fulfilled in a relationship anyway. I certainly never did feel fulfilled in any of my relationships. Not with Asher, not with my parents, nor friends or even my daughter. No one gave me a sense of completeness. It was something I had heard about from other people and the movies but I never imagined it being a real thing. With that experience, I can understand why I didn't think God could.

Six

"It's not that hard or as easy as it seems. Pick up the pieces of your dreams." -Nat Jay

As time wore on, everyone around me went back to their normal lives. They no longer acted or spoke carefully around me. In my mind, they were less considerate. That happens. When something traumatic takes place, everyone rallies around the cause, but their feelings are not yours. They move out of the crisis quicker than you do.

I once had a dear friend tell me, "Sariah, you are going to go through this for a long time and probably a lot longer than people think you should." He was right. After 6 months of grieving, I was sat down in my Vice President's office to discuss how they could "get the old Sariah back." It seemed as though my employer thought I should be done grieving and getting back to my old hustle and punchy ways of doing things. I couldn't gather my thoughts fast enough as he was talking. I'm sure he intended it to be some sort of a pep talk, but I was legitimately offended by the opinion that all I needed, as far as Management was concerned, was a positive conversation to set me right.

I left his office feeling like I was being examined under a microscope. People doubted my abilities. That put added pressure on me to do more, but I didn't have "more" to do more with! I grew depressed about my performance on the job. My depression was compounded by routine tardiness to the office. No one, including me, could figure it out. Did I just not care anymore? I wanted to care, but the daily burden I carried was too heavy to take on anything else. I remember a conversation I had with my mother during one of these times of feeling oppressed by my own emotions.

"I want to buy something really expensive," I told her.

"It still won't make you feel better," she replied.

She was right. Nothing I purchased was going to take away my feelings. It didn't stop me from trying. With the gigantic hole in my heart widening, I started trying to fill it with material things. Handbags, new shoes, trips, fancy dinners, and nights out with friends consumed my finances. I craved anything that might make me feel happy, but nothing soothed my crying soul. Sure, I was excited to get something new, but it only made me feel good for the first day or two. Then it was back to being miserable and not appreciating what I had.

I switched gears and bought Katie a new wardrobe. I figured seeing my little tot all dolled up in the latest trends would make me feel better. However, Katie didn't care what she wore, and that emotional quick fix wore off quickly, too. I bought her the biggest new swing set I could find. She loved it, but by then it was getting cold, and we were readying for winter, so she really didn't get to use it. I bought a Mercedes. I liked the idea of being a luxury car owner, but it brought me no joy. It grew to be something I felt guilty about. I felt ashamed when I considered how pretentious it looked sitting in the driveway. Was I really a person who wanted to chase after status symbols? I'd given it a try and found it wanting.

I took a couple of trips out to Austin, Texas, to see my dear friend Al. I always loved to go visit her, especially since we still had a good time and a lot of laughs, and not to mention, a lot of drinks. I was in great need to forget my pain, and a long weekend of entertainment and alcohol did the trick. I had fun, but I came home feeling guilty for taking 4 days out of my life and away from my daughter to sit on a boat and drink. It seemed as though every worldly thing I used to try and fill the hole in my heart had some sort of guilty backlash attached to it.

I didn't like adding guilt to my pain. I felt as though God had done so much for Katie and me, and I was failing Him and my daughter. I wanted to be a happy, energetic mom who had it together and excelled in her new surroundings. I was trying to find that superhero cape, but I couldn't. I wanted to hide; I wanted just to exist. I was desperate to do anything to feel better. I wanted this pain to be over. Couldn't I do anything to shed this misery that was now my daily waking life? What would do it for me? I decided I would choose to be done with it.

I was meeting with the couple in charge of family counseling at my church. It was the same couple who counseled Asher and me when we were married. We had been meeting once a week for dinner and talking. It just never got off the ground as far as making headway with me or my feelings. I wouldn't talk about what I was really going through. I felt disconnected and unable to articulate anything. I was tired and overwhelmed all the time. I was not up to the task of diving into my feelings. I was constantly sending my daughter off to play with their children and losing my train of thought in the process. I couldn't relax and connect with what I needed to discuss. I showed up one night and announced that I was ready to move on. They seemed surprised, but I was confident in my speech. I went on to say I was prepared to pursue a new life even if no one understood. I wasn't nearly as ready as I had convinced myself that I was; I just didn't want to feel like I was scared and miserable all the time.

I came home to an empty house every night. When I put my daughter to bed, it felt even emptier. The nights I would drink and smoke the hours away grew more and more frequent. I lost myself in alcohol, using it to cope with the life-changing event of losing my husband. It felt calming to let the alcohol numb my feelings for just a little while. I understood why people would want that feeling, especially someone like me.

However, it also started to scare me. I felt like I was putting my head in the lion's mouth to get a good look at his tonsils, all while hoping he didn't snap his jaws shut. I was ashamed of what I was doing, so I didn't talk to anyone about it. On Friday nights, especially, I made sure I had plenty of wine in the house for after Katie went to bed. I seldom drank to overt intoxication, but the amount grew increasingly with the passing weeks. My cigarette smoking skyrocketed and so did my shopping. I didn't want to see how out of control I really was with almost everything in my life. Why couldn't I just feel better? Wouldn't anything make me feel better? I went on more trips. I went to the spa. I bought more new clothes, shoes, and handbags.

Some lovely women from my church circles gently told me that God had to be my husband now. I couldn't wrap my mind around how that worked. I couldn't fathom a relationship with God that would equate to the intimacy of marriage. It seemed fairytale-like and silly. I would have loved to feel that way about my relationship with God, but I didn't. My relationship was one of reverence, awe, gratitude, and fear. I don't think I was afraid of God, but I was very aware of what God could do in and to my life any time He wanted to, and that scared me sometimes. I had a great sense of His Omnipresence and His great majesty as The Creator, but a loving, tender, endearing relationship with Him seemed foreign. It was kind of like a grizzly bear trying to hug an ant. That fatherly sense didn't resonate with me no matter how much I heard it. No matter what songs about my Heavenly Father I sang on Sunday Morning, I didn't feel any different. I had plenty of nights of sobbing on my bed, telling God how lonely and sad I was, but I wasn't expecting Him to do anything about it personally. The alcohol became my lover.

It so happened that a friend of mine was getting married that fall in Siesta Key, Florida. I had received the informal invitation to travel to the November wedding over the phone before Asher died. I wanted to go, but when I discussed it with Asher, he didn't seem interested. He and the groom weren't exactly simpatico. He did reluctantly agree that we could look into traveling there for the wedding. After that, we didn't talk much about it. When he passed, I decided to book my travel plans. My mom said she'd take care of Katie.

I went back and forth after booking, trying to figure out if I was up to attending a wedding or going somewhere tropical and fun without my husband. I bought travel insurance just in case. I wasn't sure what would happen. I let my employer know that I needed a four-day weekend and decided I didn't have to go if I didn't want to. On the other hand, I argued how nice it would be to be on an island getaway with so much negativity going on in my life. Maybe I deserved to go and enjoy someone else's happy moment for a change. I wanted to celebrate with my friend as I knew not many of our mutual acquaintances would be going either. I wanted to share my support. As the time came, many friends and coworkers beamingly relayed what a great vacation spot it was. "Make sure you come back," they'd say, half smiling and half serious. It couldn't be that nice, could it?

When the day came to go, I was a bit anxious. I thought of having to leave for Katie for a few days, and whether or not I wanted to. I thought of going and not having a good time or feeling lonely. I still packed my bags and Katie's belongings and headed up to my parent's house, where I would stay for the night and leave early in the morning for my flight. I couldn't believe I was really going. I kind of felt more grown-up taking a little vacation by myself.

The conversation I had with the bride a couple of weeks ago kept ringing in my ears. She was excited about my RSVP and said she had wanted to ask me something. She and the other attendees were discussing me and wondering whether or not I was bringing a date. "No," I said as I stifled a laugh, "I am coming alone." She seemed a little relieved to hear it and a bit embarrassed for feeling like she needed to bring it up. I smiled and chuckled as I made my way to the airport before dawn on a sparsely populated highway to Boston. The air was chilly, so I was glad to be going somewhere sunny and warm. The thought of the turquoise beach and the sound of the surf made me smile with anticipation.

I parked my car and headed for the terminal with all of my heavy clothes, my handbag, and wheeled suitcase in tow. I was certain they purposefully put my terminal in the exact opposite place as the long-term parking garage. I wound down and around corridors and hopped on and off moving hallways until I finally reached the ticketing counter with about 500 other vacationers also waiting to check-in.

I rifled through my purse to be sure I had everything. I rifled through it again when I forgot if I had checked for my ID. *Where was is American Express? Oh, there.* I read my itinerary fifty times and still forgot the times to board and checked again. Finally, I got to the counter. After that, I headed off to be interrogated and thoroughly searched at Security. I had traveled for business several times, so I didn't hesitate on arrival to the X-ray machine to methodically strip myself of all accessories and outer clothing, putting them in little bins and lining them up on the belt in an orderly fashion. I did hate the idea of being shoeless on a floor I can only imagine hadn't been mopped in forever, not to mention how many dirty bare feet had tread there before mine. My skin crawled with the idea. I pursed my lips and tried to get it out of my mind. I am not one for dirt or unsanitary things.

Once through the search of my belongings, metal detectors, and had redressed myself, I headed to the nearest Starbuck's kiosk for my beloved coffee. With my brew in hand, I called my mom one last time before I boarded. I shed a tear as I spoke to her; already I missed my Baby Girl. I talked to Katie and told her how much I loved her and implored her to be good for Nana. Then I awaited the boarding call. I tried to think of the new experience as an adventure. I had no idea what Siesta Key would be like.

Perhaps there would be swaying palm trees, warm breezes, a light salty smell to the air. Could I walk everywhere? Everyone told me how small it was. I was hoping I could just flip-flop it wherever I needed to go. My daydream was interrupted by the cattle call announcement over the speaker. I gathered my things, trying not to spill my coffee, and carefully shuffled down the gangway. Once all of my stuff had been stowed and situated, I sat down and tried to relax. I sat for quite a while back on my imaginary island, fixating on pleasant thoughts. I was hoping to get a tan, to be able to sleep in past 7 a.m., and a casual meal without a demanding 3-year-old who's beloved little arms became octopus-like whenever she sat at a restaurant table. Dare I even consider a nap? By the time the plane took off, I was looking forward to my mini-vacation with high expectations. I rested in my seat and waited to arrive in Miami.

On arrival to Miami, I was instructed on where to catch my next flight. All I could think about was Fantasy Island. I made my way to the correct terminal, also situated on the opposite side of the airport from where my first plane landed. I headed downstairs to the tiniest terminal I had ever been in. I couldn't help but laugh as I was pointed to a bus that drove us out onto the runway to our propeller plane on the outskirts of the tarmac. This loud, puny plane was the chariot to my destination. In no time, and because it seated so few, we were off and flying down to our island destination. I marveled out the window at the beautiful white coral sand that outlined little green islands, surrounded by varying colors of crystal-clear turquoise waters. It was a fantastic view to behold. I silently thanked my Creator for something so beautiful to enjoy. The flight was quicker than expected. I walked out of the door of the plane, down the stairs to an airport that wasn't much bigger than some houses. Everything seemed cute and makeshift. I couldn't take this airport seriously. I found the fact that it was called Siesta Key International Airport hysterical.

I made my way to a pink taxi and got in. The air was nice and warm, but the sky was a bit overcast. I checked into my economy hotel and set up camp in my spacious, but rather ordinary room. It was good enough but lacked the tropical dazzle I'd imagined. It did have a pool.

I freshened, primped, changed my clothes to something more fun and island-casual, and called the bride and my mom to let them know I'd arrived safely. The bride and I made plans for later, and I headed to the front of the hotel to find a cab. I was eager to check out the downtown area. It felt nice to be outside in heeled sandals and no coat. I felt festive and light. I hadn't felt this content in my own skin in quite a while. I could get used to this! Even though the island was a small, a four-mile by two-mile patch, it wasn't small enough to walk everywhere. I called for another pink cab, and off I went to the famous Diamond Street. I hadn't heard anything about Diamond Street before arriving. As soon as I sat down in the cab, the driver said, "Diamond Street?" I figured if everyone headed there, then it must be the best place on the island. I promptly said, "Yes."

I was dropped off on the corner of Southern and Diamond. I was overwhelmed by the noise and the lights. It was just after sundown, and the town was coming alive with tourists, locals, and revelers. I walked to the corner and sent my eyes down the streets in every direction. Where to start? The road was flooded with people and music pouring out open windows and doors. It was party-like and chaotic. It took my mind a minute to focus on a place I could wait for the bride, groom, and whoever else came for the pre-wedding festivities.

I found a little outdoor bar called The Tree House. It sounded like a perfect perch to taking in surroundings and get in some good people watching. Plus, it was about the size of a living room, so I could sit and be able to see my friends approaching. I ordered something exotic and islandy to drink and lit up a cigarette. I immediately made friends with three gentlemen there on a business trip. It seemed an odd place for a business trip. When I asked what they did, they said they were in the hospitality industry, so it made sense. We bantered on about the island and what they had done that day. A little golf and a little fishing for them. I said I just arrived today so hadn't had time to explore. I explained why I was there, and then we recounted our own wedding days of the past.

I was still wearing my wedding rings, so I didn't have to explain anything grim about recent life changes. It was nice not to feel like people were looking at me through that black widow's veil I felt like I was permanently peering out of. I could just be me, and no one had to know I was in pain.

The drink settled into my senses, and I became jovial and funny. I almost felt like me again. I felt glad I made the trip. My cell phone rang, and my friends and fellow wedding-goers came up behind my barstool. I bid goodnight to my Tree House companions, and we made our way down the sidewalk lined with bars and clubs to find the one we could all agree on. We decided that our landing spot needed to have food so we could eat dinner and catch up. Every place had its own theme and catchy name. McIrish's Pub was a natural fit as it was lined with Boston Sports paraphernalia. It had the usual bar menu, and we ordered what rang with appeal. We were not disappointed. I munched on buffalo wings and celery while the bride beamed and went on about the day and the plans for her beachside wedding. I smiled and listened. I knew that excitement, so I was happy for her. I met the groom's father, a lovely older man who was also widowed. He had heard of my plight, and we spoke on it briefly. He offered his condolences.

I hated when people said, "I'm so sorry." It was an unwelcome interruption to hear it and reply as if he'd died last week. I wanted to feel like "Widow" was not my title for the rest of my life. We ate and moved on to the next resting spot. I was enthralled by the atmosphere and light tap in my chest of live music as we passed by bar windows. We checked out several spots that night, a sampling of what was around. We made sure we checked out some famous places and then found a quieter haunt later on in the night where we could sit and chat about what the next day entailed. The bride's mother, father, and stepmother would be arriving tomorrow along with the rest of the guests. I was looking forward to a massage and facial I had booked for the morning. It was a little treat I arranged for myself before I left for my trip. As we walked the streets, I became aware of the dwindling crowds. It was getting late. I headed for a gelato stand and everyone followed. I happily spooned my frozen treat as we stood on the corner of Southern and Diamond once again.

I wondered where we would go next, being careful not to direct any plans. I wanted the bride to feel in charge. This was her weekend. As I stood, I was passed by a tall, smiling, handsome man. He was dressed in shorts, flip flops, a windbreaker, and a visor. He didn't notice me, but his face caught my eye and gave my senses a start. I decided it was the drinks and the atmosphere that made my insides tingle. I put the notion of passion out of my head. I, of course, had noticed handsome men when I was married. I thought nothing of it. It was normal to take notice of attractive people, but now when I did, I felt a little ashamed. I thought I should be mourning and lonely for my lost spouse, not getting giddy about other men. I was confused and exhilarated by the rush.

We walked on to another place to celebrate. It had no glass in the windows or doors on the frames, and the bar had saddles as chairs. Since we all had a few drinks, the idea of sitting on a saddle was appealing. In we went and found an imaginary horse to rest on. I was in the middle of lighting yet another cigarette when a street urchin-like man came up to my side. I was uncomfortable with his over the top fawning over my beauty. I was trying to figure out how to end this conversation and dismiss him from my presence when his cousin came over and apologized for his behavior. I was startled. It was the handsome man I had seen earlier. I fumbled a little to regain my confidence; I wasn't expecting to have to be charming. Thankfully, I went right into Business Networking 101 Mode and started asking him questions about himself to keep any awkwardness out of the conversation.

His name was Boyd. He told me he worked in the restaurant business and said, "So, I know good food." His cousin of less-than-average social skills stuck around and tried to insert himself into the conversation, but he was buffered by his debonair cousin. He'd send him on errands to the bar or to talk to someone they knew. He informed me that they were locals. I launched into questions about the best entertainment and, most importantly, where to go for the best place to eat. He straightened up as if to crow like a rooster and said, "My house."

I repositioned the conversation to restaurants, and he gave me the names of a couple of places. He then countered that he would love to make dinner for me at his place tomorrow. I did not answer. He asked for my phone number. I told him I'd take his. I didn't want him to contact me if I didn't want him to. He gave me his number, and he and his cousin asked me to come with them to their next destination. I politely said no, and they both kissed my hand and went on their way. I was flattered by the attention and a bit embarrassed. My friends didn't know what to make of the exchange, and neither did I. I hadn't entertained the attention of a stranger in quite some time. We all silently agreed not to discuss it. Shortly afterward, decided it was best to disperse to our respective hotel rooms.

I took a cab back to my hotel and made my way down the dark outdoor hotel hallway and into my room. I was still illuminated from the attention. I quickly washed up and settled into my rented bed with sheets that smelled faintly of bleach and over-drying.

The next day was laid back. I was looking forward to my appointment for a massage. Since wedding preparations consumed the wedding party and attendees were coming in at scattered times, we were on our own for the day. I was relieved to be released to roam and explore the island without having to consider anyone else's schedule. It was a warm, picture-perfect day with a comforting breeze. I felt invigorated by the weather and the hustle-about on the streets. I wandered in and out of stores, had a lovely vegetarian lunch at one of the funky, independent cafes off of Diamond Street, and then made my way to the most exquisite and intimate day spa I had ever encountered. It was a converted conch house with lots of eastern decorations, wood, and incense smells flowing out of the rooms. The hallways and rooms resonated with the soothing sounds of tranquil music and trickling fountains. The lighting was subdued, but in a sheer curtain sense, not dark or cavern-like.

My shoulders relaxed as I headed down the hallway to my treatment room behind the therapist who was explaining where to find the showers and held out the fluffy white robe that would be my cocoon for at least 3 hours. *Heaven*, I thought. I sank into my surroundings and enjoyed the pampering. An hour and a half massage, a foot wash and massage, followed by a facial. I floated out of there without touching the ground. I felt profoundly well.

I headed back to my hotel room for a shower and a nap. All was right with the world if only for a day. A couple hours later, my phone started ringing about dinner plans. I rallied from my euphoric seclusion and put myself together for another night of celebrating the soon-to-be-married couple. I was looking forward to meeting people in the bride's life that I hadn't had the pleasure of knowing yet. I thought of Boyd, the man I met the night before and his invitation to dinner. I quickly dismissed it. The thought of going to a stranger's house made me very nervous, and I felt smarter for deciding against it. Lots of bad things end up happening to people that way. I especially didn't like his creepy cousin, the street urchin. The thought of being in his company, especially, was very unappealing.

We went to an average place for dinner. It was nothing special. The conversation and the movement from the table signified that it was time to head to Diamond Street to find somewhere to carouse and mingle amongst ourselves.

I thought of Boyd again and felt bad that I hadn't responded to his invite. I quickly texted his cell phone. "Sorry, I got cold feet." He tried a few times to respond to my text message, but I didn't reply. He then started calling. I had forgotten that texting someone supplied them with my phone number, but at the time, I was not concerned. After a few calls, I finally answered.

"Oh, are we going to answer the phone now?" I heard upon answering.

I laughed, and he asked what we were doing. He was in the same area, so he asked if he could meet up with us. We were with a large crowd, and I thought it would be fun to have a local around to tell us the best places to go. I think my friends thought he happened to run into us out on the town because no one asked how he came to find me. He was lighthearted and friendly with the wedding guests. He eased right into the group without any effort at all. Our group of 10-plus went up and down Diamond Street, first one bar and then the next. I was getting bored with bar-hopping, but it was what everyone wanted to do.

Not wanting to be the crybaby of the group, I smiled and silently went along. It wasn't my party anyway. Boyd kept trying to convince me to leave the group and go somewhere to talk alone. I kept refusing. We went on to another outside club. It was a large, open-air spot with a big asphalt dance floor and a long bar that ran alongside it. I made my way to a stool and sat down. Boyd parked himself right next to me. I was flattered and feeling silly from both the drink and the attention.

Next, the rest of the wedding party wanted to go to a "gentlemen's club" next door. I refused to subject myself to that environment no matter how entertaining everyone thought it would be. They shrugged and went inside, leaving me outside with Boyd. We chatted, drank, and sang along with the songs that came across the PA from the DJ booth. I was entertained at his attempts to be funny. I noted that somehow, without me noticing, he had managed to turn his chair around so that his knees were straddling mine. As I looked down, he placed his hands on my legs. I jumped, shrinking my legs back away from him. His expression reflected a note of disappointment, but he recovered quickly and restarted a light-hearted conversation about the island that we had shared earlier.

I was feeling awkward and unsure of the attention. I felt like I was doing something wrong. I wondered what my friends were thinking of me, sitting alone with him at this bar. I felt as though I was being disrespectful to my husband, even though he was deceased. I felt strange. I wondered, How much time has to pass after someone dies before you can do something like this? Mid-conversation, I leaned forward to adjust my position on my stool; Boyd grabbed both sides of my head and kissed me. The small kindling of passion inside I'd been ignoring all night suddenly ignited. It felt so good to be kissed. As much as I wanted to stop the interaction, it was satisfying a very real need to be touched and admired as my husband had done. The first-kiss experience is always such a powerful one. It wasn't that I wasn't attracted to him, I just couldn't get over the uneasy feeling that my husband was watching me from Heaven in disgust. I ended the kiss.

The rest of the wedding party exited the club a few moments later. They were ready for the night to end. The wedding was in the afternoon the following day, and there were tight schedules of hair, makeup, dressing, and photos to consider. I decided to leave with them. Boyd followed us out and tried to coax me to go with him. I refused. He then switched gears and suggested we go back to my hotel and hang out. I would not agree. He held my hand for a bit as we walked along the sidewalk, and then I sent him on his way. Looking rejected, he left down a different street.

I was relieved to have warded off my new love interest. My friends and I regrouped and opted for late-night snacks of sausages from a local vendor on the corner. Greasy and delicious, the vendor prepared my sausage without a bun per my request, slicing the sausage in half and putting the onions and peppers inside and making a bun out of tin foil for me. I was thrilled. Turns out, upon asking us where we were all from that, the sausage guy, too, was from Boston. We all prattled on about Boston and what we liked about it as we munched and wiped mustard from our mouths in between bites. No one asked me about Boyd, and I was happy to not need to answer any questions about it. The collective group seemed to have decided not to involve themselves, and I went along with the apparent silence on the subject.

After our snacks, we poured ourselves into our own cabs for the night. I felt as though I had a bit too much to drink, but was content to be laughing and joking with whoever was around me. I went back to my hotel room, glad to be going back to my hotel room alone. As I settled in for bed, I thought about the kiss. I felt proud of myself for making a sound, smart decision to leave Boyd on the sidewalk. I fell asleep, comfortable with my decision, even though the empty space next to me made the bed feel bigger than it was. I still hadn't gotten used to that.

The wedding day came and everyone was energized. I met my friend Daniel, one of the wedding guests and best friend of the bride, for breakfast. We ate and discussed the events of the weekend so far. We decided we should try to find the spot on the beach where the ceremony would be so we wouldn't be late and frazzled. After all, neither of us knew where we'd have to meet for the nuptial witnessing. After one last cup of coffee, we started our walk down a busy road toward Smith's Beach. All we knew was the wedding was to take place at boardwalk #6. *No problem*, we thought and started on the journey with full bellies and being properly caffeinated to ward off any tiredness from last night's festivities. We stopped briefly to admired the beach and walked on to find our boardwalk. The walk was farther than we anticipated, but we passed the time chatting about this and that, life, dreams, plans, the wedding, and all kinds of things. Daniel was a great pleasure to talk to and he was good company.

We finally made it to the boardwalk section of the beach and started with the task of finding sign #6. We walked a bit slower, carefully looking for our number on each sign we passed. As it turned out, the #6 boardwalk was the only one without a sign. Go figure. When we finally realized that when the numbers jumped to #7 and 8. At last we found #6 and walked down the boardwalk to survey the surroundings. The spot was a lovely small beach rimmed with palm trees. It was precisely what one would hope a tropical beach would look like. The water was as clear and as stunning as a finely cut aquamarine gem. It was a picturesque setting for a beachside wedding.

Silently nodding that we were both satisfied that not only had we found the correct location but that it met with our expectations, we turned back to the boardwalk and walked out onto the hardness of the cement sidewalk lining Siesta Key's busiest thoroughfare. It was a stark contrast to the picturesque scenery we just took in. We headed back toward our hotels together. We continued our conversation about life, invigorated by the unexpected exercise session of the long walk. I was also happy to be getting some sun as well. No sense in going back to Boston without a tan. Sporting a tan in the late fall and winter brags to the world of the frozen Northeast that you've been somewhere fun. I wanted to come back looking and feeling the part. I had a sense of buoyancy as we walked. I felt pretty good. Daniel never mentioned my recent turn of life's events, and I was relieved to escape the subject.

Daniel walked with me back to my hotel. We picked up a real estate paper and sat by the quiet, secluded pool on the quaint, but hotel chain-like property. Pulling up lounge chairs, we sat in front of the unoccupied water, perusing the paper. We looked at the real estate offerings and fantasized about what it would be like to buy a house and rent it out as an investment. Neither one of us was serious, but it was fun to act like a couple of big shots who had that kind of financial flexibility.

I remembered my dress was a little big when I tried it on that morning. I thought of Boyd and wondered if he knew of a local tailor so I could get it fitted last minute. I wasn't sure if I wanted to call, though. I had been satisfied to leave him the night before without much expectation for a later meeting. I wasn't sure if I wanted to see him either. I felt as though the flirtation and attention pushed my boundaries. I wanted to feel safe. I didn't want to take any chances, and I didn't want to be taken advantage of. Still, the thought of things going a bit too far was thrilling. I dismissed the notion as reckless and decided not to call.

As Daniel and I were talking, my cell phone rang. It was Boyd. I decided not to answer it for fear of being asked if I had any plans for later. I didn't want to commit or give away anything, so I let my voicemail get it. I smiled a bit, feeling a tad smug that I was being pursued. It was nice to think I was occupying someone's thoughts. I was quick to retrieve the message on the phone. I wanted to know what he had to say. I hate when people don't leave messages. To me, it said, "I wasn't sure I really wanted to call anyway." The message was sweet. He invited me to come to the restaurant where he worked for lunch, promising me a lunch of grilled lobster. I liked the idea, but I still had the morning's omelet and home fries occupying my stomach, so I decided not to take him up on it or return his call.

Starting to feel the effects of our walk, Daniel decided to return to his hotel for a nap. I liked the sound of that idea so I opted to head to my room to do the same. I showered and drew the shades. Slipping into the coolness of the sheets, I relaxed. I don't think a second of time passed between closing my eyes and drifting off.

I was awakened by the sound of my cell phone ringing. It was the bride. Excitedly, she rattled on about the chain of events before the wedding ceremony and asked me to participate. She'd already been to the hair salon, so it was just a matter of helping her dress and keeping her company before it was time to head to boardwalk #6. I let her know I'd be down to her room shortly and ended the call.

I looked back at my cell phone to check the time. I had slept for 3 hours! I sprang out of bed, feeling excited to be in the court of the bride. I felt a twinge of sadness for myself, being unaccompanied by anyone, not even Boyd. He had offered to be my date on my voicemail earlier, but I thought it would be a bit awkward for everyone else, so I dismissed the offer. I had to forget about alterations on the dress. Life would go on without a perfectly-fitting dress. I rinsed my hair in the shower and started primping for the ceremony.

The attire for the wedding was casual. We were told sundresses for the women and Hawaiian shirts for the men. There was a clear expectation of no shoes. The only acceptable footwear at this event would be flip flops. I found no problem with that request. After much fussing, partly because I wanted to look good for pictures and partly because I wanted to look my best in case I changed my mind about meeting up with Boyd later, I grabbed a small handbag and my camera and started off down the hallway to the bride's room. I prayed briefly on my walk, asking God to bless the couple and the ceremony.

I knocked on the door and opened it to find a room full of women, everyone moving about to help with dresses and the bride's headpiece. A kaleidoscope of onlookers snapped pictures. I felt like I was in the way and out of place. I stood to the side, reflecting on my own wedding day. I smiled quietly and admired the commotion and the bride's nervous excitement. Those moments before the wedding are so exciting. I recalled putting on my own dress with my Matron of Honor at my side. I remembered thinking, *This is it! I really get to be the bride,* as I put my dress on.

I was very happy for her. I really was, but I felt a lingering sadness because my marriage was over as hers was just beginning.

Time at last! We all snapped our final pictures and piled into waiting cars with the bride in tow, heading for the wedding site. I had butterflies in my stomach, hoping this would be a very memorable and special time for her. We parked and found our sign-less boardwalk. I could feel the anticipation as we climbed the stairs of the retaining wall and on to the boardwalk. The bride sought the location of her groom. There was an electric charge in the air the moment their eyes met. I relived that moment of my wedding as I watched hers happen. I suppose every former bride does that. It's a good feeling.

The ceremony was short, as I expected. The pictures took about three times longer than the vows. Once pictures were complete, we headed for a nice meal at a local restaurant. Then it was time to change clothes and head out to celebrate and experience our last night on this four-by-two-mile island. The bride and groom, the parents with their companions, and now Daniel and a guest, Kelly, had paired up. That more or less left the groom's father and me. He was a nice man, but I started feeling lonely and isolated. I knew I could have some easy company if I would just call Boyd, so I did. The great thing about a small island is that no one is too far away to meet up with you.

Boyd was happy to hear from me. I had already had a few drinks, so my guard was lowered enough to tell him where we would be. He was there in minutes. I relaxed as I saw him, happy to be with someone who would make me feel special even if only for one last time. We settled on a place to continue the festivities at the suggestion of Boyd. It was an outdoor venue with local bands and lots of places to sit amongst the flora of Siesta Key. Since everyone was paired up, and feeling like no one would take offense, I sat away from the crowd with my new friend. We sat together closely, discussing music. He repeatedly pled his case to take me off somewhere else, leaving the wedding party behind. When I wouldn't relent, he dropped the subject. The bride decided she needed to check out one last bar that we hadn't gone to, so we collectively headed off in that direction.

A few more drinks and I was chattering like a songbird and flashing my perma-smile. Boyd got a little friendlier, and I got a lot more willing to let him put his arm around me. It felt strange to have a different man so close, but at the same time, it was like a warm blanket on a cold night. I didn't want to take him off. He kissed me sweetly, and I felt my whole body go warm. He asked me to dance, and I obliged. I felt free, pretty, and desired. That was a pretty powerful combination for someone in so much pain. Another drink and he asked to take me back to my hotel room. I agreed after a small deliberation. I left my bag of souvenir t-shirts for my daughter and me on a stool at the bar. I never even said goodbye to my friends. I felt a little precarious and self-righteous. *Didn't I need to feel some excitement?* I knew it was irresponsible, but I didn't care. I knew God would not approve, but I shook my fist at him in those contemplating moments and decided I would do what I wanted to do. I knew, even in the alcoholic haze, I was wagering a massive bet against God's ire, but I surprisingly wasn't too concerned. It was a dangerous game to play, and I reveled in the excitement of it.

We poured into my room from the cab and instantly became entangled in one another. No words were even exchanged as passionate kissing landed us together on the bed. The room was as dark as pitch. Neither one of us had given thought to turn on a light. The line of intimacy with another man was crossed in a matter of minutes. It almost happened too quickly to pay attention to or to change my mind. I wanted to stop, but at the same time, I wanted to feel physically close to someone again. I became enveloped in the excitement and emotion and sold myself out to the only bidder.

The next morning was awkward. I didn't know what to do with him. I hadn't even planned on talking to him again. Interestingly enough, he asked for the ongoing communication plan. I chalked it up to politeness and his probable assumption that I would ask for it. Maybe he wanted to beat me to the punch. I casually agreed to hear from him again, pretending to be as distant and non-committal as I had been from the beginning, unswayed by what had transpired.

I had an early flight to catch, so I showered and dressed hurriedly and asked him to do the same. I didn't want to miss my plane. The guilt was starting to settle in my guts so I didn't want to be around him anymore. I shoved my belongings into my suitcase and supervised as he collected his things. As soon as I assured myself that I was not leaving anything behind, I ushered him out the door. I called for a cab as I walked in front of him, towing my suitcase behind me. He carefully took my bag from my grip and wheeled it towards the front of the building.

When my cab arrived, I quickly hugged and kissed him goodbye and slid into the backseat of the SUV. I wondered how many times the cab driver had witnessed this scene before. *Probably too many times to count*, I thought. If I were him, I would have sarcastically rolled my eyes. I wouldn't have been surprised to catch him in the act.

We drove away, and as I looked back at the storage area of the SUV, I noticed a sleeping young woman dressed from the night before curled up in the back. Not sure if I should panic or laugh, I asked the driver if he was aware of his extra passenger. He nodded in the affirmative and gave me a look that said, "Of course, silly woman." Since he appeared unconcerned, I nodded back and looked out the window, trying to hold in a belly laugh. I decided to take in as much scenery as my hungover mind would take in on my drive to the airport. The morning was as hazy as I was. Thankfully not many people opt for an 8 AM flight out of Siesta Key, so my check-in and embarkation was without hassle. I flew off the island, wondering whether or not I should allow myself to believe last night had never happened.

Like a gentleman, Boyd messaged to see if I arrived in Boston safely. I was a little flattered that he feigned caring. I called him to say I was on my way home and that all was well. We made small talk as I drove down the highway. I tried to be more focused on the road than Boyd, but the conversation captivated me. Not because it was so intriguing but because I was being willingly lulled into believing that this was more than a friendly exchange and it wouldn't be the last one between us.

We chatted until I pulled into my driveway. I ended the conversation quickly as I knew my precious little girl would be eagerly waiting to greet me. I missed her so much. I hurried up the stairs. In my mind, I expected her to be so much more happy to see me than she actually acted. Perhaps she was but I was too surrounded by remorse over what had transpired to notice. I felt as though I had betrayed her by sleeping with another man.

Even though my husband was dead, I felt like I had cheated on him. I felt like I cheated on her. I had a secret that I had to keep, and it wore on me like slime I couldn't wash off. As much as I wanted to forget my secret, it continued to ooze out of my soul. Every thought became consumed by either the excitement of reliving it in my mind or cringing from realizing what I'd done. When friends and coworkers would ask me if I had a good time, I'd grimace. I wished I had just gone, enjoyed my friend's wedding, and come home unscathed.

Almost a week passed when my cell phone rang. Surprisingly, it was Boyd calling. I was astonished and relieved all at the same time. I was tired of seeing myself as a cheap, desperate person. In my mind, Boyd had seen me as an easy target. I had cooked up a story in my mind of a man who picked up unsuspecting tourists nightly. He acted out his disguise as a nice guy who just happened to meet those tourists by chance only to find that they'd been scammed.

I didn't want to realize I'd been scammed, so I never bothered to contact him. I thought if I didn't try to reach out, then I wouldn't have to feel worse.

"I just wanted to say hi. I can't stop thinking about you," he sang into my ear.

I blushed at those words. I was trying desperately to fend off any ideas that made me feel like he thought I was special. *He does this all the time,* I thought. *Just be friendly and thank him for calling and get off the phone quickly.* I reminded myself not to give him the upper hand in my emotional war.

"I thought you forgot about me," the sentence slipped out my lips before I could close my mouth.

"How could I forget about you?" He said in a giggle-like chirp.

There it was, the start of something new. Something that I thought I didn't or shouldn't want, but he made me feel good just by calling. I couldn't stop it. It was already too late - I wanted more. I wanted to feel good again, and he met that need. I became addicted to the attention. He soothed my wounds with his words. He was attentive and complimentary. He was eager to call and always did what he said he would. We talked for hours, way into the middle of the night. He would listen when I cried. He comforted me. He cheered me on. I listened to every word he said.

I became very interested in him. He described the restaurant he used to own along a bustling seaside sidewalk in a little tourist town. He crowed on about how successful it was and how much everyone loved his cooking.

I imagined in my mind what the restaurant must have been like. To me, it was a warmly lit room with gleaming old plank floors and white walls. Maybe some of the walls were exposed brick from being situated in a historic building. I tried to see the kitchen, a starch white one, with brilliant aluminum everything that flashed in the light. I could see him intently fixed on his craft, sternly directing his staff to help him with exact timing. I could practically hear the jolly hum of the dining room full of patrons all enjoying their experience in his bistro. I wanted to be there. I wanted to have a glass of wine and watch this all take place. He said he had sold it when he divorced his wife. It was an unfortunate situation. He moved to Siesta Key to be close to his daughter when his ex-wife decided to move to there. I found it almost romantic that he wanted to move to be near his little girl. We would gush to each other over our children. I took comfort in the fact that he was also a parent. To me it meant he was more responsible than other men, having to help provide for her and be involved in her life. He was proud that he did so much for her. He said he loved to show up to events and help her with her homework. I pictured him as the perfect divorced dad. He even taught her guitar and how to sing. It was a lovely vision.

As the weeks went on, the conversations got more and more frequent and went on longer and longer. Some days he would text message me all day long. I was drunk from the daily attention. It provided a little hideaway from my pain. The problem I encountered was that I wanted to live in my hideaway. To be jarred into my real life was unpleasant. I didn't want my life anymore; I wanted my escape. This emotional drug had its withdrawals. I wasn't sleeping. I lost interest in eating. My rigorous schedule, the regimen of taking care of my little girl as a single mom, and the many nights of three hours or less of sleep were catching up to me. I was drowning, and I was finally noticing, but I didn't know how to come up for air.

Seven

"Why can't I breathe whenever I think about you?" -Liz Phair

Boyd and I continued our torrid love affair fantasy over the phone for 3 months. Part of me was disappointed in myself for letting it go this long. The other part of me would rather live in the dream that our relationship was real, rather than go back to being a sad, lonely widow. I longed to be swept up in passion again. When I could stand the thought no longer, I brought up the idea to Boyd of going back for a visit for my birthday near the end of the month. He practically burst with excitement over the phone when I asked him what he thought. He then asked how soon I could get there. The next day I booked plane tickets and a place to stay. I wondered what my parents would think of me returning to the island so soon, since no one back in Boston was aware that Boyd even existed besides my friend and her wedding party. I made up some stupid story that I was looking at property to buy and rent out. No one challenged me on that excuse, so the plans were finalized. My friend Tanya agreed to watch Carli, so I had a babysitter. Nothing left to do but wait until the day of my trip. I could hardly focus on anything else.

I rushed with emotions on the days up to trip back to see Boyd. The anticipation of seeing him again was intoxicating. We spent the days up to my trip going on over phone about what we would do while we were together. I also spent nights lying to myself that maybe it was meant to be between me and Boyd. *Maybe this whole terrible event in my life was supposed to bring us together?* Even I couldn't get myself to buy into that one. The day came and I became anxious to hurry up and get down there. Plane rides can feel like days when you are impatient to arrive somewhere. At last, my plane arrived on Fantasy Island.

I felt fluttery as I made my way out of the little plane and onto the tarmac of the tiny airport of Siesta Key. A text message came in as soon as I turned my phone on. I was scrambling to gather my things in a plane no bigger than a walk-in closet. Suitcases, elbows, and sun hats were seemingly tossed in mid-air as passengers negotiated each other and their luggage to disembark.

"I think I saw you land." How sweet. He saw a plane come in for a landing and thought of me; it was, in fact, my flight. He let me know he would be arriving via bus to meet me. My stomach was restless as I fussed with my hair and makeup in the mirror of the bite-sized women's room next to the only luggage carousel. It was as spacious as the top floor of a raised ranch-style home. I rushed to be ready and presentable before he arrived. However, the funny thing was, in those kinds of situations, even if I had a hair and makeup team at my side, I never thought I looked stunning enough. Being stuffed into a coach seat all day wasn't going to help me find satisfaction with my looks. I gave up before I worked myself into a frenzy.

As I exited the bathroom, the carousel was slowly spinning black suitcases, so I lined up alongside my plane-mates to find mine. I thought how miraculous it was that anyone gets their luggage, considering most of the free world has only black suitcases. I found mine surprisingly fast and oriented myself to the exit after carefully quadruple checking tags and stickers. I left the carousel with the suitcase rolling behind me. I needed to get a cab for us, so I stood outside near the rest of the passengers in need of transportation. I pretended to be entranced by my cell phone and busy on the internet, purposefully not looking up to see him coming. In minutes, I heard his voice. I gazed over as if I was only half-interested to see him walking toward me with a lazy, happy grin.

He was tanned and casual. His hair was a little windblown, which worked for him, and sunglasses perched on his face like he was born wearing them. I didn't know how to approach him. Should I hug him?

Kiss him? I quickly made the decision to let him lead. He leaned down and kissed me gently on the lips.

"Hi, Ma'am," he sweetly whispered into my ear with a southern drawl that made my knees weak.

I was comforted by the greeting. My face was starting to twitch from too much smiling. We made our way to the cab line. It stretched for several cars. Mostly bright pink taxis of different shapes and sizes lined the walkway. To me, the taxis looked like flamingos waiting in line for a snack from the zookeeper. As we stood in line, we made the usual small talk when greeting someone at the airport.

"How was the trip?" He started off.

"Good, not too long. Uneventful, really." I always said, 'uneventful' when anyone asks me about traveling. It summed up the trip in one word; after all, running in and out of airports all day isn't really considered a good time.

We got into our flamingo car, and I told the withdrawn taxi driver where we were going - Elizabeth Street. I stayed in bed and breakfasts before, all of them drastically different then one another, so I had no idea what to expect. This one had a pool. I probably wouldn't get into but it was there. I was sure it wouldn't be as lovely as the one Boyd suggested, but that one was unavailable for this trip, and it was the most expensive one on the island. I was a little put-off by the suggestion, considering its expense and the fact that Boyd wasn't be contributing to the room cost. He'd quit his job weeks before on a whim after a dispute with the restaurant owner didn't resolve in his favor.

I remember him telling me this over the phone as I was standing on a street corner outside my office building, trying to locate my boss who was taking me to a meeting. I was craning my neck down the street to see if I could make out his silver Saab Sedan and trying to pay attention to what Boyd was saying. He relayed the chain of events and the conversation he'd had with the restaurant owner earlier that day. He sounded almost giddy.

"We never got along," he started out. "She was always on me about things. Nothing was ever good enough," he trailed a little. I waited for him to continue. "She told me that I'd need to take a two dollar an hour pay cut, so I told her goodbye."

"Oh, but what about supporting yourself and your child support?" I asked. According to him, his ex-wife was a very demanding and unforgiving woman who was unwavering in what she required of him. I alighted with fear for him over having to convey this story to her because, in my estimation, she'd still want her support or else.

"I can get a job in a matter of days." He sounded condescending in his tone as he went on to assure me that he was well-known and greatly desired by the restaurants in his area. He didn't care about the fact that he was out of work, and neither should I. As he was talking, I had the feeling that he was being a bit immature in his response to his former boss and quite irresponsible with his finances. I chided myself. I wasn't being affected by it, so why was I so concerned? *Because I'm going to visit someone with no income*, I thought, but I had dismissed the worry just as quickly as it came.

The cab pulled up to our bed and breakfast. We got out of opposite doors, and the driver made his way to the trunk to retrieve our bags. As the bags came out, Boyd's hands went into his pockets and stayed there. I paid our fare and tipped the driver who hadn't even looked me in the face or spoken a word the entire time we were with him, but I always tip. It's the right and expected thing to do, even if the service is mediocre to terrible.

I felt a little slighted by Boyd for not even attempting to pay for the cab, but then I decided he probably didn't have much money. I realized I shouldn't expect much in the way of monetary contribution to the weekend. Well, I thought, I signed up for this. I knew what I was coming down to.

We were greeted at the office door just off of the main front porch by an overly smiley woman with well-bleached hair up in a ponytail and leathery, worn skin. Whether from life, age, or the sun was irrelevant. The results were the same. She made too much small talk and perky chatter as she collected my information.

"Where are you from?" It was the usual opener of a question.

"Boston," I replied.

I wasn't actually from Boston proper, but no one cares about North of Boston, Massachusetts. It is only a short car ride north of the city, so it's close enough.

"Oh, I've been to Boston once before, about 25 years ago!" She flashed an ear-to-ear grin with the ability to relate to me. "You must like the Red Sox!" Anyone from somewhere other than Boston always says that to me.

"Sure." The truth is, I don't. I don't like baseball at all. I didn't want to get into the fact that I don't care about the sport. It is nothing against the team, and I can respect the fans and the players; baseball moves too slow for me. I'd rather watch football. I just didn't have the energy for the conversation, and we were having much more discussion than I wanted the first place. I kept my responses short and didn't ask questions.

She turned her attention to matters of business and my credit card number. After that was finalized, she dug for the room key in a chaotic mess of paperwork on the desk. Two miniature Doberman Pinschers peered out from underneath her chair. As they crept out from under her legs, she introduced them with a high pitched, squeaky baby voice. I couldn't have cared less. To her, they were her children. She appeared a little frustrated by my lack of interest in them. Almost like I was saying she had two ugly, small, hairy, creepy-looking babies. When I didn't address them or, for that matter, even look in their direction, they ceased creeping toward me. They probably realized I would not be stooping down to pat them. Just as checking in started to get a bit awkward and long-toothed, she found the key. She happily sprang up from her seat when she found it and plowed through the two of us standing in the office doorway to usher us to the room.

It was a secluded room near the pool at the back of the property. The large home was an L-shaped, beige, two-floor house. It had a lagoon-like backyard in the crux of the L, with a small dip pool at the foot. Our room faced tropical plants and the pool. It was perfect. The room itself was very non-descript, mainly because it was decorated in all beige and similar tones and with very little detail. She quickly pointed out the features - bathroom, mini-fridge, and TV with remote.

Satisfied she had done her job correctly, she nodded and said, "Have a great day and holler if you need anything!"

I briefly entertained the idea of yelling at top of my lungs, "I need more towels!" I figured she wouldn't appreciate that. Without talking, we settled our things in their proper drawers and places. Boyd commented that the bedspread was the same as his ex-wife's. I wondered how he had been in her room long enough to know that and then quickly dismissed my train of thought. I didn't need to start myself on that downward spiral.

Once things were put away and the two of us had primped a bit, we decided to head down the street and out to Diamond Street. Boyd felt it necessary to announce that he would take me the usual sites he liked show people when they first come into town. I thought it was charming that he was about to start me on his unofficial tour of Siesta Key. It felt special, kind of like the insider's guide to the island. I was privy to things that the regular tourists weren't. First stop - the bar where we met. It was a perfect, sunny day. Even in the beaming sun, it was not too hot. It was a tepid day with no breeze, and the whole town seemed to glow with a golden hue.

I made my way to the saddle I had been sitting on when Boyd introduced himself to me. I patted the top of it and smiled up at him. We had a little chuckle and made our way to the bar. A good friend of Boyd's was bartending. He was a tall, slim, smiley guy with big brown eyes and dark hair. He sort of looked like a Spaniard. He had a crew cut that was growing out, and he was fully painted with tattoos from neck to wrists. It was fun to try and survey them. I was trying to be polite and not stare, but I wanted to take note of the detail and color. It was beautiful work. He was friendly and chatty. He was the kind of person who made you feel instantly comfortable, the mark of a good bartender. Boyd introduced us, and we all had a good conversation about country music playing. The Bartender had the CD book out and was skimming titles to find the right song in the player. Boyd loved country music. Sometimes he broke out into song a bit too loud, often interrupting whoever was talking while we were there.

"Lucky guy, man. Beautiful day, a pretty girl with you. Lucky guy." The Bartender complimented Boyd as he turned to fix drinks.

The Bartender shared that he had lived in Boston some years ago after he found out where I was from. I was having a good time letting him reminisce about Boston, but Boyd started to look bored, so we finished the exchange. We spent the rest of the afternoon with The Bartender and rounds, trading stories about nothing in particular. It was a heavenly day except for the fact that I had no idea what to do with Boyd. I was a little uneasy about how to posture myself. I felt so close to him on the phone, but now that he was in front of me, the dynamic of our relationship seemed to evaporate. I felt as awkward as any first date. I wondered if he was pleased that I came. He was congenial, but he wasn't looking longingly at me or showering me with compliments. I surmised that we would both feel more comfortable as time went on that weekend.

I started feeling hungry so I brought up the idea of a late lunch. I also thought it wise to grab a bite since I'd already had 4 drinks by then. It's a marathon, not a sprint when you're going to spend the day drinking. We decided on Mexican food and said our goodbyes to The Bartender as I settled the bill. We simultaneously slapped sunglasses on our faces as we exited out into the light. Boyd pointed to the right and we headed down the road to find our lunch.

As we walked, he became more animated. Maybe he'd become more relaxed around me, or perhaps it was the booze, but he seemed eager to get me to smile and let my guard down a little. He made funny short remarks about the places and the people as we passed, and we soon found ourselves at another bar that served Mexican food. The place itself was another country bar only larger. We strolled into the dimly lit, hollow room with lots of empty tables and chairs. Any attempt at ambiance gave way to a cave-like atmosphere. It was not my idea of island tropical settings for lunch.

I was fascinated by the fact that they wanted to offer Mexican food instead of something more American, being a country venue. I appreciated the random selections; I ordered soft tacos and another Crown Royale and Ginger Ale. A short time later, our lackluster entrees arrived. I stared down at my letdown of a lunch. I thought since he worked in the restaurant business, Boyd ought to know good Mexican. The heap of food on my plate was a mere substandard replica of real Mexican food. It tasted exactly how it was presented. Having lived in California, I knew good Mexican, and it is admittedly hard to find unless you are in an area densely populated with Mexican natives. I ate it to fill my stomach, not satiate my palate, and hoped if I was going to keep paying for meals, he would pick a better places while I was there.

"Not bad?" It came like a question.

"Yeah, not terrible," I replied. At least I wasn't lying.

After my fifth Crown Royale and Ginger, the rest of the day blurred into the nighttime. We chatted up tourists, wandered from place to place, until I was worn out from walking, talking, and I was done drinking. We made our way back to the Bed and Breakfast. Boyd helped himself to the mini-fridge as we entered. A stash of beer was chilling inside from an earlier trip to the convenience store. I was done. I chain-smoked cigarettes as we sat outside and had a drunken, hazy conversation about nothing serious, although riveting when you are in that kind of condition.

I don't know how or when I got to bed, but the morning's first minutes felt like a bus driving over my head. My tongue was pasted to the roof of my mouth, and my brain felt like a rung-out sponge that had dried on a sink ledge overnight. I was afraid to lift my head from the pillow. Just as I suspected, instant dizzy nausea slammed into me. I scuffed to the bathroom and got into the shower to wash the queasiness away. Despite protests from my stomach, I managed to maintain my intestinal integrity and got dressed, leaving my hair wet and my face without makeup so I could hurry to the convenience store for my hangover elixir, PowerDrink. Had I been smart about it, I would have bought it ahead of time and downed one before I went to bed and then another one upon waking. It is the only thing I know that will make you feel moderately okay when you spent the night drinking like it‘s going out of style.

I quietly excused myself from the room and pounded down the pavement to find any store I could find to get my fix. I finally found a CVS and headed in. I scooped up a shopping basket and found the PowerDrink. I filled the basket with blue bottles. Six of them would be a lot to carry, but it would be worth it. I got lost for a few minutes trying to get back to the Bed and Breakfast but managed to find my way. I took big gulps of PowerDrink as I walked. It almost spilled out of my mouth. I was trying to get as much fluid as I could into my body before I got back. My headache was dissipating, but I had the all-too-familiar sweat going. Perhaps a greasy breakfast would also help with my testy stomach. I thankfully made it passed the little office without the Inn Keeper seeing me. I wasn't in the mood for idle conversation. I had to repair myself fast!

Boyd was feeling about the same as I was but he was ready to take on the day. I handed him a bottle of PowerDrink. We had a short conversation about which place on the island made the greatest breakfast. He eagerly suggested a restaurant, but it was too far and probably had a very long wait. We found a sweet little diner with only about a handful of tables, and it had what I needed - home fries.

Our second day was more of the same. We went back to see The Bartender and did the same walk all over again. What happened to the tremendous local tour I had been promised, I couldn't say. Apparently, based on my guide, the only thing locals do in Siesta Key is drink at one of four bars.

The final night in Siesta Key came almost as a relief. I was sick of drinking and done having someone else spend my money. He thanked me profusely with every credit card transaction and promised to pay me back, but I knew those pledges were empty. I believe he knew it, too. Maybe he thought it was just polite to say. I would have rather heard, "Hey, I had a great time. Thanks for treating me to everything, but I have no intention of keeping any promises, and I am just using you like every generous girl who comes back to visit me." I felt foolish for coming on this trip in the first place. What was I looking for? He was fun, but he wasn't the love of my life. He was very handsome, but he overwhelmingly knew that, and at times, it was obnoxiously obvious.

My final day was marked with his constant joking about doing something to make me miss my flight. He'd make pouty faces at me and whine at me, "Stay, Sariah." His puppy dog eyes and protruding lip were cute at first, but as the morning wore on, I got a little annoyed. I was ready to go home. I was tired of drinking and paying for everything. I like to be treated well. He acted like a gentleman when it suited him, but this guy hanging out and sponging off of me wasn't what I wanted.

Breakfast that final morning was followed by one more trip to see The Bartender. I looked for an excuse to separate from Boyd, so I stepped outside to check on my flight status. I dialed the numbers and punched in all the required information. "We're retrieving your information now. Thank you for your patience," the recording said while I stood watching tourists stroll by me on the shaded sidewalk. A Birds of Paradise printed shirt here, a woven straw fedora there, and lots of sunglasses. I almost forgot I was on the phone, dazed by the clichés wandering by me. The air sucked out of my lungs as the recording regained my attention. "Flight 2245 is on time and due to depart at 2:00 PM Eastern Standard Time..." I checked my watch, but I already knew what it was going to say. It was 1:10 PM. I hung up before the recording finished. I was convinced all morning that my flight left an hour later. It was too late. I looked behind me to see Boyd talking to The Bartender. I didn't want to relay the news.

I now had the embarrassing job of calling my friend to tell her I needed to have her watch Katie for another day. I would have given anything not to make that call. Would she even believe me? I swallowed hard and called my mom first for practice.

"Mom, I missed my flight."

"How do you do that?" Her voice elevated as she spoke. I tried to explain to her that I thought it was an hour later, but she kept interrupting me. "Well, what are you going to do about it?" She was trying to stay calm but demanded an answer.

"I'll see what I can do about getting another flight out today," was all I could offer.

"Okay, call me back then." She wanted to end the conversation partly because she wanted me to get more information before she got mad and partly because she wanted me to call and get this situation straightened out. I hung up and walked back into the bar. The sideways smirk on my face announced my plight before I could utter a word. I saw two pairs of eyebrows raise as soon as Boyd and The Bartender turned in my direction.

"My flight is in 40 minutes," I said.

"You'll never make it," Boyd assured me as he laughed.

"I thought it was at 3:00," I huffed, and the two of them exchanged a round of high fives.

"What are you going to do?" The Bartender asked.

"You are going to have to stay another night. I have a friend that manages a hotel down the street. I'll call him and see what he can do about a cheap room," Boyd quickly volunteered.

My instant relief and gratitude turned to resentment as I realized he could find inexpensive accommodations well before now but was content to spend my money carte blanche on an upscale bed and breakfast. I focused on the task at hand - getting off this island. I called the airline and explained my emergency to the Customer Service Representative on the other side of the phone.

"There is no other flight that I can put you on that will get you back to Boston today, Ma'am."

"But what about connecting flights?" I offered up a resolution even though I was sure she'd tried that.

"I am sorry, Ma'am, but the problem is getting you from anywhere to Boston. There isn't anything to connect you on."

"Ok, what about tomorrow?"

"I can book you on a flight that leaves at 12:00 PM," she said, her voice half question and half trailing answer.

"I'll take it."

What other choice did I have? I had to be on that plane. We finished up my booking, and I thanked her profusely and ended the call. Just as I turned to walk back inside, I was stung by the realization of what I had to do next. I had to call my boss to tell him I wouldn't be in on Monday. I exhaled and emptied my lungs. Should I lie? I could make up some terrible story about flamingos eating my wallet and stealing my license, rendering me unable to board any flight home. I felt willing to offer him any reason other than the fact that I was irresponsible in not correctly checking my flight times. I had to admit and succumb to the truth. I had to call my boss and tell him what had happened. I felt foolish as I left the message. He probably wouldn't buy it even if it was the truth. Who would? Oops! I missed my flight and had to stay another day in Siesta Key. Shucks! I wouldn't believe me either.

With all of my business resolved, I had to call back my mom. She took the information shockingly well and offered to go to my friend's house and retrieve my daughter. I called my friend and got her husband on the phone. I sorrowfully offered up the details and the resolution.

"My mom will come to get Katie. I am really sorry." I felt like such a terrible mother.

"Don't worry about it. Worse things could happen other than having to stay another day in Siesta Key!" He tried to reassure me that all was well and it wasn't a big deal. I didn't feel any better.

He accepted the plans and said they would have Katie ready to go when my mom got there. I hung up at least feeling like I had fixed the problem. I just didn't want to stay.

We had already been out all day, but I made him go back to the room with me and shower. I wanted to feel pretty and dressed up for my last night. In the last few hours, he took me to an outdoor place that had live music. I like live music, and I love being outside. Perfect. Why didn't we go there before? We met up with a few of his friends who were already parked at a long, intrusive, rectangular bar. The size was overwhelming for the space, but it was situated parallel to the stage, so it was a good spot to sit and watch the bands and the tipsy dancing crowd.

I was ushered to a seat at the bar. Boyd told me that he'd be back in a few minutes. He left me with a word of caution. "Rosie has a thing for me, and she might be a little jealous that you're here with me, so don't talk about me to her."

That struck me as strange, and my earlobes tingled with his words. Who was Rosie? I didn't believe his story. I wanted to disregard his words to find out what the reaction would be, but I also didn't want to hurt someone inadvertently. Were they together? Had they been dating recently? Trying to dismiss the notion and focus on enjoying myself proved fruitless. The words hung on a vine in front of my face all night. I wanted to go home. I wanted to leave him at the bar. *Why did I come here? What a mistake.* He became nonsensical and paranoid as the night went on. After much prodding, I convinced him to leave. I was now not only angry but embarrassed to be seen in public with him.

We found our way back to the hotel. I tried to have a conversation with him, but it was a merry-go-round of topics and drunken promises to always be there for me, no matter what. I wanted to believe it. Alcohol has a way of signing me up for things I never intended to do. It also had a way of making me forgive and forget when I shouldn't. I don't know when we fell asleep.

I woke in the morning, lying across the bed in the clothes from the night before and with the lamp still on. The pasty feeling on my face told me my makeup was still on. I was so glad to be going home.

Boyd accompanied me to the airport in the cab I hailed. I gave him money for his return trip back to his apartment. I knew he needed it, and I was sure he'd ask for it anyway, so there was no use in holding out. I checked in, and he waited for me, begging me not to go. It felt good to have him say that over and over again. His face looked so sad and sincere. Perhaps if I'd had a different life and no responsibilities, I might have stayed, but reality was calling me home. I had a little girl, a great job, a big house, and lots of things I had to show up for. I got in line for security, and he wandered next to the cordon, still whispering to me to stay. He kissed my hand over and over as he said it. My heart was pounding with each touch. I knew he wasn't speaking the truth but I didn't care. The perception that I was valued and needed was worth listening to the lies. It was intoxicating to be told I was wanted. Just hours before I was unsure if I wanted this relationship to continue. I had expected more excitement from him and had been sorely disappointed. Now I didn't know if I'd be able to tear myself away. I felt like I jumped into cold water. I stepped forward in the line, leaving him behind. He stood and watched me until I couldn't see him anymore. I went home in disbelief and longing to belong to someone again.

Eight

"Blue Morning, Blue Day. Won't you see things my way?" -Foreigner

Tuesday morning felt like God took a food processor and minced everything I did to get ready for work. No matter what I did, I couldn't get out of my own way. I had the goal of getting me and Katie fed, clean, dressed, and out the door in a timely manner. However, I had the added bonus of being a single parent, which meant I needed to get her to daycare and me to a train without a moment to spare. I was already mediocre at it, but this day was pathetic. I missed the train by a solid ten minutes. Ten minutes late equates to two hours in commuter time.

Now not only did I miss Monday because of my tomfoolery, but I was going to be late to return on Tuesday. I knew this would be an awkward conversation, and I prayed as I dialed the boss's number that I'd get his voicemail. Luck being what it is, he answered. I was blunt. No need to mince words. "I missed my train. I'll be in at 9:30" it was the truth.

"Ok, see you when you get here." He wasn't interested in a long conversation about it either. That was a relief. I knew there would be a more extended dialogue later, but I was glad to put that off. I had to focus on the task of driving into Boston.

The commute by car into the city is a lot like standing in line at the post office within hours of the Tax Day deadline. You find your spot at the back and slowly inch your way to your destination. You don't really drive. It's more like a slow roll. First, I stopped at my favorite coffee shop for a large one and made my way to the highway. This morning offered no mercy. The line started at the beginning of the exit. I lightly touched the button on the car door to crack the window. I opened the lid to the coffee, lit up a cigarette, and settled into my seat.

My mind wandered as the car inched along. I looked around me at all the cars waiting in line. There was a silver Lexus, a blue Acura, a late-model green Honda, a dented brown Toyota. I wondered if their drivers were happy. Were they looking at me? I was driving a brand new silver Mercedes. Did they think I was happy? I flipped open the visor mirror flap and examined my face staring back at me with flawless makeup and designer sunglasses. My face was framed by the black fox collar on my beautiful black wool jacket. Did they look at the person I saw in the mirror and wish they were me because of what they saw?

My upper lip went numb and started to sweat. My lower lip stiffened against my bottom teeth. Tears rose to the surface and flowed down my cheeks. I couldn't stop the emotions from spilling out. My tears turned to sobs, and I finally admitted what I hadn't allowed myself to proclaim. I had reached the breaking point. I was so sick of being tired and sad. I couldn't fabricate one more positive attitude and try to grind out another week. The thought was absolutely unpalatable. I wanted to hold it all together, but I buckled under the weight.

I dialed my mother on my car phone. Thankfully, many sounds are muffled with the imperfection of that technology.

"Hi!" Her voice boomed from the dashboard. She sounded cheery, but her tone implied that I never call this early. "What's up?"

I attempted to gain some composure, but my voice cracked with the straining. Words spilled out faster than tears flowed. I could hardly see through my tears. I recounted aloud what I had been thinking only moments before.

"So, what do you want to do?" she asked.

The question struck the air with such audible force that I stopped breathing. What did I want to do? I knew how I wanted to answer, but I feared the consequences of saying it aloud. Once it passed my lips, I was going to be held accountable to follow through with it. I wasn't entirely ready to marry that commitment. I inhaled to capacity and let it fly, "I want to write a book."

"So do it."

So do it? My mother said three words that left my head spinning for lack of anticipated debate on what I had just declared. She repeated before I had a chance to respond, "So do it!"

"Ok then!"

What had I just signed up for? When I was new in my widowhood, I was frustrated by the lack of books to which I could relate. I told myself that I should write a book about what it is like to be a young widow since I couldn't find one. I was certain there were other young widows like myself. Why didn't they want to tell their story? I thought it could be a service to God and to others out there to offer comfort where I had none. I had just committed to making that dream a reality. My hands shook and my palms turned clammy. The quivering in my gut told me I had just taken a dive before I had a chance to look at the bottom of the pool. My mind created random thoughts and scenarios during the remainder of my tedious drive. I parked the car in a daze underneath the building and rode my elevator to the office.

I had just put my briefcase down on my desk and unbuttoned my coat when the sales assistant scurried over to me and, in a hushed voice, said, "You're needed in the conference room."

I always appreciated her. She had the worst job a person in a sales office could have, cleaning up the paperwork mess that representatives left when they closed a deal. Salespeople are not known for paying attention to details, and it is the misfortune of their assistants to fill in the missing blanks. Many sales assistants sour towards their jobs and the representatives they work for, but not so with her. She approached every day and dilemma with the same pleasant smile and fortitude as the last. She made every directive her mission, and she did it with excellence. Therefore, when she approached me, I knew she'd been told to find me, and she would have scoured every corner of the office to do it.

She offered no other details and hurried off to her desk with a half dozen beige folders full of half-completed paperwork. I huffed and straightened my suit jacket, buttoning it as I walked to the back of the office, as was customary to do when you are requested by management. No time for questions on my extra-long weekend as I opened the door to find two levels of brass sitting at one end of a long, empty table. There were no smiles, and I sat down at the closest, most appropriate spot near them, keenly aware that I did not come with a notepad and pen, a faux pas in management meetings. I didn't even feel like improvising. I folded my hands in front of me, and one of my supervisors stared down at the table as he began to speak.

"Sariah, we know you've been through a lot."

Patronization was always the start of a long, hard conversation in these situations with them.

He continued, "We've done a lot, and I think you'd agree, to help you out while you've been trying to get to some level of normalcy in your life."

My other supervisor remained silent and fixed her gaze on anything but my face. I knew they were working their way towards the description of my shortfalls.

"But it's now come to a time where we need you to step back into your role as manager here and take the reins again."

I understood what he was saying. They would carry me no longer. I knew this would come one day soon. I just couldn't believe this was happening within a half-hour of my meltdown in the car! "Ok," was the only reply I could offer.

"Do we have your 110% commitment to rebuilding your department?" As soon as he said that, four pairs of eyes and raised eyebrows stared at me, awaiting a response.

"No," was my simple reply.

If I'd broken into song and started tap-dancing on the table to 'When You're a Jet,' I couldn't have gotten more of a look of shock on either of their faces. "No?" he asked.

Apparently, my reply needed verification. After all, I was a new widow, a single mother with a great career at a terrific company, and this one little word was going to end my relationship with them and dash the high hopes they had for me. I knew I was letting them down.

I took a deep breath. "No. I just can't do it anymore." I choked on my tears and grappled with my emotions as I continued, "I need a leave of absence or something. Either way, I can't do this anymore."

There, I said it. It was the truth, but hearing it still surprised me as much as them. I was sent to go have coffee and see what needed done while my Regional Vice President called the President to deliver the news. It must have been an interesting conversation because he was in his corner office behind closed doors for an agonizing amount of time. He spent half the day calling people on my behalf to try to honor my request for an extended leave. To be honest, I had no intention of coming back when it was over. I think in my own way, I was trying to be polite or let them down easy.

At the end of the wearisome and emotional day, I was called back in to have a final conversation. An extended leave was not an option. I needed to resign but under the assurance that I could come back at any time. I had the full blessings of upper management to take the time I needed, regroup, and rejoin when I felt I was up to the task. I was relieved. It felt less like lying to simply resign and leave.

"What are you going to do with your time?" he asked now that the gritty details were over.

"I'm going to write a book," I said with a smile.

"About what?" My supervisors shot looks of astonishment at each other across the table.

"About me!"

I wasn't yet labeled by society as an Author, so I wasn't surprised when my announcement was met with a mixture of amazement, disbelief, feigned encouragement, and suppressed laughter. I realized I was going to have to get used to that type of reaction because it was probably going to happen a lot.

With nothing else to cover, I left the room to pack up my desk. The rest of my team was waved in from the door and ushered to find a seat as I exited. Everyone looked anxious as I walked in the opposite direction. My non-participation in this impromptu gathering meant only one thing. I was no longer part of their team.

It didn't take me long to pack up the few personal photographs and trinkets on my desk. I was swarmed with strained smiles and wrapped in hugs. In keeping with tradition, once I was packed, I was rushed out the door. Management didn't like to extend emotional situations and garner any more attention from officemates than necessary.

A profound rush of calm encircled me as I headed toward the elevator with a box in hand. I looked up at the numbers over the doors as they closed and laughed to myself. I had really done it, but what had I done? I declared myself an author of my first book but hadn't written a word of it.

Sure, I was a semi-faithful online writer. I'd been a regular contributor to a couple of online magazines, but to write a novel was something wholly different. Did I have the stamina and endurance to complete it? What would I do with all of my time now? The questions swirled around and around in a tornado of inner dialogue. Finally, the elevator bell chimed, signaling that I'd reached the garage.

The corner of my cardboard box full of office belongings was starting to press against my the inside of my wrists painfully. I struggled to hold it steady while balancing my briefcase and purse on my shoulder. The last thing I needed was to send all of it spilling to the ground. I walked quicker when I spotted my car flashing its lights in response to pressing the button on my key chain. I popped the trunk and sent my load tumbling into the compartment with great relief. I hastily freed myself from my suit coat as I rounded the back of the car to the driver's side door. I wouldn't need the corporate uniform any time soon. Hallelujah!

I sat for a minute behind the wheel. I felt the leather as I gripped and twisted my hands around it. I couldn't get my mind to settle on an emotion. Was I more excited or scared? First, I checked myself for any profound signs of mental illness. Had I any hallucinations? Heard voices? Did the devil make me do it? Then I daydreamed about what it would be like to live the life of a Writer. In my daydream, I fashioned myself in an eclectic outfit, dressed in whatever I felt like putting together with an odd Bohemian flair. I'd play guitar, drink exotic herbal teas, and color my hair whatever shade fit my spirit. I'd always wanted to feel that freedom to live my life out loud. I'd been hemmed in by my work and career expectations so long I didn't know if I'd have the courage anymore. I recalled one time when I dared to wear red leather patent heels with my black pin-striped suit and overly starched white dress shirt. It was a little too avant guard for my crushingly conservative Vice President's taste. I thought I'd never hear the end of it. Forget about cutting edge hairstyles. I would have had a full-fledged war on my hands had I had the nerve to allow someone to create such a thing out of my tresses. I realized all those regulations were gone, hopefully forever.

I interrupted my own fantasy with the realization I was still sitting on the bottom floor of a garage underneath one of Boston's largest high-rises. It was time to say good-bye to Corporate America and let it go. I was overwhelmed with emotions as I wound up the ramp to the exit. Was I really leaving for the last time? I assured myself that I could call and beg for my job back if I woke up in the next few days with the realization that I'd lost my marbles and made a horrible mistake.

As soon as I could see daylight, I dialed my mother's number. "I did it!" I bellowed into the car mic.

"You did what?" she asked. I sighed. Didn't she remember anything we talked about this morning?

"I took a leave of absence from work." It was a little lie, but I wanted to lessen the blow. I think that was more for me than her.

"Oh," she replied. That was all my mother of many words could offer? "Are you okay?" came after a brief pause.

"Yeah, I am better than I have been in my whole life!" That was a total fabrication and aligned more with what I thought I should be feeling than reality, but I went with it.

"Do you want to come over for dinner?" I instinctively knew she didn't want to feed me so much as she wanted me to dish on all the details.

"Yeah, when I pick up Katie, we'll head up."

I was trying to wind down the conversation. I was feeling self-conscious because I didn't yet have my mind wrapped around my new circumstances. We agreed to see each other later and hung up. The silence that followed the dial tone hung in the car like a curtain in front of the windshield. I could see outlines but no detail. My mind was elsewhere. It was on the death of my career.

I pulled so much of my self-worth from my business accomplishments. I felt as if I had nothing of merit to offer other than the skills and awards displayed on my resume. I was so caught up in the desperation of my life that I hadn't even been scared enough to consider what I would be like without being able to puff out my chest and grin while explaining what I did for a living. My sense of importance came in extending my hand to the recipients of my business card. If the clothes made the man, then for heaven's sake, I'd spend every dime. I looked like no less than a million bucks. I had the look, the smell, and the poise of success. After all, I spent enough money on it.

My most significant self-inflation came from an accidental invitation to participate as a judge in the MIT Sloan School of Management's

International Sales Competition. I had been asked by a colleague whom I greatly admired to apply to be a judge. Judging the loftiness of the reputation of the university letters, I took him up on his request as more of a lark. I never dreamed I'd actually be accepted and thanked for electing to participate. I acted I though I won the Mega Lottery the way I told everyone within earshot about what I'd be participating in. Once the novelty wore off after a few days, much to the relief of my coworkers, I plunged back into the ordinary, telling myself that the competition must not be a big deal if they accepted me as a judge.

I was asked to give a talk about my experiences and life lessons in my sales career. I envisioned sitting on a stool in front of barely interested participants as they munched on boxed lunches and tried to talk quietly so as to avoid being detected by me during my presentation. I'd gone home that day and told Asher what I'd been asked to do.

The morning came when I was to present my speech in Boston. I was escorted to the faculty dining room where the speakers would present. The grand lobby opened to a sea of white linen table cloths and a multitude of table settings. I made small talk with the attendees and fellow judges and tried not to focus on the river of people pouring in.

The luncheon got underway as a Director from Google thanked us for coming and announced the lineup of speakers to come during the meal. The first, was a Vice President from Microsoft. I would follow the VP. Instantly, I stopped listening to the list of other speakers. As soon as he announced the VP from Microsoft preceding my time, I started to look around the room at name tags. The names blurred against the titles and logos. I was in the company of some of the best of the best in business. As this set in, my mind numbed and my vision tunneled. I struggled to swallow. I felt a faint dampening on my forehead and the back of my neck. I felt nauseous.

Never in the history of my sales career had I been afraid to speak in front of a group of people. I felt so small and inadequate. "Get it together, Diersch," I said to myself. Mr. VP of Microsoft was halfway through his speech. I had no time to choke. I was going to have to deliver, whether I was prepared or not. In all actuality, I wasn't prepared. I hadn't even thought of what I wanted to say. I hadn't practiced and I didn't bring note cards as prompts. Nothing. It was only me, figuratively stripped naked in front of Google, Microsoft, Sun Microsystems, etc.

Suddenly, my vision returned to normal and calm overcame me. As the clapping died down, I made my way to the podium about 20 feet away. The silence was so intense that if someone had dropped a fork onto their plate, someone would have had to peel me off of the ornately painted ceiling. I was pleased that I didn't trip on my way to the podium.

I opened my mouth to speak but I heard myself saying things I hadn't even thought to mention before. God presented himself in my brain and told me what to say. I know this because I was too nervous to focus and yet it flowed seamlessly as if I'd rehearsed for hours. God's words spilled forth to nodding heads and attentive eyes. I finished and sat down.

Upon sitting back in my chair, I was greeted by a VP in the financial industry. "You, lady, are a rock star!"

As my mind played the movie reel of that moment, I was snapped back to the present, realizing I was still waiting for the red light to turn. I began to wonder how I would package the news of my day to my dad. He's not much for entrepreneurial spirit, especially mine. I pressed my left foot into the car floor, thinking of the look on his face when I'd tell him that my financial livelihood was now history. I imagined the disapproval on his face when I described my new project. I could almost hear him say he was sure it would fail.

My expectations were met that evening when I blurted the news across the dining room table in the direction of my father as he leaned against the back of his chair. "I left my job."

I couldn't believe it actually came out. He stared intently and sucked air through his teeth, a habit he has when he's irritated. I continued as the sucking and lack of verbal response grated on my nerves like nails on a chalkboard. "I've decided to take some time off to write a book."

I had no idea if that would help recover my status in his eyes, but the continued lack of speaking assured me that it hadn't gotten there yet.

"What about Katie?" He asked.

That one question felt like a punch in the stomach. I knew with the benefits I was collecting for being a widow with a dependent that I could care for Katie, but not in the way that I had been accustomed to. I sensed that he considered my decision to be irresponsible. It felt that way, but at the same time, it felt like a huge prize was suddenly within reach.

"Can you go back?" He asked as he stared at me without even a pause or a blink.

"I can whenever I want to," I assured him. I knew he wanted to hear that, and it was the truth, but I was hoping never to find out if my boss would make good on the promise. He walked away and thus ended the conversation. He didn't speak to me for the rest of the night or several weeks after. I, his golden child, had disappointed him. He had put his hopes and dreams into my successful lifestyle, and in return, I had thrown them to the ground. He hated me for it.

Nine

"I'M GOING OFF THE RAILS ON A CRAZY TRAIN." -OZZY OSBOURNE

It was day one of my new career. My sole source of income would be social security benefits while I embarked on my writing journey. I was on a fixed income; I was willing to make the sacrifices if it meant I could finally have some rest and some version of a normal life. I could spend time with my daughter, finally, like I always wanted. Sure, I'd have to cut back on my spending, but we'd be fine. If necessary, I could supplement with the money I had in the bank from Asher's life insurance. I looked forward to the concept of a good night's sleep. I was thrilled with the idea of being a stay-at-home mom. I needed a little sunshine in my life and a slower pace.

I hadn't slept much the night before. I was up late filling in Boyd on my day's events. We tried earlier in the evening to converse via text message, but between my comings and goings, not to mention my Cold War showdown with Dad, I hadn't been able to get much across. I was maniacally high on my bungee jump of a life change, and he seemed a little intoxicated. For every statement, I made he went on a little too long in response and seemed obnoxiously jovial for nearly midnight on a Tuesday. To me, he had been drinking a lot lately, but I chalked it up to being unemployed and living on an island that didn't stop partying. Most days when I'd talk to him on the phone, he'd either have just woken up sometime that afternoon, or he'd phone rather early in the morning to talk - obnoxiously early. That type of early morning call that told me he hadn't yet gone to bed. The late-night chats romantically intoxicated me at first, but they got a little annoying when they occurred too many early mornings in a row and without regard for what I had to do the next day.

His state of intoxication made it difficult to gauge his reaction to my news. His response felt like a congratulatory veneer over disappointment. I had a glimmer of feeling like he thought I had made a mistake. This was quickly replaced by my confidence that I could do anything I set my mind to. I was determined. When I have the right focus, I can accomplish any goal placed in front of me. I reassured him that I knew what I was doing and that I would be able to take care of myself and Katie. He halfheartedly accepted this declaration and ended the call. He had to go. Where he had to go, I didn't know.

As my first stay-home morning progressed, I found I couldn't shake the conversation with Boyd. It rubbed against my emotions like fine-grain sandpaper. I wondered why he wouldn't have faith in my decision. The truth was, I wondered if his feelings were more selfish, considering he had been regularly asking me to loan him money since I left Siesta Key after our visit. He asked a couple weeks after I left. He asked if I could wire him $300 to get him by. The next month he asked for more money, and, again, I sent it. I didn't start questioning his intentions until the third time he asked. The sums were getting more substantial, and instead of pleading for money, he was matter-of-factly asking. He had grown accustomed to my agreeing to help him. I started to feel like I was wading into something that could prove dangerous. During our conversations, he casually mentioned his need for things, and I would surprise him by buying them and shipping them to his apartment. He was dependent on me. I couldn't admit, even to myself, that he was probably using me and I was buying his affections.

In return for my financial charity, I exerted my entitlement. Since I was a major support to him, I started asserting my will. He didn't seem too phased until I announced that I was coming to Siesta Key for a few months to chill out. "I think I am just going to pack up the car and come stay down there for a while. I'm going to go online and look up some long term rentals," I announced during one of our evening calls.

I never asked if he wanted me to come. As far as my announcement was concerned, I wasn't looking for approval. I was looking for his reaction, and I expected it to be thrilled.

"Wow. You can get in the car, just like that?" His voice rang with nervousness. I had a faint tingle that my plans were invading his space. "What about Katie?"

Did he think I would leave her behind? "She'll be with me!" I replied.

"Oh, well, that's cool." He said it like I just told him I never wear deodorant. "When would you come?"

I sensed that his mind was in planning mode. I stated I would probably come in about a month. We ended the call soon after, and I hung up the phone with my heart lightly tapping on my sternum and a faint dew around my hairline. *What was I doing?* I had the distinct impression that my choices were not too smart, but I didn't want to care. I wanted to live on the edge. I wanted to feel alive. I wanted to feel anything but absolute, desperate, constant emotional pain. I was willing to do anything to escape it.

My next hurdle was to tell my mother of my plans by giving her as much information as possible while offering up as little detail as I could. She didn't know much of anything about Boyd, other than I had described him as a passing acquaintance I met while in Siesta Key on my first trip. On my second trip, she overheard him in the background while I was on the phone, checking in with her. She became alarmed and started firing off questions like bullets out of a machine gun as I stood there on the sidewalk in downtown Siesta Key with him standing within feet of me. She seldom waits for an opportune time to get answers. I bristled at her barrage and dismissed him as someone with whom she need not concern herself and tried to smooth her porcupine quills.

"Tell him to keep his hands to himself!" Those were her parting remarks that evening.

It was too late; the damage was done. Sorry, Mom. Feeling starved for attention for so long, I wouldn't hear of it anyway. It was like rain to a thirsty man lost in the desert, and I was parched.

My mind went into overdrive, struggling with how to spin this announcement. I knew she wouldn't approve, and she didn't, but she took it better than expected. The speech - okay, lie - I came up with centered on a road trip to visit friends and family. I'd see my cousins and some of my old friends who had moved to Maryland. I said I wasn't sure how long I'd be gone, but maybe I'd last only a few days if Katie wouldn't tolerate the car. I assured her there was no need to worry because I was going to have fun. She settled into the idea that people she knew would be seeing me and that I wouldn't be driving at night. With Mom out of my way, I could move forward without a fight. Calm swept over me. It must be God's hand. Things were lining up like dominoes.

I had lots of time to talk to Boyd now. With neither of us working, our texting and phone conversations hit an all-time high. He kept asking if I was serious about coming to Siesta Key and how long I thought I would stay.

Finally, sick of his interrogation, I responded, "Do you not want me to come?"

I was almost hoping he'd say no, but he didn't. "Of course I do, Sweetheart. Of course, I do."

He called me Sweetheart a lot. I tried to believe it was my pet name, but I was jolted out of that fantasy when I overheard him on the phone one afternoon call a store clerk Sweetheart. It wasn't special. It was what he called women when he wanted to win their attention. I decided to ignore my disappointment. I'd win him over. In the end, he would think I was his only sweetheart.

Boyd and I spent many late nights talking and drinking together on the phone We planned our pretend future together. Maybe Katie and I would stay forever with him in Siesta Key. Perhaps we'd all go to Maryland where he was from. He wanted me to meet his parents. He was certain they would love me. He kept dropping breadcrumbs, and I gobbled them up before they hit the ground. "When something seems too good to be true..." is the most practical life statement ever made, and I ignored it like a pro. I was so busy feeding the emotional addiction with his attentions that I dismissed the fact that Boyd was intoxicated every time he called me. There were nights he was so drunk that he'd be ranting into the phone about nothing. I saw the freight train coming, but I thought I could jump out of the way when I heard the whistle blowing.

I was so sure I was doing the right thing. This is what God wanted for me. Ironically, I barely told anyone I was leaving for Florida, and I would "forget" to mention that I was in a relationship. I actually didn't know what to call my status with Boyd. It was hard to define since I had only seen him twice. The first time I met him was amazing. The last time I saw him, I was relieved to leave and wondered why I came. Yet, here I was, leaving my home and taking my toddler down to the southernmost part of Florida to be with him. Many people asked about my goal for my trip. I told them I was embarking on an adventure with my daughter on the open highway - no destination in mind, simply going where the road would take us. Some thought it was crazy. More than a few thought I was full of it and just not 'fessing up. They were the smarter ones. I offered no information. "It's none of their business" I would catch myself whispering to no one when I replayed conversations in my mind from concerned friends.

I even lied to myself. I told myself that I was an adult, and I didn't need anyone's permission to do anything. I felt like a little girl standing in front of her mother, with her hands her hips, yelling, "You're not the boss of me!" I always needed everyone's approval. Seldom had I ever done anything without a proper quorum of people telling me what to do. Now, I was doing the craziest thing I had ever done in my life and ignoring the opinions and concerns of those closest to me. I felt ashamed. I tried to convince myself that I was feeling misplaced guilt. I deserved to be happy. I figured, given time, others' objections would be laid to rest when they could witness how good and caring Boyd was to me. I convinced myself that, in the end, all would be well. Besides, everything was lining up so easily and neatly to make this happen. I was convinced that this expedition wasn't just my idea. It was part of God's plan for me.

However, I was so far from God that I barely prayed. I didn't want God's discerning. I knew what He'd say about my current lifestyle, and I didn't want to hear it. I had tried to do things His way. I had been a good Christian, and He'd rewarded me with a tormented marriage that ended by losing my husband too early and not on my terms. I was now left alone with a baby who would likely not even remember the father who loved her so tenderly. I was done with God's plan. It was my time. I was going to grab the brass ring. God was just going to have to go along with it. He seemed to see things my way since I hadn't run into any hiccups or snags in my plans. I also felt distant from my church family, so much so that I didn't want to be around them. They didn't understand. They were too blinded by the rules and regulations of the church. I had the real line on things. I wanted what I believed I deserved.

I lined up places to stay on my journey down to Florida. I only needed one night in a hotel with Katie. I planned to drive the distance in two days.

I hadn't ever taken a trip for more than two hours with her in the car. I wondered how she'd fair and started worrying. I started having anxiety as I imagined a screaming, flailing toddlers in the back seat in traffic. I went to the store to get DVDs and a portable DVD player. I compiled toys, books, and anything else I thought might hold her attention. I knew she would nap, too. She was an excellent car napper. I tried to keep my anxiety low by steering clear of thoughts about the dangers of a single mother driving down the interstate highways of the east coast and relying on rest stops for bathroom breaks and lunch. Whenever my mind wandered into an awful scenario, I'd rationalize if God didn't want me to go He'd make it impossible for me to leave. I knew if I prayed for Him to bless this journey, I'd get the answer I didn't want. Therefore, I didn't bother praying.

With only a couple of weeks remaining before my journey, I still hadn't found a suitable long-term rental on the island. Boyd told me about a motel with kitchenettes and spacious accommodations for a reasonable rates. I hadn't asked for his help, but I was thrilled to have him include himself in my plans as far as living arrangements were concerned.

I tried to avoid guilt, but there were times when I recalled the many nights that I spent shedding tears on my bed, begging God to help me live a life my daughter would be proud to emulate. I had all but abandoned that prayer, and my life looked nothing like what I'd want for her. My thoughts turned to hope that she wouldn't remember any of this. Boyd had a daughter that he loved to talk about. The stories he told about his relationship with her sounded like the father I had hoped for and seen in my husband. I was sure Katie would grow to love Boyd. I wasn't considering her happiness for one second. It was all about me, and I convinced myself she'd benefit in the end as well.

One evening, while looking at a calendar as I planned my journey, it occurred to me that my period was late. I lighted with fear but quickly reasoned that it was probably the stress of planning the trip. I gave it two more days before I bought a pregnancy test to ease my nerves. I laughed to myself as I took the test stick out of its packaging. Once I proved I wasn't pregnant I won't have to worry anymore. I peed on the stick and waited. After a minute, I checked the results. Then I read and re-read the directions ten times to make sure of what I saw. I was shocked. My thoughts raced - *How could this be happening to me?*

I was sick from trying to take it in. *Oh God,* I thought, *You wouldn't possibly have the nerve to put me through one of the worst trials of my life in the middle of one of the worst ordeals of my life, would You?* I bristled at the memory of the fateful night of instructing God that He was no longer going to tell me what to do because I could take whatever He dished out. Except this. I hadn't counted on this.

I let the news settle into my mind for a day before I called Boyd. *How am I going to broach this topic?* I wondered. I called but he didn't answer. I left a message, and he returned the call an hour later.

"I'm pregnant," I spit out as soon as he answered.

"Oh, wow…oh, wow, wow, wow…oh…Are you sure?" he asked in disbelief.

"Yes, I took a test. I am pregnant."

"Okay. Alright. You are going to have to give me a minute here. This is big news."

"I know."

He said he'd call me later and quickly got off the phone. I reeled from his reaction. There was no finality to the conversation. I couldn't gauge from his reaction if he felt anything other than shocked. I was in complete denial. I was positive it was some kind of mistake. This wasn't real. The test was a false positive. His return call was one of the biggest 'about faces' I'd ever experienced.

"You know what? I am happy," he gushed.

I was stunned. "You are happy? I don't think I am happy."

"You know what, you'll come down here, and it will all work out. You'll see. I am happy."

I wasn't happy at all. I was concerned about my image. *How am I going to tell my parents, my in-laws, and Asher's friends?* I suddenly felt dirty and like a bad person. I was a phony and a fraud. I billed myself as a good Christian woman, but in reality, I was a disgrace. *What do I do now?* My head screamed.

I started out wanting to follow God's plan for me, to let Him use me for the greater good of others. I wanted to write my story as a young widow and show people how God worked in my life to heal my pain. Instead, I sent Him packing; I closed the door to my heart. I had decided to write my story without Him, and now I was disqualified by my actions. The enemy wouldn't let me forget it. Time after time, the phrase "damaged testimony" popped unbidden into my thoughts. I was unusable now. I was glad to be going far away from judgmental eyes.

Finally, everything was in its place. I had nothing left to do; no one left to talk to about my plans. Katie and I headed out pre-dawn on a Monday morning. I packed the car the night before. I stocked the cooler with enough juice boxes and snacks to occupy a toddler for several days. I was ready to take on the road. I prayed for safety on the drive. I knew I could at least ask for safety, if not for my sake, for the innocent bystander in the car seat behind me. I backed out of the driveway and took a look at my beautiful yellow home with the sun just starting to lighten the roof. I sighed and put the car in drive.

I had a habit of gripping the steering wheel and twisting my hands so the leather squeaked under my palms. On that morning, my hands gripped the steering wheel so tight that it made no sound. The car was eerily quiet. Katie fell asleep, sipping on a juice box, still in her pajamas. The guilt and sadness kept pinging my conscience. My motherly conscience wouldn't let me forget that someone who had no choice was on this trip with me, and I was embarking on something God would never rejoice in. *Are you trying to tell my something, God?* I wondered. Then I purposefully put my guilt and God out of my mind.

The journey was uneventful. I expected at least one major I'm-done-with-the-car meltdown, but Katie handled the traveling like a pro. First, we visited my friend and life mentor, Ned, and his wife, Chandra, on the first night. They are a couple that I met through mutual friends. I had made a regular habit of consulting and clarifying most of my life's affairs with Ned. He was a wise man with many insights, and I loved to talk with him. He held me accountable and, on more than five occasions, saved me from the bitter abyss when I'd fight with Asher.

We arrived at their home, and my daughter sprang when I released her seat buckles and ran up the walk to Ned and Chandra's door. To her delight, a sweet, gigantic Great Dane greeted her. My daughter, occupied with her new furry friend, allowed Ned and I to say our hellos and small talk about the drive. Knowing Ned and Chandra were Orthodox Jews and that I'd be in their home, I respectfully chose a long dress to wear, as is the custom for women. Ned thanked me for my thoughtful and considerate dress in their home.

I gave the same road-trip story to Ned that I gave everyone else. The person with whom I could be the most honest, I didn't even tell the truth. My soul cringed at this realization. How great was this relationship with Boyd if I wouldn't share it with Ned? My mind wrestled, and my heart spoke to me. *Who are you kidding?* The question flashed across my mind. It felt like lightning was in my fingertips, and my emotions stirred — the jolting hurt. I was going to be leaving early in the morning, so I wouldn't spend much time avoiding the subject. However, Ned knew me. His forehead wrinkled in concern, and his eyes a little saddened. He knew something was wrong; he just didn't say so. I pretended not to notice his concerned look.

I said my good-byes the next morning and headed off to my cousin's house in South Carolina for a day. After visiting them, the following two days of driving ran together. I became laser-focused on getting to Siesta Key. Katie and I had a good time singing songs and checking out various little places along the way. I knew I was south of the Mason-Dixon line when there was a Cracker Barrel at every highway exit. The last stretch from the top of Florida to Siesta Key was the longest. My last two hours involved driving in the dark. Katie was tired, but we had to press on because I hadn't made plans to stop at any other hotels. Boyd was texting me every hour on the hour during the last day. He seemed anxious for me to arrive, leaving me with a feeling of rekindling passion. This would be the first day of the rest of our lives together. Our romantic story started here.

Finally, my tires rolled into Siesta Key. I called Boyd, who was downtown, and we coordinated an intersection to meet up. I'd pick him up, and we'd go to the hotel he picked for our first night. As I neared the designated spot, my breathing got shallow, and my heart rate picked up. I suddenly felt silly and out of place. My mind quickly shifted from excitement to anxiety, and I wondered if he'd be disappointed in my shaggy appearance from driving all day.

I parked along the side of the street to wait for him while the anxiety continued to build. I jumped at a sharp tap on the passenger window. I had been straining so hard to find him in the dark through the windshield that I didn't see him approach from the side. My head snapped in his direction.

He let out an open-mouthed laugh as I unlocked the door. He had a half-empty drink in one hand and a cigarette in the other. He leaned in and started to sit down. "Um," I started.

He hesitated, lifting his cigarette. "Oh, this? How about I just meet you at the hotel so I can finish this."

Without waiting for my reply, he shut the door and walked away. So much for the orchestral climax I had composed to signify our long-awaited kiss. I pulled my car away. I knew where to find the hotel. We stayed there when I missed my flight during my last trip.

I pulled into the hotel parking lot. Boyd sauntered down the sidewalk a few moments later. My body felt heavy as I realized he was very intoxicated. His overly-friendly demeanor and annoying boisterousness gave him away. Katie shied back, wrapping her arms around my leg.

"Is she shy?" He asked.

"Not usually, but it's been a long day. We're tired and need to go to bed," I replied. I knew she was acting shy because he was loud. She wasn't around drunk people. I didn't tell him because I didn't want to make him feel bad. I felt dismayed by his condition. I wanted him to go, but he didn't. I ended up falling asleep to him snoring next to me on top of the covers.

The next day signified another beginning. We checked into a lovely villa-style motel with big rooms, seating areas, and a spacious bathroom. Boyd redeemed himself. I beamed over our temporary home as I walked around and showed Katie every nook and cranny. It had a pool and was quietly tucked away from the main strip. It was private and quaint. *This is good*, I thought. *I can stay here.* I set up camp, unpacking our suitcases and arranging our toiletries in the bathroom. I started to relax.

That first day was all that I hoped for. We walked Katie in her stroller down Diamond Street. My mind fashioned the fantasy that we looked like a happy family. That fantasy was erased when Boyd picked out our lunch location. He chose the large, dark bar with the lousy Mexican food. I was not happy with his choice, and I tried to steer him in another direction. It felt irresponsible to bring my daughter into a bar to eat in the first place.

He tried to make light of it and talk me into staying. "It's no big deal!" he said with a smile, shrugging his shoulders. "This is a tourist town. People do it all the time when they come off the cruise ships. Lighten up!"

Was I just being too uptight? I wondered. *I am from New England and it's common knowledge we are wound tight.* I breathed out and sat down. I took a long pause to look at the face of my daughter as I unbuckled her and plunked her down in her seat next to me. She was more interested in the bustling around her than me trying to save face with her for bringing her into a bar for lunch.

With such a beautiful and enjoyable day, aside from the as-predicted lousy Mexican food, I couldn't wait to see what our first magical night on this gorgeous island would bring. Would we quietly sit out in the seating area outside our room? Would we simply watch TV as Katie slept? I was eager for our time alone. As we made our way back to the motel for rest and a swim for Katie at the pool, Boyd announced he had something to do and would meet up with us later. I agreed, still glowing from our walk. Katie and I left Boyd on the sidewalk, and I wheeled her to our motel.

Time flew by because I was distracted by Katie's love for the water and her need to make me the 'Water Horsey' on whose back she rode while I galloped around the pool. I realized Boyd had been gone for 2 hours. I checked my phone but there were no calls or texts. I tried not to feel rattled and forced myself to pay attention to my daughter instead of the clock hanging in full view of the pool from the window of the motel office. Three hours passed. Pangs of anxiety started to gnaw at my stomach and my nerves, but I resolved not to call and check in on him. I didn't want to seem like a pain in the neck, worrywart, or control nut. I decided to wait for him to call, even if it killed me.

Hours later, Boyd arrived, drunk and loud with his equally-inebriated cretin of a cousin. Katie had already been fed and put to bed, tired from the sun and her long swim. I had ventured to a local fast food place for dinner when it became apparent that Boyd wasn't interested in supper plans with us and Katie was hungry. I grew increasingly frustrated by their amplified slurring banter and lack of concern for my sleeping baby. When they ignored my requests to control the volume, my temper got the better of me, and I snapped at both of them. They apologized and Boyd announced he was going out. He quietly kissed me on the forehead and walked out the door with his snickering sidekick following behind. I was hurt that he left me sitting by myself on our first real night together. Waves of anger, disappointment, disrespect, and contempt washed over me. I felt the corners of my mouth turn down as tears started filling my eyelids. I washed up for bed in slow motion. I told myself, *Tomorrow is another day. There's lots to do to find a place to live. Get some rest.* I spread out on the king-sized bed, but I couldn't sleep. I tossed and turned, waiting for Boyd to return from his night out. He didn't.

The next morning, I focused on the task of finding a long-term place to stay. I didn't know how long I was staying. Part of me was hoping I'd never want to leave; the other part was cautious. I still hadn't seen Boyd since the night before. However, my excitement got the better of me when I found what sounded like the perfect place for rent in the local paper. I eagerly called and the landlord said I could meet him to see it in an hour. I quickly agreed to the time and hung up.

I arrived at the appointed time to see it was a second-floor apartment in a quaint and tidy four-unit condominium house. It was newly remodeled. There was a granite and stainless steel galley kitchen and beautiful crown molding through the neat but compact space. I was smitten with the balcony entrance. It had just enough room for a wicker chair and a palm tree that hung a frond lazily over the railing.

After my brief tour, I announced that I'd take it. The landlord asked me to fill out a rental application at the counter and told me he'd call me to let me know the outcome of my application later on that day. I shook his hand and left with a big smile on my face. I was hoping he'd call with a "Yes."

After we returned to the hotel, Boyd materialized hungover and apologetic for not calling. I didn't want ruin my good mood by asking too many questions, so I asked where we could go for lunch. Boyd knew just the place. It was a local Cuban lunch spot and he thought we'd all like it. We decided to make our way there and check it out.

Katie, Boyd, and I were sitting in the small Cuban sandwich shop when I got the call an hour after the tour from Bob, the landlord. At the words, "It's yours if you want it," I felt my muscles tighten in my cheeks from smiling. I didn't pause to consider consequences before telling the landlord that I'd take the year lease. I agreed to come back and sign that day.

I was ecstatic. We had a place to stay. I had very little to put into it, but it was ours. I looked at the two loves of my life, eagerly awaiting a proportionate response to my emotions. Katie, too young to care, just stared at me as she stuffed too much bread into her little chipmunk cheeks. Boyd hardly looked up from his plate as he nodded in agreement and gave me a one-handed thumbs up. "That's good, Baby," he finally choked out as he tried to swallow and talk at the same time.

"What do you have that we can use in the new place?" I asked. I started inventorying what we'd need for our bungalow in the trees.

"I don't know; I'd have to check. Don't want just to leave my cousin with nothing in his apartment." He shrugged and looked at me for understanding.

His deflection told me he didn't have anything of merit to offer. I would be the one supplying what we needed. I pondered this realization as I watched him finish eating the lunch I had purchased.

"You are going to need to get a job," I stated matter-of-factly. As one side of my brain tallied my list of living needs, the accounting side was quickly calculating the costs for upstart and monthly maintenance.

He threw his hands up and huffed, looking away from me and toward the glass doors of the restaurant. "No kidding. It's not like I haven't been trying, you know, but that silly restaurant manager I used to work for is telling everyone around here bad things about me, so I decided I should just lay low for a while before I start looking again."

My veins ran cold, and my breath got shallow. Thoughts crowded my mind. *Lay low? How long is he going to lay low? How long since he worked? Is he assuming I'm going to take care of him? Is he under the impression that my bank account is open, and he can make withdrawals any time he wants?*

Boyd took note of the look of indignity on my face. He twisted his mouth into a grimace and nodded, "Okay, we'll pick up the paper on the way back to the motel."

The apartment was immediately available, so without further hesitation, we moved out of the motel and into our new place. Next, it was a trip to the only discount department store on the island, Reggie's. The three of us headed into the store, grabbed a cart, and started wandering down every aisle. Katie visually inspected every dish, piece of cheap artwork, coffee mugs, towels, and other household items that we hurled into the cart behind her as she sat in the child's seat. She squealed when I put a pink plastic princess lamp into the cart for her room. Materials or quality made no difference to Katie. She just loved the chandelier lamp shade.

"Sparkly," she said as she touched the hanging gems on the shade. If I bought her nothing else, she would have still been thrilled. I found myself still smiling ten minutes later from my daughter's simple contentment with something so inexpensive. I was glad to have made her happy.

We set up our home in short order. With only three rooms, the condo came together quickly. I was practically manic as I stormed International Imports and purchased most of their inventory for my home. My most prized find was a beautiful, dark brown, sixties retro egg-shaped, wide-weave wicker chair. I fit perfectly in the chair. I put my feet up on the matching ottoman and closed my eyes so I could imagine the right place for it on my precious balcony.

I was more at ease now that the condo looked like a home. I didn't want my little girl squatting in some hovel. I wanted her to feel like we lived there.

By now, my mother's calls were more frequent. I could touch the edginess coming through the phone. She was not satisfied with my blasé answers and changing subjects. I refused to elaborate. My forehead would tighten each time I saw her name come up on the screen of my cell phone. I would clamp my jaws, waiting for her to bring up the subject of my intentions in Florida. With every call, she became more and more insistent that I tell her the truth. I couldn't bring myself to do it. I warred inside, part of me screaming to tell her the truth and the other slapping duct tape over my mouth and threatening me if I uttered a word.

I didn't want to lie to my mother; I also didn't want to tell her the truth. She would say what I already knew but chose to ignore. *You have no business being here, in this situation!* I wouldn't admit I was conscientiously sinning against God, my daughter, and my body by living with a man to whom I was not married and pregnant with his child. My guilt kept me silent. My ego kept me from the ones who would readily tell me the truth. Inwardly, I argued that I didn't want or need to be judged.

I lost sleep, and I worried about how this would affect Katie. The calls from my mother went from pointed discussions to heated conversations and then screaming matches that ended with hang-ups and volleys of angry text messages for the rest of the day. The ugliness was hard to live with, and she was 1800 miles away! I could almost feel her watchful eye on me no matter where I went. I lost sight of the fact that her angry words were those of a mother who was desperately hoping her daughter was okay. I saw her as an attack dog who barked at me with every call, and I was wondering when she'd break her chain and come to Siesta Key.

After much coaxing and encouraging, Boyd finally found a job. Though he felt it was beneath him and his skills, it came with a paycheck. He stated he would get used to it but he couldn't keep himself from lamenting. I listened to him complain that he should be running the kitchen at this restaurant, not relegated to the lowly position of sauté cook.

I was relieved that he was finally going to contribute to the household income. I believed the responsibility of a job would curb his drinking habits. He'd spent too many nights going out to meet friends at the bars downtown instead of spending time with me. He also didn't seem too remorseful for borrowing money from me to fund his habit. The financial tally was mounting, and he had stopped promising to pay me back. I wasn't foolish enough to think he would anyway, but I had appreciated the feigned attempt at humility. His former kind demeanor was replaced with entitlement and the expectation that I would meet his demands. Somewhere the dynamic changed. He went from being at my mercy to feeling like I owed him something. I didn't recognize when it happened or how I agreed to it, but this new change left me feeling insignificant and objectified. I was being voluntarily held hostage.

My relief was short-lived. Boyd's work schedule of 2 PM to 12 AM Sunday through Thursday lasted only a short time. For the first week, he came home at 12:30 AM, stinking of fish and garlic, tired and ready to fall fast asleep after a hot shower. That first Friday morning, he asked me to take him to the restaurant to pick up his first paycheck and take him to the bank. He exited the bank with a wad of cash in his hand handed it to me.

"I'm not good with money," he said. "Please take this from me and keep it until I need it."

I was surprised by his trust, but he owed me a lot of money. Upon returning to the condo, which I had named the Tree House because of the palm tree that encroached on our balcony, we divvied up his cash. He required child support for his daughter which he paid in a weekly sum to his ex-wife. He needed money for cigarettes and some spending money. I would hold onto the rest. I thought it prudent to ask what he intended to pay me for the bills, food, and rent.

"Let me get on my feet first." He moaned out this statement as if my question were an imposition and I was raining on his parade.

"How long will that be?" I asked. I felt justified in my expectation that he would share in the expenses.

"Okay, okay. I don't know, maybe in a couple of weeks. I have to go somewhere. I'll call you later." He quickly picked up his stack of spending cash, folded it, put it in his pocket, kissed my forehead, and jutted out the car door. I didn't see him again until 4 a.m.

Boyd's late nights of drinking increased with his newfound coworkers at the restaurant. They enjoyed alcohol just as much as he did, and none of them seemed to have any interest in considering how they would feel the next day. Within a three week time span, Boyd went from calling to say he was going out "for a couple of beers" to no calls and no explanations. Within a matter of two months, his after-work arrival at the condo went from 12:30 a.m. to 6 a.m.

The ramp-up to full-blown disregard for me, my feelings, my graciousness, or his sense of responsibility in paying his way was so fast that I never saw it coming. It seemed like once he received the extra key to my front door, he turned into someone I never met before.

Hoping to be incorrect in my assessment, I sat down Boyd one afternoon after he awakened, blurry-eyed, and reeking of perspiring booze on my couch. I started talking while he stared at the floor in the opposite direction. "When are you going to start contributing to this house?" I could hear the elevation and frustration in my voice, trying not to lose my temper and alarm Katie.

"Do we have to talk about this now?" he whined. I knew he was not feeling well. He'd been out until almost dawn earlier that morning. When he came in, he collapsed on the couch and passed out in his work clothes, crusty from dried sweat from working in a hot kitchen. He wanted sympathy, and I had none. I felt manipulated, and I wanted to be convinced otherwise.

"Sariah, I don't have a lot of money right now," he said. He shook his head, and his eyes remained fixed on the door.

"I know because you drink it all as soon as you get it!" I snapped. My nostrils flared, and my hands started shaking. My inner voice screamed *I want answers, you bastard!* as I waited impatiently for a reply.

"What do you want me to do? Stay in every night with you and Katie?" The implication was that family life, which he claimed he was looking forward to only weeks before was now unappealing.

"One night a week, even?" Now I was the one whining. "You don't even spend one night a week with me. You tell me you are going out for cigarettes, and you don't come back until 3 AM!" I started to cry and felt angry with myself for showing such weakness. "You promise and promise me things and never follow through. You've not given me one dime toward any of the expenses here. You eat my food, sleep in my bed, and with nothing in return, and not even one measly night to spend with me. It makes me feel used!" The tears and emotion, like raging water, exploded out of me.

The masks were off. I was finally seeing him for who he was, and he was starting to understand that I wasn't going to go along with his behaviors.

"I have to get ready for work," he muttered. He rose from the couch, walked by me without a glance, and went into the bathroom. I heard the shower start as I stood there, blinking tears off of my eyelashes. I realized that my mouth was open from the shock of his callous response to my outpouring.

I had convinced myself that I could make this life look good and then present it to my mother as a blessing in disguise. As I looked at the closed bathroom door, that feeling poignantly wore off. I knew I was going to have to tell her what was happening. I shivered as I thought of the moment I would say, "Mom, I'm pregnant" and her reaction. I had expected God to take this garbage that I turned my life into and gift wrap it to look like a blessing.

My thoughts reminded me of a conversation with a woman a few years ago. She was married with four children and had recently, after much deliberation, decided to leave her husband for the man with whom she was having an affair. She was suffering through a lot of emotional fallout from both sides of their family, and her anguish over dealing with the constant barrage of communication was exhausting her.

"Doesn't God want me to be happy?" she'd asked me in desperation.

"No. He wants you to be content in His will!" was my reply.

The memory of that conversation stayed with me and firmed my resolve to get the news over with. I asked God to make my mess into a masterpiece. I figured He wouldn't do it.

I dialed, inhaled, and hoped she wouldn't pick up. She answered on the second ring.

"Got a minute? I need to talk to you about something important," I said, trying to sound cheerful.

"Okay, what's up?" her voice trembled a bit into the receiver.

"Mom, I'm pregnant, but I have a plan. I am going to pursue adoption." Silence hung in the air after that sentence. After a minute, I continued. "I just can't do this with Katie and everything else I am going through. I don't know what else to do. I can't raise her by myself, and Boyd isn't going to be a good father to her."

I wanted to spill the truth and flood her with information, but I didn't want her to worry about Katie and me. However, I kept my emotions and the reality of our life in check. I needed to feed it to her piecemeal so she wouldn't get overwhelmed.

"Have you done any research or called an agency?"

I filled her on some information-gathering searches I had done on the Internet. I had reached out to a few agencies and settled on one. My mom had questions, but I couldn't answer many. The situation was new to me, too.

I had threatened Boyd with adoption if he didn't straighten himself, but he didn't seem to think I was serious. I knew he wasn't going to take me seriously. I was debating on whether or not he even cared. What had initially been such a sweet adoration for this man had now become a bitter taste in my mouth. I had become nothing more than something he retained out of necessity, not desire.

One evening the whole charade came crashing down in front of my face. It was a weekend afternoon, just like any other. Boyd pretended he was going to the store. He said he'd be back in 10 minutes.

"See you tomorrow," I said without turning in his direction.

"No, really, I'll be right back," he countered.

"Right, see you tomorrow."

He'd gone out and returned drunk and crying at 9:30 at night. I was at a loss for words when I saw the upset state in which he presented. I got off the couch and asked what was wrong.

"I saw Amanda," he said through sobs.

Amanda was his former girlfriend. A girlfriend he initially felt "inclined to marry," but as he got to know me better, he waved her off as nothing more than an intimate friendship. I could see that had been a lie. I asked why he was crying.

"You don't understand. I loved her, Sariah. I loved her so thoroughly." His tears were now practically outright wailing.

"I don't understand. What happened?"

I was asking what had happened that night to put him in such a hysterical state, but he misunderstood and started talking about the past. "Nothing. I had to tell her about you when you decided you were coming down here. She was supposed to move down here at the same time, and I had to tell her I hooked up with some tourist girl, and she got pregnant."

He looked at me for sympathy, but I wanted to smash him across the face. I felt rage build up from my toes, and just as it crested, it broke my heart into a thousand pieces. I gasped to inhale, but suddenly calm poured over me.

"That's it, isn't it," I whispered to him as I stared straight into his pupils. "I wasn't the one you loved. I was the one you wound up with."

The reality settled in as my own words pierced through my ears. He couldn't deny the truth. He turned away and headed right back out the door again. The game was over. I had my answers. Boyd was a drunk and a user. He didn't now and never had loved me. He did what he needed to convince me. I was so desperate that I was willing to buy affection. I had the faint feeling that I had taken up with a prostitute. I wasn't living with my boyfriend. I was paying for a service.

Over the next several days, the weight of this revelation almost overcame me. My decision to seek adoption for my unborn child cemented.

Ten

"Is someone getting the best of you?" Foo Fighters

If ever there could be a haven in a spiritual hail storm, it was the Main Street Baptist Church in Siesta Key, FL. The only thing I did right when planning my fateful trip was research churches I could attend. There was a smattering of churches that categorized themselves as Christian, but this one's website mirrored my beliefs. I added attending a service to my to-do list. I sent an email to the church through their website. After a couple of exchanges with the church secretary about the services, stuff for kids, and the pastor, I felt like it was the place we'd attend church, as long as people weren't too loony in their zealousness.

One overcast Sunday morning, 2 months into my stay, I decided to make good on my unspoken promise to attend the Main Street Baptist. Wanting to make a good first impression that everything was normal in my life, I got Katie and I dressed in the best clothes I brought. I fashioned our hair and accessories and drove to the church in my shiny, clean car I washed the day before under the concrete knowledge that it was sacrilegious if I showed up in a dirty car.

The church was located, not surprisingly, on Main Street. The street represented a line almost smack in the middle of the island, cutting it in half. In an area so small, everything is only 5 minutes away so I was early. I planned to wander in unnoticed. That plan was derailed when Miriam appeared in my path as I entered the sanctuary. A bright smile and flowing long brunette hair, she greeted us warmly and asked about Katie. "Are you looking for Children's Church for her?" Miriam smiled down at my daughter, whose eyes were roaming about the new surroundings, rather than at the person talking to her. She was unaware that anyone was even addressing me.

I shook her hand to get her attention, "Say hi, Katie."

Upon speaking to her, I became aware that I was asking Katie to break the ice for me. I smiled. "I'm sorry, my name is Sariah James. This is our first visit." Katie smiled weakly up at Miriam and then returned to the visual surveying.

Miriam was not offended. "Let me introduce you to Angel. She can help you with finding children's rooms upstairs and talk to you a little more about what they do there."

Miriam quickly walked toward a petite blonde woman standing in the right aisle of the humble yet pretty sanctuary. I promptly followed her with Katie trailing behind, holding on to my hand for guidance but still distracted.

Miriam touched Angel's shoulder and she turned around to greet all of us with a beaming grin. Angel's soft, gentle voice and twinkly eyes disarmed my usual apprehension when faced with someone new. Her face blushed with hospitality as she introduced herself and bent down to address Katie, face-to-face.

"Do you want to see where all the kids are?" Angel asked. Katie smiled and nodded eagerly, and we followed Angel to the room where Katie's age group attended the Children's Sunday School. I kissed my baby good-bye and slowly turned around in the door, glancing back to make sure she was settled and engaging.

I heard Angel's voice in front of me. She was waiting for me to finish up with Katie. "She'll be just fine. We have a great Children's Sunday School program, and the teachers are wonderful!" She smiled reassuringly. "My kids are older now, but they were all raised in this church."

We walked back to the sanctuary and parted ways. I said, 'thank you' and made my way to an empty spot in a pew. In widowhood, sitting alone in the church was something I never wanted to get used to, and it certainly didn't make it easier when no one knew me.

The church was a stucco white building with a long, narrow steeple top. It was a moderately sized building by usual standards but large for the small island. It seated about 500 people. The decorations were modest, but the building grounds and rooms were clean. It looked well-cared for.

I made myself comfortable and tried not to look around. I wasn't looking forward to introducing myself a hundred times, and I didn't want anyone to get to know me. I thought if I could fly under the radar and not make any friends, then I wouldn't have to explain my situation. I saw myself as damaged goods amongst church-goers. I didn't want to share my life with anyone because I didn't want to see looks of disappointment or judgment. I believed God wanted me to sit in the corner of my life and be quiet. So that is what I planned to do.

The singing ensued, and I felt a little lighter. I enjoyed good praise and worship music, especially from southern Baptists. Unlike their Northern brethren, they sway and clap to the music. I was only one of seven people at my old church that had the nerve to do that. I felt right at home, clapping and raising my hands. I wasn't feeling particularly joyful, but it was my way of trying to break the silence with God and see if He would be willing to be friends again.

After the opening song, the pastor made his way to the pulpit and announced his intentions to the congregation. "Today, we will begin our 9-week study on Christian suffering."

My stomach knotted, and I felt like someone just punched the wind out of me. I couldn't believe what I just heard. I certainly felt like I was suffering, like I had suffered, and that it would never end.

The pastor continued. "There many reasons that Christians suffer. Sometimes we suffer at the hands of the sins of another. But often, we suffer because of our own sins."

Did he know I was coming today? I wondered. I felt ashamed, convicted, and mostly called out by none other than God Himself. It was as if He was letting me know He knew all about what had happened, and He wanted me to understand, in full color, how my choices landed me where I was. If I could have waved a magic wand and made myself disappear into thin air right there and then, I would have. But I had no choice. I had to listen.

He gave an excellent sermon. I couldn't help but take it in. By the end of the service, I was looking forward to the next week. I wanted to know more. I wanted to hear what God wanted me to understand. If He still wanted to talk to me, I would pay attention.

As everything came to a close, and everyone filed out of the sanctuary, Angel found me and asked me what I thought. I wanted to burst into tears and tell her the reasons for my profound sense of grief, but I withheld and said, "It was really good."

"Let me give you my number," she said as buried her face in her purse, looking for a pen and a piece of paper.

As she busied herself with writing down my information, I opened my bag and pulled out one of the business cards I made up when I quit my job. I handed it to her without speaking.

"Oh, you are a writer," she commented as she read my card.

"Yes, I am writing a book," I replied. I felt like I had to add some validity to the title underneath my name.

Next, she asked the million-dollar question - the one I hated answering and everyone asked once they heard what I was up to. "What's your book about?" She raised her eyebrows and paused for my answer.

I felt like a fraud. What was my book going to be about? How about when God totally messes up life, do Him one better and make it all that much worse? That probably wasn't message anyone needed to hear. "I'm a widow. The book is about my husband dying and my journey in the first year."

"Oh, I'm sorry," she murmured.

Everyone was always sorry. What she didn't know was the person who should have been the sorriest was standing right in front of her, pregnant and living with a man who was taking advantage of her while dragging her daughter through the whole ordeal. I was the one who should be sorry, not Angel. We agreed to connect with each other soon, and I went on to fetch my daughter from Children's Church. Katie greeted me in her usual way, jumping up and down, screaming "MAMA!" and running at me with her arms out. Nothing in the world felt better than that. She showed off the pictures she drew and the sticker she got for coming that morning. We could belong here. I decided we would return.

Prior to my arrival in Florida, Boyd made promises to come to church with me. He said he'd love to get into church again, even bring his daughter. He never lived up to his promise. His perfect excuse was that he worked on

Sundays. He had an alibi. Honestly, I was relieved I didn't have to bring him; I left him and my reasons for being with him at home when I came to church. We had a mutual agreement without ever having the conversation.

After Boyd's confession about not loving me, things continued to decline. After many more nights in a row of coming in after 4AM, yelling obscenities, and staggering into things, I was done with his behaviors. One late morning, I confronted him and told him to move out. He plead for reconciliation and promised to mend his ways. He begged for me to give him a chance to change. He stood in front of me with palms open and eyes pinned on me as he spoke. I simply swept the floor around him and told him I wasn't changing my mind.

"If you can stay sober for 6 months and I am still interested, then we will talk, but for now, you have to go," I stated. "I can't have you here like this with my daughter. I am pursuing adoption for the baby. You are in no condition to be a father and I wouldn't want you around her anyway."

He continued to coax me into a different decision. He stopped just short of agreeing not to drink any more. He said he'd cut back, but I had lots of experience with alcoholics in my family, so I knew cutting back never cuts it. It's all or nothing when it comes to alcohol. He wouldn't hear of it. I continued sweeping as he spoke, and he started to get angry when he saw this conversation was not going his way.

"I'm not leaving," he said. His voice lowered and his tone was stern. "I'm not leaving, Sariah, and you are not putting this child up for adoption. You'd never go through with it."

He stood with his hands on his hips, committed to his ultimatum. I felt as though prison gates were closing in on me. I didn't know how to respond. I stood there, clutching the broom in my right hand, staring intently at his face and trying to think of something sarcastic and biting to retort with, but nothing came.

"I want your key by the end of the week." It was all I could get out. It sounded like how I whisper to Katie in the store when she gets all riled up, and I need to correct her without nearby shoppers thinking that I am yelling at her.

I thought of having the police remove him immediately. It would be best for both of us and less embarrassing if he'd just give me his key. I wanted him to leave quietly, but after a couple of days, it became apparent that he was taking no steps to go elsewhere. Again, I asked for his key but he refused. He said he would never relinquish his key to my Tree House. I revisited the idea of calling the police the following week as my morning-sick stomach rebelled from the stench of garlic, fish, cigarettes, and putrid alcoholic sweat permeating from my living room couch. Boyd routinely fell asleep on my couch still in his cook's uniform, which was always encrusted with some sort of food paste from constantly wiping his hands on his clothes.

The idea of being held hostage in my own home was revolting. *How could he treat me with such disregard, after all I had done for him, and in the situation I was in?* I stood in the doorway of the living room, watching him snore. Suddenly, I realized I was treating God in the same way Boyd was treating me. Tears began to fill my eyes as I continued to watch him. The regret was so unbearable I could scarcely choke down my coffee. I heard Katie stirring in her bed, and I got off my chair to kick Boyd in the shin to rouse him and shoo him into the bedroom so she wouldn't see his appalling display in the living room. He growled and stumbled toward the room. I snapped at him to get out of his filthy work clothes before he got into my bed. He grunted and shut the door.

My sweet Katie missed all that happened that morning. She usually did. This kind of morning had been happening nearly every day. I did my best to hide Boyd and his ghastly behaviors from her. My guilt for adding to her already traumatized life was squeezing any sense of joy out of me. I realized I had only thought of myself and what I wanted without any regard for her emotional well-being. I felt like a neglectful mother and a failure. The waves of emotion felt certain to capsize me. I couldn't do this anymore, but I couldn't do this alone. I knew I needed to be truthful with myself and others and start to deal with my choices. I wasn't Catholic so I couldn't participate in confession; therefore, I did the closest thing a Baptist could do - I called up Main Street Baptist Church and asked to meet with their pastor.

I was scheduled for the next day. I planned to take Katie to her preschool, which she was now attending on weekdays. That way, I could fall apart without her witnessing it and she would have as little exposure to Boyd as possible. I had a glimmer of hope for the first time in a long time that something might go right or somehow get fixed. I was willing to hold on to it with all my might. Tomorrow morning someone would know what I was enduring. I was praying to be held accountable.

The next morning had an air of accomplishment as I prepped, preened, and took my daughter off to school. I came home to shower and found myself standing there, letting the water hit me with my mind wandering, wondering what I would say to the pastor. I was eager to just come out with it. Maybe he would think I was a total loser who imploded my life like an old building, but I couldn't keep it in. I was tired of feeling like a prisoner of my own choices.

The pastor was a kind man with a quiet demeanor and a friendly, inviting face. He was older, but more of a fatherly age. His title and his stage of life gave me the impression of being able to trust him and his judgment. He hadn't even said anything more than, "Hi, I'm Pastor Harry."

After I introduced myself, he escorted me to his quiet and spacious office above the sanctuary. We sat down and he gave me a kind, non-judgmental look and asked the question I was waiting for. "So, what brings you here today?"

I spilled my story without missing a beat - the death of my husband, how I met Boyd, the pregnancy, what I was doing in Siesta Key, and what my wretched living situation was like. I word-vomited all my problems onto the floor between our two chairs. Our chairs were positioned side-by-side with an end table between us, so I didn't need to look at his face. This made it easier. When I was finally done emptying out 20 minutes later, he asked if I wanted to repent.

"Yes," I whispered. I did. Repenting meant that Boyd would need to move out immediately so I wasn't continuing to live in sin, and I was dying for someone to make me do it.

I wept quietly as I prayed with Pastor Harry. The relief was instant. I felt like I had lost 50 pounds in an hour. I felt my jaw loosen, and the tension in my neck started to unwind. I thanked Pastor Harry and headed down the stairs to exit the church. My breaths were deeper. Something had changed. My determination to rid myself of the leech was unwavering. He was going to be gone, whether he liked it or not, and he'd never see it coming. Perfect.

I didn't mention my visit with the pastor at Main Street Baptist to

Boyd. The next morning I took Katie to school, as usual, and came back to shower and start my day. Late morning, like clockwork, stinking and hungover, Boyd rousted himself, asked if the coffee was made, and scuffed out the front door onto the balcony for his cherished morning smoke. There wasn't coffee made, but I cheerfully offered to make him some. I knew it would be the last thing I would do for him.

When he was ready for work, he asked if I could drive him. He decided not to ride his bike to the Tree House the night before because he was too intoxicated to make it. I obliged and gathered my things. If he spoke during the drive, I heard nothing. I was too fixed on my goal and wouldn't have cared if he'd told me the winning numbers for that night's Lotto. I just wanted him gone. I pulled into the parking lot and looked at him. He thanked me and kissed me on the lips for the first time in weeks. How ironic.

My mind was scrambling. I only had a few hours to pull off my plan, and I felt unprepared. First, there was a locksmith. It occurred to me that I changing the lock on a door I didn't own without so much as a word to my landlord, but I didn't have time to change my mind. I was sure he'd thank me later. I anxiously parked my car on the street outside my Tree House and hurried up the stairs to the door. I found the tiny island phone book on top of the refrigerator and called the first locksmith I found under that heading in the yellow pages.

"Can you come today? It is kind of an emergency. I need the lock changed." My heart pounded in my chest as I awaited his answer.

"Sure, I can be there in a couple of hours. Is that okay?"

I told him I'd be waiting for him and hung up the phone. One thing down. Next was the big task of gathering Boyd's belongings. I piled clothes and random belongings on the bed and dumped them carelessly into garbage bags. As they filled, I robotically marched them outside and down the stairs, plunking them onto the platform floor near my entrance gate. I filled and plunked until I was satisfied that nothing was missed. Then I found his guitar.

Boyd was a talented musician, but no one knew it. He hadn't played or written anything in years. He said he was too busy or didn't have the right people around him. I knew the alcohol had taken his gift from him, but he wouldn't admit it. He had a prized loose-leaf notebook filled with pages and pages of lyrics and chord diagrams. He hid it underneath my bed so it wouldn't get anything spilled on it or destroyed by a toddler innocently looking for paper to draw on. He said it was the collection of every song he'd ever written. When I retrieved the cherished book from the under the bed, I let out a sinister giggle as I imagined him coming home and seeing me pour lighter fluid on it in the driveway and then dropping a match on it. He had taken something precious from me. He had taken advantage of my grief over my husband, and I wanted to make him feel like he made me feel - helpless and ruined.

I scolded myself by asking if God would want me to burn this book and make him suffer. I knew He wouldn't. I sighed and placed the book into a shopping bag, picked up the guitar, and took them both downstairs. I put them on top of the washing machine and dryer on the landing so they would be safe until he came to pick up his stuff.

The locksmith came and went with little fanfare. It cost me eighty dollars to change the lock. I wanted to pay him twice as much because I was so overwhelmed with gratitude.

I was practically ready to dance a jig. I wouldn't have a leech in my condo anymore! Locks were changed. Boyd's things were gathered and removed. The only thing left to do was to let Boyd know he was evicted.

I picked up my cell phone and texted him the news as bluntly as possible. "I changed the locks. You can't stay here anymore. All your stuff is at the gate downstairs."

I had trouble swallowing, and my hands were shaking as I pressed send. For an agonizing two minutes, I waited for a reply.

"Don't do this. Please don't do this. I have nowhere to go."

My millisecond of pity was replaced by the feeling of justice being served as I typed, "You should have thought of that 3 weeks ago when I asked you to leave. I'm done. We are done. I called an adoption agency too. I am going through with the adoption."

I read it 4 times before I sent it. I needed to see the verdict in typed form, "We are done." Sweet release, it was over. He tried many times that evening to reach me via text and phone calls but I refused to answer every one. I didn't need to. There was nothing left to say.

My last official duty of the day was to let my landlord know what I'd done. That meant telling him why I had to do what I did and what kind of condition I was in. Every time I thought about having to explain myself to others, my esophagus tightened. I felt like a sketchy single mother who doesn't care about anything but herself and can never really get it or keep it together. I didn't want people to think of me that way. However, only one word came to mind when my thoughts circled around my decisions: Loser.

An hour later, I heard the front door of my landlord's condo downstairs shut. He always went immediately onto the front porch with a cigarette upon returning, so I knew I'd have a few minutes of his time if I went right down and got it over with. My legs slowed as I walked. I felt heavy, but I kept going. I rounded the corner at the bottom of the stairs, sidled up to the side of his porch fence, and made my entrance known. I sighed and put my hands on my hips, and stated my agenda.

"I had to throw Boyd out today," I stated.

Bob raised an eyebrow, "Oh?"

"Yeah, um, he has a drinking problem, and I just couldn't deal with it anymore, so he had to go. I asked him to leave but he refused so I had the locks changed today. Sorry." My head bent down in response to my words.

"I'm glad you told me. I wished you had come to me sooner. I could have done something about this if you needed me to." His tone reflected fatherly concern. "Thank you for being so pro-active. How much do I owe you for the locksmith?" He asked unexpectedly.

"Oh, Bob. No, this is my fault. I'll take care of that." I didn't want anyone being put out for my poor choices.

"Split it?" He countered with a half-smile.

"Okay. Split it," I agreed.

I wasn't going to ask for the 40 bucks, but if he wanted to hand it to me, I'd take it. Bob and I ended up talking on the porch for a little over an hour. His wife arrived home, and I repeated my story to them. She said she had a suspicion that I was pregnant but didn't want to pry if I didn't want to say anything. That was a relief. With this cloud lifted, I felt free to let them get to know me. We talked about where home was for the both of us and what we loved about Siesta Key. Bob stated he used to be a club owner in a big city back up North. Now, he was working with troubled youth. He didn't immediately offer how he made such a big transition from one career to the next, but I had my guesses. I was pleased to hear he decided to use something in his life to make the world a better place for the next generation. I've always admired people like that. Bob had been concerned for Katie and me all along. He hadn't felt comfortable approaching me since I really didn't take any time to get to know him. Since there was no yelling or anything violent, he had waited to see how it panned out.

"Are you okay financially with him gone?" It was a valid question for a landlord to ask.

"Yes, yes, Bob. I am totally fine."

"He never gave you any money for anything, did he?" He had him pegged.

"No, nothing." I was disgusted and laughed as I spoke.

"I didn't think so. Are you okay?"

I was soothed by their words and kind attitudes. We parted with a sense of levity and understanding of one another. I felt cared for, and it was a great feeling to know that my landlord and now friend, Bob, was downstairs watching over Katie and me even if I didn't realize it.

I picked up Katie and took her to McDonald's for a treat of McNuggets for dinner. We went home, and I unpacked her dinner. As I arranged nuggets and fries on a plate for her, I told her that Boyd would not be back.

"No more?" she asked with a smile on her face.

"No more, Baby."

"He's all gone? All gone?"

"Yes, Baby. All gone."

I wondered why we needed the extra verification when she let out the most overjoyed "Hooray" I ever heard come out of her mouth, raising her arms and hands up like I just scored a touchdown. Apparently, I hadn't kept anything hidden from her. She was just unable to tell me how unhappy the arrangement had made her. I was relieved to know that she was contented again but heartbroken to realize that all this had been affecting her sense of well-being.

Much to my delight, the following Sunday, Angel asked me if I'd like to get together for dinner when I saw her at church. I sighed with disappointment and put up my hands. "I would but I don't know anyone to babysit for me."

"No worries, I know some girls at the church. We'll find you someone."

She did. With a proper church-girl babysitter to tend to Katie, Angel and I headed out for a delicious dinner on the water on our gorgeous island.

We sat outside alongside the yachts that were docked in the marina as we dined on freshly caught fish and amazingly-prepared vegetables. It was nice to be out conversing with an adult, take in the atmosphere, and watch the swaying palms.

Angel asked me all the typical new acquaintance questions. I volleyed the same ones right back at her. I felt safe with the conversation; it was a familiar routine and I didn't have to answer difficult life questions. We got into a spiritual discussion from there. Christians have a gage to see where the other one is in their walk with Jesus. I am always interested in spiritual conversations. I always have been as long as I can remember.

Prior to our dinner date, I vacillated over whether or not I should share my situation with her. Once we got done with spiritual check-ins, I felt comfortable enough to open up about my reason to move to Siesta Key and what had happened. I braced myself for rejection but none came. I continued to elaborate on the events. Maybe she doesn't get it, I thought. As I continued, she seemed to take longer to look at my face. The only thing I saw was a comforting assurance that she understood and had compassion for me and the road I had been traveling. I knew then that Angel and I would be good friends.

Now that I had a friend in church, a caring and authentic pastor, a sweet little church family that I was getting to know, and Boyd eradicated from my life, I could breathe a sigh of 'Thank God.' I looked forward to Sundays like a kid waiting for Christmas. Whatever event was taking place there, I was volunteering and present. I wanted to be at church all the time. I was drawn to something. I was not sure what it was, but I had a longing to be around people who shared my faith.

As we continued to study Christian Suffering, I took copious notes in and outside my Bible. I looked up and examined every verse that Pastor Harry suggested from the altar. I wanted to seek and understand. As I continued to study, my hunger grew. I wanted to know more. I was never satisfied. I have always been a student of something. I love to research everything about what interests me, but this was different. I wanted to really comprehend what I was feeling and to hear what God was trying to tell me in this church. There was hardly a day that I was not sitting in my living room with my nose in my Bible, reading chapters at a time, and pausing to meditate and pray. I felt like God liked me again, and maybe He was interested in being around me more. I wanted to hold onto that notion. Inside I was begging God to forgive me and to love me. I wasn't sure He'd be willing. I felt like I had really killed my relationship with God this time, and while He'd forgive me, it wouldn't be the same. I envisioned myself in a group of people He had to keep around because they said "the prayer" and they were trying, but they messed up all the time. I was a wayward child.

One morning, as I drove Katie to preschool, a song came on the radio. It was Casting Crowns' *Does Anybody Hear Her?* It is a song about a girl making her way to church after a night of bad decisions. The song is a confrontation to the Church asking whether or not we go out of our way to show compassion to those suffering and struggling to know Jesus. I'd heard it before, but this time I saw myself as the woman in the song. I felt like Mary Magdalene coming before Jesus. *Would anyone see me as forgiven?* I wondered.

I changed the channel because my emotions were threatening to spill out and regained my composure. I didn't want Katie to see me upset. I parked the car and bounced my sweet girl out of her seat, kissed her on the head, and set her down. We walked hand-in-hand, as we always did, into the building and down a long corridor to the outside playground where the children started their day. As I walked her, I noticed a set of pictures lining the right side of the hallway. "Jesus loves me when I eat" with a cartoon picture of a little boy eating dinner with his family. The next one was "Jesus loves me when I am sleeping" with another cartoon picture of a little girl asleep in her bed. The next picture said "Jesus loves me when I am bad." I don't know what was in the picture because the words stabbed right through me. "Jesus loves me when I am bad." I was so overcome with emotion that I hustled Katie out and on to the playground, kissed her quickly, and waved good-bye to her teacher. As I felt the tears start, I took my sunglasses from their perch on top of my head and fastened them to my face. I scurried with my head down so no one could see that I was now flowing large, sorrowful tears.

I jumped into my car, and started driving back to the Tree House. I turned on the radio to distract myself. I was humming the melody of a song as I drove and my ears caught the words, "Can you show me just how far the East is from the West?" I remembered a verse that I read:

"As far as the east is from the west, so far has he removed our transgressions from us."

Proverbs 103:12 NIV.

"Because I can't stand to see the man I've been rising up in me again." I was listening intently, fixing on every word being sung. "In the arms of your mercy I find rest." Tears started to flow again. I felt like I needed Him to show me how He forgives, not just tell me that He does.

I parked in my usual spot at home with the car running for 5 minutes, sobbing and taking in what happened that morning. Jesus still loved me, and He wanted me to know. He never stopped. I was heartbroken that I had walked away from our relationship, and so was He. The sorrow over what I'd done to Him and the relief that I was not one of the condemned washed over me as I cried. With every tear, I was being cleansed. The release was nothing short of a spiritual awakening. God had reached out His hand to me.

Two weeks later, I was again volunteering at the church, this time as a helper for Vacation Bible School. Angel had asked me if I could help. I wasn't sure I wanted to teach kids, but I did want Katie to attend, and it was another opportunity to be around my church family. Angel was the teacher, and I was helping her out. The children were participating in an organized game with some other volunteers, and Angel and I sat and watched our little group on the front steps of the church.

"Have you ever read, *The Shack*?" she said.

I waved my hand like I was erasing the question. "No, my pastor didn't like it. He had some bad stuff to say about it, so I never read it. Isn't it for people who don't really know about God anyway?"

Angel stood up on the stairs and looked down at me. "I think you should read it."

I wanted to please her, so I said, "Okay".

"I'd really like to know what you think about it. I'll bring it on Sunday."

It made me feel good to know that she valued my perspective on it, even as I knew she wanted my opinion as a way to hold me accountable and to make sure I read it.

As planned, Angel produced the book after Sunday's service and placed it into my hands. I took it and filed it into my large satchel of a purse. It disappeared into the abyss of folded papers, lipsticks, sunglasses, and other 'have to haves.' Not wanting to dishonor my agreement, I took the book out later that night after Katie had gone to bed. I wanted to at least start it, maybe skim through it a little and get a feel for what it was all about. I began to read and found I couldn't stop. Every time I tried to put the book down it would nag at me to continue reading. I read the entire book in less than 3 days.

The idea behind the book, I think, is to discuss the common misconceptions that people have about God as He relates to Christians in The Trinity. In this book, the main character has discussions about this with God, the character. They'd have tea and talk about who the main character thought God was and what He is in actuality. I was intrigued by this because a lot of the misconceptions that were brought up were the same ones that I had. At one point in the book, the discussion comes around to the main character's broken relationship with his father and how that affects how he sees God's character and intentions. The idea struck me. My mind raced to figure out how I saw my own father, and if I had misplaced any of those defective notions and put them on God.

My father is a man who loves practically. If someone's furnace was on the fritz, he'd be right over to take a look. If someone needed advice on a car or a situation, he was happy to share it. If someone was looking for a huggy-bear of a guy who lavishes kind words, my father was the wrong person to ask. My dad did provide; he gave us things, he let us do things, but I wouldn't say he was one who blessed. I was constantly in need of earning his approval. His comments about what he thought about how I dressed, what I did, my friends, and zero encouragement left me feeling like I started off my day at a disadvantage with him. I would spend the remaining hours trying to please him and getting him to like me for a little while. I never felt of sense of him being proud of me. I saw myself as someone having great potential but still falling short. I was someone he didn't care to know, and we had nothing in common. I realized this was precisely how I saw God; I had transferred my perspective of my father onto God.

I finished the book as I was sitting out on the balcony of the Tree House on a relatively mild summer afternoon. I smoothed the front of the book and tried to wrap my mind around all that I had read and processed.

I looked up at my palm tree's frond bowing down over the railing as if it were extending its hand toward me to offer comfort.

I looked up at the clouds above the tree and breathed in, starting to cry in my desperation and disgust at how small I felt at that moment. I offered a confession to the only one who could hear me. "I don't think I know you like I thought I did. Who are you, really?"

Eleven

"You just call out my name, and you know wherever I am I'll come running to see you again." James Taylor

Asking God who He is both a dangerous and powerful question. When I asked God who He was, I wasn't prepared for the answer. The truth of God, as I have come to understand, lies in this question. It is the one question that He wanted me - all of us - to ask so he could show His awesome power. I asked in all sincerity. I was tired of the God I had designed. Because I had my own ideas about God, I was often confused by teachings about Him that didn't match my understanding. I didn't want to know Him; I wanted Him to fit neatly into the box that I created for Him. That way, He couldn't interrupt the plans I had for my life.

I didn't expect any grand revelations right at that moment as I sat on my balcony, but the question remained on my mind for days. I was looking for an answer, but I had no idea when it would come or how it would show up. God's answers usually come in unexpected ways. Mine arrived the day I needed to call my investment bank to withdraw some money.

I was living pretty well by most people's standards, even after I quit my job. I had my earnings in the bank, Asher's liquidated investments, life insurance money, annuities, and money market accounts, all at my disposal. Whatever I wanted, I bought it. I didn't give much thought to it running out or that my quest for a luxurious living was sinful. I dialed my investment bank, seeking a couple thousand dollars to help with my rent and also pad my account. I dialed up the customer service representative number and waited for help.

"Mrs. James. It appears you moved recently," the representative stated, her voice slightly bored.

"Yes, I did." A few weeks prior to this call, the bank mailed a letter. The letter stated the postal service had informed them of my new address and if the change was correct, I could throw the letter away and disregard it. That's what I did.

The representative continued, matter-of-factly. "What we need from you is a letter of your change of address with a medallion stamp signature from your bank."

"A what?" I asked. *A medallion stamp, blah, blah, blah? What in the world is that? Why? It is my money, and I need my funds!* I thought. I countered the representative's statement, feeling defensive. "The letter you sent me recently said that you were informed by the postal service of my new address and not to do anything else. Why would you say that if I needed to do something else?"

"I understand that Ma'am, but we need to prove that it was you that moved and that it's okay that we send checks to your new address. It is a security procedure." *Are you human? Could you sound any more robotic as you say that?* I wondered.

"Okay, so I'll get that done tomorrow."

The representative's voice brightened. "That would be great. Once we have that, you just have to wait the 30 day waiting period, and then you can make a withdrawal request."

What? Did I hear that correctly? Thirty days? This money was needed to cover rent and whatever else I wanted. The social security money wouldn't even cover my basic needs for the month, never mind anything extra. I tried the representative to budge, asking for managers and pleading my case, but it was no use. I couldn't access anything for a whole month.

My legs went numb, and I found it hard to breathe. *What do I do? How can I make rent or my car payment?* My mind swirled, and flashes of Katie's face kept coming in front of me. *What about Katie? How do I feed her? What about her school?* The reality of my financial situation was closing in on me.

I picked up Katie from school, took her to the park, made her dinner, and tried to distract myself, but the thoughts wouldn't leave. The only thing I could focus on was what an idiot I had been with my money and the foolish decision I'd made leaving Boston to end up in Siesta Key, alone, pregnant, and overextended.

I tried to make the best of my situation on my own. I went to my bank the next day and requested the medallion stamp and began my 30-day countdown. I bought as little food as possible to make meals that would satisfy and be healthy. There were many nights I traded a healthy meal for freezer burnt breakfast sausages and instant potatoes for Katie's dinner, much to her delight. I didn't want her to have to do without on a count of her ridiculous mother.

My thoughts constantly battered my self-esteem. *If I am so smart, like I've always been told, how come I make so many dumb and thoughtless decisions? The 'Mother of the Year' award would not be mine.* I imagined the shame and disappointment that Asher would have in me. *Here I am with his one and only child, having promised to make him proud as a single parent and carry on in good faith. Instead of fulfilling that promise, here I am in Florida, having left everything, including my career, and dragging Katie through it all.* I pictured him on the edge of a heavenly cloud, shaking his head while watching me sit at the kitchen island with his daughter. While she enjoyed her macaroni and cheese, I ate flavorless breakfast meat and 'just add water' mashed potatoes. I had indeed made a pitiful mess of myself.

One morning I rallied of my own volition. I made a declaration to myself that I would see this through. I would make it. I took a look at my expenses and made decisions about the ones I had to put off for a month. The credit cards would have to wait. It was going to hurt my credit, but this was survival time. I needed to figure this thing out. I decided I could be a few weeks late on my car payment. I had to pay for Katie's school. After all, I needed to have time to write. Writing was the one positive thing I had going. I made a skeleton budget for my weekly grocery allowance. We'd have to live on canned vegetables, pasta, and sauce. We could do it. Other people did. It was not the time to be proud, just resourceful.

After all my scheming and reconfiguring, I was still short. I knew I would have to swallow my pride and ask my parents for money. That meant telling the truth about what had happened and my loved ones would learn exactly how immature and irresponsible I'd been. I would have to explain how I was dipping - diving - into my money to make ends meet. I envisioned yelling, scolding, disgust, and maybe they'd be so upset with me that they'd say, "No." I deserved it. It took me days to find the courage to call them. I lost sleep.

Finally, I couldn't put it off any longer. I felt humiliated as I dialed the number and prayed for their voicemail to pick up. My mother answered. My tongue felt like sandpaper as I tried to speak through the barren desert that my mouth had now become. We made the usual pleasantries, but I wanted to get down to the agenda. My anxiety was skyrocketing. My forehead was dewy, and my stomach tossed like the surf after a storm.

"Mom, I'm in trouble," I blurted out.

"What's wrong?" I heard the alarm in her voice, and she was breathing heavier than usual, so I launched into my explanation. I always conveniently left out the fact that Boyd had been living with me and I still didn't fill her in on that bit of information.

"I made a mistake, or I didn't understand the directions, I don't know. But I went to take money out of my investment account, and I can't because I didn't fill out the proper paperwork with them when I changed my address." I could hear the despair and desperation in my voice.

"So, did you fill it out?"

"Yes, but I can't access anything for 30 days, and I need money to cover my rent," I stated, feeling close to tears. "I thought about how I wouldn't have to ask you for anything, but I can't make it. I even considered selling my engagement ring." I choked on those words, my throat tightening and sobs threatening to cut off my ability to speak.

"NO! No, Sariah. Don't even think about that," she interjected. "That's for Katie. We'll give you the money. How much do you need?"

The tears finally broke through their dam. I don't think she heard me break down on the other end of the phone. I was so relieved that help was coming. There was no lecture or scolding. I told her how much I needed and she said it would be in the mail the next day. I thanked her in the most sincere and humble way I could to let her know that not only did I really need it but that I was, most assuredly, grateful. We ended the call with 'I love you.'

The help from my parents wasn't going to solve my problem, but it meant I could make it until I could get money. The days waiting were nearly unbearable for me. I felt so ashamed. It was almost as if I wore a sign that everyone could read around my neck that said: "I'm a mess." I continued to assault my self-esteem with negative thoughts. *What a failure I've made of my life. I had a great husband whom I hardly appreciated, a fantastic career that I threw away, and a plan for my future that would have been unbelievable. The only thing I have left is my beautiful Katie, and I'm not even getting that right. She deserves a better mother than I'm being. How did it get this bad? How did I fall so far down?*

The money from my parents arrived several days later, and I paid what I could. I had little to nothing left over, aside from what I needed to feed us. I decided to avoid using my credit cards. I had to make it without them. I settled into bed that night and said a heartfelt prayer, hoping God would hear my cries as a desperate mother.

I prayed, "Lord, just help me to take care of Katie until I get my money. I need you to help me." I settled into bed and fell asleep quickly. I was exhausted from too many days of emotion.

The next day I got up as usual and took Katie to school. I came home and opened the mailbox at the bottom of my stairs to take out the mail. As I opened the gate to head upstairs, I started sifting through the mail, removing the junk mail, and dumping it into the recycling bin next to me, while pulling out the important envelopes.

With my mail sorted, I sat down on the steps and opened the envelope belonging to the only worthy piece of mail - my cell phone bill. My cell phone was the only form of communication I had. I didn't see a need to get a regular phone because everyone I cared about knew my cell phone number. However, living on the other end of the Eastern Seaboard from my family and friends resulted in a lot of long calls. My bill was usually greatly enhanced by overage charges. I unfolded the bill and looked at the total near the bottom. In bold type, at the bottom right hand corner displayed my tally, $324.69. I gasped as my hands lightly shook. I didn't have more than twenty extra dollars for the next month, never mind $300! Tears started to form, but surprisingly, I started laughing.

My reaction was not a small giggle. I had a full-on, from the tips of my toes, out loud and without muffle, belly laugh. I hadn't had a good roll in such a long time. It felt good to look up at the sky and just let it out. When my vocal cords and cheeks started to hurt, I calmed down and threw my hands in the air.

"You can send me whatever you want, Lord. I am just going to have to trust You."

It was like a light switch in my head. When I said that, I had truly let go of the worry, the distress, the fear, and the judgment against myself. I had finally arrived at a place so desperate, so disparaging that I had no choice but to trust God. I was so low to the ground that the only thing I could do was look up.

This is what I learned, purely from my own experience and void of anything outside myself, is that when I start walking to God, He started running to me. He was willing to knock everything out of the way that stood between Him and me. Things like toxic relationships, the pride of self-sufficiency, bank accounts, careers, and anything else are no match for Him. The Bible was providing a path for me to follow, and God was leading me. At that moment, I adopted my life's motto:

"Come to Me, all who are weary and heavy-laden, and I will give you rest." Matthew 11:28 NIV

There was something so simple and beautiful in giving my trust entirely over to God. I regretted that it took me so long, and I had to suffer so much to learn. I allowed myself to accept His forgiveness for what I'd done. I stopped judging myself and agreed I was worthy of saving. By accepting God fully into my life, my heart became lighter. The burdens I had unfairly laden upon myself, even after He had said, "As the East is as far from the West," that He would cast away my transgression. It was as if I wanted to wrestle them from Him as if to say, "No, you can't forgive this. I won't let You." I had to agree with Him. He had forgiven me. However unbelievable though it seemed, it was true. As He was nailed to the cross, the last thing He said was, "It is finished." And so He bore the burden of sin for the world and my transgressions so that I could be His.

My relationship with God was brand new again. I needed to see Him as the loving father He always wanted to show me. I had a clean slate, and I was eager to let Him show me His love and adoration. I wanted to feel precious. I wanted to feel like I was made for a purpose, just like it says:

"I praise You because I am fearfully and wonderfully made; Your works are wonderful. I know that full well" – Psalm 139:14 NIV

I plunged headfirst into my Bible every morning, searching for scripture that would tell me how much God loved me. If He loved me as much as I was always told, then it had to be in there. It was as if I had never read the book before. I had so much head knowledge of the Bible. I spent hours and hours doing research all those years in my spare time. I dazzled Bible study participants with what I knew and what I could recite, but it was between my ears this whole time and not within my heart. I felt as though it were all undoubtedly true, but I didn't have any proof to back up my beliefs. Now I had experienced He forgiveness and love. I needed more.

I listened intently to the sermons that Pastor Harry shared with us on Christian Suffering. I was disappointed when he finished the series, but I was lifted as he announced the new series. We'd be covering all of the names for God in the Bible. He explained how God has many names and they all have different meanings. The meanings represented God's character attributes, rather than simply being one more thing to call Him. I almost leapt out of my pew. I could find out more about who God was by studying the names. I couldn't wait for next week.

It was staggering to realize I had asked God to show me who He really was only a couple of weeks before, and here He was, answering my request. Could it have been the breeze I felt on my balcony and in the palm tree the moment I asked was actually Him showing up as requested? I liked to think so. It is awe striking to pray and to see Him respond with such passion. *Why me, Lord? Who am I that You should harken Your ear to me?* I asked and waited painstakingly for the answer.

Our journey on God's names took us from Genesis forward. First, we studied God's names in light of how God chooses to address Himself. That was pretty interesting. I had never stopped to consider how God refers to Himself. 'I AM' stuck out at me. When you slow down and think about it for a minute, it doesn't need any explanation. I appreciated His philosophical approach to His name on that one.

There was one name that had the most impact on me. It was in the story of Hagar in Genesis. Hagar was a servant in the home of Abraham and Sarah. Abraham had been called by God to be Abraham instead of Abram and Sarah from Sarai. God made known to Abraham that he would have a son. The trouble was, Abraham was as old as dirt, and Sarah wasn't exactly a spring chicken herself. Abraham and Sarah decided to hurry

God's plan for a son and use Hagar to conceive Abraham's child. Hagar became pregnant, and soon disaster erupted in Abraham's home between Sarah and Hagar. In the heat of the situation, Hagar fled, pregnant and not knowing where she was going. She stopped to rest at a well, probably crying. I could relate, and I knew I would be crying in her situation. The Angel of the Lord appeared to her to ask where she was going. She answered she was fleeing her mistress. The Angel went on to address her, saying she was pregnant with a son, what to name him, and he instructed her to return to the house of Abraham and Sarah.

I admit, I was jealous. An angel appears out of nowhere in the middle of a crisis. He speaks kindness and truth and describes what to do to make it right? I wondered how I would have personally reacted to such a visit. I also marveled at the fact that Hagar was an Egyptian. The God of Abraham was not the God of her understanding. She was so overwhelmed by God's concern for her that she named the well, "Beer Lahai Roi," which in Hebrew means "The Well of the One Who Sees Me."

Pastor Harry elaborated on the need to understand that the name that Hagar had given the well was based on a personal encounter with God and a knowing that He saw her in her current situation. He knew exactly what was going to happen so she could trust Him with the outcome. I almost dropped my pen. The person sitting next to me probably saw me sitting there with my mouth hanging open. Not only did God make me a wonderful creation, He saw me as a unique creation. He cared about me and my life. To Him, I was not just a cog in the wheel that we call the Universe. I was an individual to be looked after. He wanted to pay attention to me, Sariah James, just like He did Hagar, who had no relationship with Him at all. God saw me, too. And if He could care for Hagar, He would do the same for me.

I choked back tears as Pastor Harry continued. The rest of my day was spent processing what I'd heard. It was true. God had loved me this whole time. He knew everything and He knew it before time began, yet He loved me. It was hard to get my mind around. I had come from a relationship with my own father that, to me, was based on earning praise and affection. I didn't have to earn anything with the Lord. He loved me; He loved me completely. He knew everything about me, and it didn't deter

Him. There wasn't anyone I had encountered who made me feel this way. I was awestruck.

My heart filled as this knowledge took root and began to take hold of me. I wanted scriptural proof of my newly discovered love and acceptance. I searched my Bible for them.

"For God so loved the world that He gave His one and only Son, that whoever believes in Him shall not perish but have eternal life" John 3:16 NIV

Few are the ones who have not read it, heard it, or have at least seen it spray-painted on a billboard or overpass. It is the most famous verse in the Bible. Of course, I was familiar with it. Didn't I have to accept this verse to become a Christian? Isn't this what my faith was based on? The verse came full-circle to me one day as I contemplated its simplicity. It was as if I'd never heard it before when a one-word question came to mind about it. *Why? Why did He do that?* Because He loves me. Such love to sacrifice your only Son? Yes. How could I refuse such a desire to call me His own?

My love for God had never been like this before. I was startled by it, overwhelmed with emotion at times, but I was not fearful. What had I to fear? He loved me completely. I looked at my relationship with God in terms of my relationship with Katie. I would never let anything happen to her if I could avoid it. I lay awake at night, filled with joy over my love for her and my gratitude that she was with me. If I naturally had those feelings for Katie, then Jesus had them in an even greater capacity for me. God's people are referred to as His children over and over again in the Bible. I was growing into its truth.

One afternoon, I was in my bedroom, putting clothes away when I heard rustling in the bathroom closet down the hallway. Only one person was around to get into things. I yelled out to her, "Katie, you're not supposed to be in there. Come out of there."

My daughter was a wonderfully curious and creative girl. This was something to behold, and it was also something that got her in an awful lot of trouble with me. Since we had too many experiments with water, soap, and things in and around the bathroom, Katie was not allowed in there unless she had official business. She knew this, but it wasn't stopping her from digging through the closet in the forbidden room.

I called out to her again. This time I was leaving my bedroom and heading down the hallway when I heard the crashing of things falling off of shelves. I rounded the corner to find my daughter, the closet, closet contents, and the bathroom floor covered in silver glitter. I had no clue where the glitter came from or why it was in the bathroom closet, but it was now decorating everything in sight. I looked down at my pouting child, looking up at me in defeat.

"Sorry, Mama," she said with her sweet blue eyes peering up in remorse.

I looked down on her face with my hands on my hips and sighed. I wasn't sure if I was more disappointed that she didn't obey me or that I now had to figure out how to get glitter cleaned up without making more of a mess.

"Why didn't you just listen to me?" I was frustrated by the disobedience and the mess.

Immediately I distinctly heard a voice in the back of my mind. It stopped me short, and all sense of angst left my body. It was the first time I'd ever heard Him so clearly. "Yes, exactly."

It was as if Jesus Himself were standing behind me, looking at this whole display in my Tree House. I felt sorrow. I was asking Katie something I had not been capable of doing. I saw my daughter, at that moment, like me. The glitter was so pretty, and she wanted to admire it. She planned to look at it and put it back without my knowing. Before she knew what to do, the closet shelves crashed under her weight, she lost her grip on the bottle, and it had emptied onto the floor. I am sure she felt helpless to do anything to clean it up, except maybe to ask me to help her.

I brushed her off, and we had a quick discussion about how we need to listen to Mama so we don't wind up in these situations. I explained to her that there are poisons in that closet that she shouldn't touch, and they could make her very sick or hurt her. I didn't want any of those things to happen to her. I got the broom and dustpan as I sent her out to the living room so that I could clean up. I reasoned this is why God doesn't want us to do the things He asks us to stay away from. He doesn't want us to get hurt or sick, just like I wouldn't want that for Katie. What a loving realization that He wasn't a 'downer' or a 'buzz kill.' He just wanted me to stay out of harm's way, out of love for me. Like any dedicated parent would.

Katie and I had a great routine of watching the Sprout Channel after she got into her pajamas. I cleaned her up for bed, and we would cuddle on the couch and watch her shows until it was time for storybooks and bed. I'd sit, with my little one under my right arm, tucked right up against me. She loved to squeeze in as close as she could. I'd practically burst with joy over the love I felt for her in those moments. We'd sit and talk about the shows, and I'd gently kiss the top of her head and stroke her arm. I'd imagine Jesus felt the same about me when I drew near to Him. I saw Him as a God who wants me to spend time with Him, not some obstinate God who may or may not feel the desire to hear me on any given day. I earned nothing. He gave His love so freely if only I would accept it.

I thought of Asher in those weeks. I thought of him being with Jesus and getting to know the full knowledge of my new relationship with Him. I imagined how Asher could see the whole picture of my life, and he was able to see me through the eyes of Jesus. Asher had no judgment or condemnation, either. My heart and my head lifted at the idea that God and Asher had the same love and mercy for me. I didn't need to sit in the emotions of my old life. I could lay all that aside and move forward.

Although I loved my friends and church in Siesta Key, I felt an overwhelming desire to return to Boston. I wanted to be with my family and put the pain of my time in Siesta Key behind me. I thought about when I should return. It was summer. If I waited until the end of my lease, I would be moving back to Boston with all of my stuff in February, and I didn't want to do that with snow looming at that time of year. However, I wanted to be fair to my landlords. I had signed a year-long lease, and I wouldn't be making good on it. After much time spent in prayer, I decided to write them a letter with my next rent check and offer to pay out the year to satisfy the lease. I hated disappointing people or making them upset with me, but the idea of waiting through the rest of the year to start my life again was unpalatable.

The night I left the letter and the check in their mailbox, they came upstairs and knocked on my door. They came in and hugged me and told me I didn't need to pay out the lease as long as I paid through November. That gave them two months to find another tenant. I thought that was fair. We chatted a bit about my need to return home. I had been through a lot and now it was time to be with people who knew me and loved me. They couldn't blame me for that.

"You shouldn't be doing this by yourself. You need your family to help you," Bob stated. He was referring to me raising Katie alone.

Now that my landlords had notice, I had a date to go home. I was a little emotional that night, realizing the hugs were their way of letting me know they cared about us. I felt sorry knowing I had missed an opportunity to get to know them better. I had been so busy with the turmoil of my life that I hadn't taken time to get to know them.

Next, I was going to have to tell Angel. My heart broke over the thought of having to move away from her. She and I had grown into close, heartfelt friends. I wondered if she knew she was the kind of friend I loved to have in my life. We had some great nights of sitting with a coffee on the couch at her house, sharing our lives, our upbringing, our past, and growing closer. I was not afraid to be a real person around her. She knew that she could tell me anything, and I would never think less of her. I felt as though I owed Angel my life, and that I still couldn't repay her for the love and support she gave me during such an unbelievable time of transformation in my life.

I broke the news to Angel gently. She knew that I'd be telling her this at some point but not so soon. We discussed when and how. She trailed off her sentences, staring off as I finished telling her my plans. I wished I could take her with me. Of course, we'd stay in touch. I was pained thinking of what it would be like to not talk to her anymore. I knew I'd keep up my end of the deal; I hoped she would, too.

Lastly, I let my church family know, as well as the scant acquaintances I'd made in the neighborhood through the commonality of parenting small children.

Now that people knew we were leaving, I was relieved and happy again. I couldn't stop thinking of returning to my roots. *Would I think of home in the same way? Would people see me as the same person? How much do I want to tell them had happened while I was down here?* They all knew that I was down here, presumably to write a book, which I was, but there was so much more. Now that I had this incredible desire to follow Jesus, how would people respond to that? I started to laugh a little when I'd think of it, only because I didn't care one iota what they thought. Truth is, most people find me a little eccentric anyway.

I picked a moving date during the first week of November and phoned my mom. My mother was thrilled to hear that I had an arrival date. She could plan for that, and she had Katie and me to look forward to. I needed to discuss logistics with her. I had things I wanted to take back with me that would not fit into my car. I'd be renting a truck and shipping my car home ahead of me.

"Mom, I don't want to take Katie with me in the truck. I don't think it would be safe."

"Oh, no. I wouldn't want that. Can't you get movers and fly home with her?" she asked.

"No, it's too expensive. I wanted to ask if you could come down here and fly back with her. I'll pay for it, but you'd have her for about a week until I can get up there. Is that okay?"

"No, that would be fine. I'd rather that than to have you try to drive back with Katie in the truck. I don't feel good about that."

We ended the call, and I was pleasantly relieved my mom was so willing to make such an effort to help me. I thought of Katie being so far away from me for so long. We hadn't been separated much since Asher died. Whenever we were apart, I was pained in my spirit until she was back with me. I thought of the Lord and how He must have hurt, too, when I was separated from Jesus. I imagined if I decided to choose anything other than Him, I'd be breaking His heart all over again. I was distressed in my spirit at the thought of causing my Lord any more grief.

Twelve

'Wherever you are, my heart is with you. Sweet dreams, sweet dreams, Mon Cher." Kelly Sweet

With Boyd's eviction came his silence. He ceased all communication with me, which frankly came as a relief. I didn't want a constant battle with my plan to put the baby up for adoption. I figured with him out of the picture and uninterested in changing my mind, by default, I would be unhindered in my decision to pursue adoption for the baby.

I contacted Bethany, the adoption counselor with whom I spoke before, asked some questions, and set up a time and a location to meet her for the first time. I had to drive up to Miami as she was near Orlando, a nine-hour drive from Siesta Key. We settled on Panera Bread in a South Miami strip mall.

With the date and time settled, I made hotel arrangements. Katie was overjoyed at the idea of staying at a "special building house." I also booked tickets online to Zoo Miami, figuring we could take in a site while we were up there. The thought of lumbering my now swollen belly around a zoo in 95-degree weather wasn't what I would have opted for, but the timing made no allowance for that. I'd have to deal with it and hope they had a lot of shade and benches. Katie had been through so much on account of me. I wanted to do something nice for her, even if I passed out in the middle of it.

The time came for our meeting to discuss the adoption plans. My nerves jangled as I looked around the café, hoping she'd see me. Bethany was a young, attractive woman, barely out of college from the looks of her. She had a fresh face, eager smile, and she took readily to Katie. In a flash, she had crayons and coloring pages out for her, engaging her in a few sentences and filling in space on the page right alongside Katie.

We exchanged a few things about the travel and any new developments before she flapped out a stack of paperwork on the restaurant table. I hadn't seen so much paperwork since I bought my first house. I started to wonder what I had gotten myself into. Was I signing this baby away today?

Bethany eased my concerns and started to fill me in on the legal stuff. She stated the courts would properly notify Boyd and instructed me on what needed to happen. I had no address or any way to reach him other than his cell phone and his work. She informed me that the courts would serve legal notification papers to the restaurant. I thought of the finality and the heaviness of that scene playing out at the little beachside eatery where he worked. I had a moment of feeling a bit sorry for him. That would be so impersonal. I wondered if I should do something different. She asked me if he'd be willing to sign papers and work with us together. I gave her his cell phone number and asked her to try.

Question after question about social history, medical history, and psychological information made my head burn. I begged God silently for the last page to come soon.

"I want to pick her parents." I blurted out.

"You can do whatever you'd like. You are the one driving this. You tell me what you want, and we'll do our best to make that happen," she replied. "I'll send you 5 profiles of couples that meet your criteria, and if you don't like any of those, I'll take back the books and get you 5 more. Okay?"

Once she was satisfied she had exhausted every page, we ended with an agreement to stay in touch by phone. She would check the profiles of couples who met my list of desires, and then she'd mail me the profiles down once she verified that.

A week later, she called to say her attempts to reach Boyd were unsuccessful and she'd be serving him the legal documents that coming Tuesday. My stomach lurched at the thought of contact from him. Once he had the paperwork, he'd have 30 days to contest the court on the adoption. Even if he wanted to go through with that, he'd have to prove to the court that he would be able to support both the child and me. I knew he'd never be able to do that, assuming he could sober up enough to actually pursue contesting. That would be a long shot at best. I relaxed and focused on waiting for the package of profiles.

Tuesday came, and the only communication I got from Boyd was, "Got the paperwork." He was served.

I thought with that out of the way, I'd feel clearer about things, but instead, I railed at his lack of participation. Wasn't he ashamed that he'd all but abandoned this child and me? Didn't he shrink at the thought of his actions towards me? I burned with resentment sparked by his dismissal of this child and me. I'd come to Siesta Key for him, only to be left on my own to deal with this pregnancy. I was warmed by the remembrance of a verse in the Bible about the woe that befalls anyone who dares to mess with God's widows and her children. "Good luck to you, Buddy," I'd whisper under my breath and smile at his demise.

I started to think too much time had gone by for my liking, and I wondered if my adoption counselor had forgotten the promise to mail the adoption profiles. However, I discovered a shipping box leaning up against my door as I returned home. I knew exactly what it was. Katie danced around me, asking if it was a present from her Nana.

"Is it for me? Is it for me?" Her head bobbed up and down as she tried to find her way around me to the box.

"No, Honey. It's for Mama." I verified the addressee and the return address.

"A present from Nana?" she persisted. To her, boxes only come from Nana, who regularly sent her surprises.

"No baby, it's from Bethany." I gripped the box, trying to figure out what to do about it. I had already decided to open it later; however, I found myself sitting in my wicker chair minutes later, ripping back the tab on the box to reveal what was inside. I thought I would just peek inside and read through them later. As I folded back the flaps on the box, the names "Brett and Kayla" leaped off of a sky blue bound book. I felt tears readily pour down my cheeks. I shoved a bucket of sidewalk chalk at Katie, who was still trying to go through the box, and instructed her to draw a picture on the cement floor of the balcony. Thankfully, she agreed.

As I opened their profile, a letter fell out of it and into my lap. It was addressed to me. I tearfully read the personalized letter which expressed their hopes on what I'd get out of their profile book. I wiped and smiled, eager to read through their album. There were pictures and captions of their happy moments in life. Descriptions of work, home, and church life flowed from page to page as I read and cried. Kayla looked like she could be related to me. That somehow brought comfort. When Katie was no longer entertained by her impromptu art session, I put the profile back into the box and took them inside. I knew I needed to give the other 4 books a fair read. After Katie went to bed, I took them all out and browsed through the other profiles, but I had no emotional feeling toward the other couples like I did Brett and Kayla. My mind was set.

I prayed and called up Angel to see if she'd look at the profiles, too. I wanted to know if she'd pick out the same couple. I went over to her house later the next afternoon, shuffled the stack, and handed them to her as we sat on her couch. She thoughtfully turned and carefully considered each page, asking questions, and pointing out things she found interesting about each one. As she finished, she neatly organized them into an aligned pile and pulled "Brett and Kayla" off the top of the collection.

"This couple," she said as she held up the book by the corner and looked to me for confirmation.

"Yup. The decision has been made." I had my confirmation.

I notified Bethany and asked if I could meet Brett and Kayla right away. I was jumping at the chance to establish some kind of relationship.

My mind swirled with scenes from movies where the adoptive couple supported and visited the expectant mother before the adoption, having dinner and going to doctor's appointments. It looked so beautiful in the movies. I wanted it to be like that for me, for us. Would they accept me? Within hours we had a day and a time back at the same Panera Bread where I had met with Bethany. I couldn't wait to see them, and I was sure they felt the same. Bethany informed me that they didn't know that I'd picked them; instead, they were told this meeting was to see if I'd still want to choose them as the parents. I tried to envision what that would feel like from their point-of-view. It sounded like the worst interview ever! After going through so much with infertility, and to wind up in front of a pregnant woman who chose to meet with them only to be told: "No, not good enough." I was dizzied by the thought of that emotional rollercoaster.

I prayed to God for Him to calm their nerves. I knew He'd chosen them, and unless they ended up being some tripped-out weirdos, I wasn't going with anyone else.

I started to feel weird about the baby not having a name. I wondered what I would name him or her if I had the opportunity. I considered several possibilities but since I could only go with one name right now, I chose Alex. Alex was a strong name, the name of a warrior, and this child was going to need a strong calling over him, so I thought it was fitting. I wanted to give Alex the middle name of Ruth if it was a girl. It was one of my favorite Biblical female characters and also the name of my paternal grandmother.

When an amniocentesis proved her gender, Alex Ruth became more of a reality to me. She was a little girl with a big plan for her life, and while she grew and tossed in my belly, I prayed over her and talked to her, knowing that my time with her was limited and precious.

I told Angel of my arrangement to meet with the prospective parents, and she promptly offered up her timeshare condo at a nearby resort. She volunteered to drive up with us and watch Katie while I went for our visit. I was bowled over by her offering. I didn't want to take up her time, but I was desperate for support and reassurance. Having someone come with me for such a big day was like opening a window on the first warm spring day. I gladly accepted it. I knew I'd need someone there for the emotional fallout that would inevitably come. Much as I tried to "Positive Think" my way through this, I could feel the emotions I was pushing down as they fought to surface.

In all of the drama of kicking out Boyd, figuring out how to return to Boston, getting the adoption rolling, and picking out parents, I ignored my emotional needs. The lack of consideration caught up to me one morning as I was taking Katie to preschool. As I drove along the shoreline, I thought of what it would be like to have to give Katie away. The mere consideration made me howl with grief. In no time at all, I was awash in tears and struggling without success to stifle my wails. Katie became frightened by her mother's sudden reaction, and I spent the rest of our drive trying to distract her from asking more questions and diverting her to another topic. I lay awake in my bed that night, whimpering into my pillow over what it would be like to hand Alex over to another person. When the whimpering became sobs, I heard a little voice, very audible to my senses, speak to me.

"Do you mourn like a woman who cannot have children?"

"What?" I said aloud. I was startled out of my tears.

"Do you mourn like a woman who cannot have children?"

"No," I answered.

I thought of the six months in which Asher and I tried to conceive Katie. I languished during that time for the day when we'd know we'd achieved conception. In comparison, it was hardly a moment next to what some couples experience. Some waited for years, spending thousands and thousands of dollars on fertility treatments to no avail. I didn't know what that pain was like because I'd never experienced it. In that moment, I decided to stop feeling sorry for myself and looked beyond me to the masterpiece God was creating for Brett and Kayla through my situation. To keep from self-focusing, God asked me to pray for Alex's adoptive mother. I thanked God for the opportunity to share a secret with Him. I imagined Kayla praying every night for a child, and only God and I knew that her prayer was already answered. I prayed for her, asking God to calm her spirit until she could hear the secret we were keeping. My heart warmed and within a few days, I was smiling as I continued praying for her.

The resort Angel booked for us was stunning. Katie and I shared a master suite that was as big as our tiny little Tree House apartment. The room featured a Jacuzzi tub the size of a small wading pool. Katie begged for a bath before I could even set our bags down, and who could blame her? I wanted to try it out, too!

After Katie went to bed, Angel and I shared girl time. We sat on her bed talking, hugging pillows, and spilling our secrets. It reminded me of teenage sleepovers. I was grateful for the opportunity to be vulnerable with someone and to have her trust me back.

Later, as I lay in my bed next to Katie, I was dozing off when I heard my phone ring. It was 11:30 at night. I looked at the caller ID. It was Boyd. My initial reaction was to ignore him, but then I became concerned about why he was calling so late. I answered.

As soon as I offered a "Hi," he started into a drunken emotional seesaw. He fluctuated between sobbing "I am sorry" to raging "I'm going to sue you! I am talking to lawyers!" I wasn't in the mood for a volley of pleas or threats, so without offering any conversation, I hung up on him.

The next morning, I was nauseous with anxiety as I drove to our meeting spot. Miami had a lot more morning traffic than I anticipated, and, as a result, I was a half-hour late. I pained with shame at my tardiness. I didn't want them to think that I didn't care about this meeting. It was one of the most important ones I had ever attended!

I waddled into the restaurant in a fluster, apologizing, and trying to avoid a direct eye contact with Brett and Kayla. I stammered with awkwardness. I was confused by my nervousness. After all, I was the one holding all the cards or, in this case, the one carrying the baby. Kayla looked sickly from the tension, and Brett looked like he was putting on his game face and hoping this turned out well for his wife. I could tell he was trying to be optimistic while holding his breath. I smiled and made small talk with them, hoping to break the ice and get us all to a healthy heart rate again. Bethany offered breakfast, and we sprang from our chairs to the bakery cases, grateful for the distraction.

Once we returned to the table with our food, Bethany asked me to share my pregnancy story and the reason we were here. I choked down breakfast and blinked back tears as I recounted. The tissues were passed around when I got to how I saw myself in this situation and what helped me keep my head up during this time in my life. I saw myself as a vessel being used by God to carry a blessing. I was being used by Him to deliver an answer to prayer. I believed God took my shame and my situation, and He wove it into something extraordinary. He was using me to carry out His loving plan. While I sorrowed that I was the one who made the decision to be in this situation, He rejoiced in life and wanted to use me for something great. I felt like one of the most special people in the world to be able to do that for Him.

After asking a few general questions I had for them, I made a long pause in the conversation. I smiled gently and looked into Kayla's eyes and asked, "So what are you going to name her?" With that simple question, Kayla and Brett started breathing again, and tears of joy flowed from both of them. I pulled out ultrasound pictures that I'd copied for them to take home and share with their family. We exchanged email addresses and left the cafe, hugging and still crying tears of joy. I felt hopeful that

Brett, Kayla, and I would grow a relationship now that I had a way to communicate outside of the agency's intermediation. I drove back to the condo, happy for them, and cemented in the gravity of what I was undertaking. I hoped it would work out. After all, Brett and Kayla, and all their hopes and dreams, were involved in the baby's life. I feared what Boyd might try to do to thwart my plans.

My mom came to Siesta Key for a visit. Thankfully, I had a pull-out sofa as our tight quarters made no allowance for a guest bed. I counted down the days until she arrived. I was desperate for some solace of home. The day she arrived, I carefully planned my outfit so I didn't to look too pregnant even though by now, I was quite obviously showing and waddling around. I wanted to hide the pregnancy so we didn't have to talk about it. My decision to put the baby up for adoption was very hard on her, and I didn't want to upset her. I also didn't want her to talk me out of it.

We kept our visit light as Katie and I showed her the sites of Siesta Key. She'd never been before and wanted to take it in. I was happy to be a tour guide, keeping the focus on the cute little island and not on my rotund belly. Toward the end of her trip, she started to ask questions about the baby. I winced with each one I had to respond to. I was never for sharing much with my mother. We never had that kind of bond, so to start now seemed awkward. I didn't want to hurt her anymore. I felt ashamed for how my choices were affecting her life. I didn't want to add to it with any new revelation in our conversations. I did my best to be honest but brief. She poured over Brett and Kayla's profile, day after day, and tried to look happy. I wished she'd just forget about it. Pining wasn't going to make it easier on her.

After my mother left, it was time to count down to Alex's arrival. There were moments when the due date couldn't come fast enough and days when I never wanted it to arrive. Boyd texted one afternoon to say that he wanted to meet and discuss things. I was cheered by his interest but skeptical of his motives. I wanted to believe he was finally taking an interest in his daughter's future and acting in her best interest. I agreed on two conditions. He could not show up to my condo when Katie was home and he had to come sober.

The day of our meeting arrived, and I waited with bated breath for his appearance. I paced and peered over my balcony, looking down the road. After fifteen minutes went by, I texted him to find out when he was coming. After a half-hour of waiting, I called, but he didn't answer. Three hours later, he texted to say he'd been called in to work a double shift. What a liar.

Boyd and I repeated this procedure three times before I called it off. I hurled a barrage of curse words and insults into the phone when he called an hour late with an excuse to cancel the third time. After I hung up on him, I fled my tiny apartment in tears and drove to go sit by the water. I was too angry to be home and too sad to stare at walls. I parked alongside the seawall and balled my eyes out. I was angry. I was angry at Boyd for not caring, at myself for being in this mess, and at God because He hadn't killed Boyd yet. When I got done with the crazy thoughts, I sat in my car and called Angel to confess my crime of cussing. The thought of "Be angry and do not sin" made me angrier. I needed to tell someone. She gave a sympathetic ear, but it was too brief to comfort me. I needed to talk to God about being upset with Him.

I was surprised by His ready comfort. I felt peace as I told Him how I honestly felt about His decisions. The more vulnerable I made myself to God, the better I felt. Why did I ever think God had no knowledge of my inner feelings? As I prayed and watched the waves roll in, I mellowed. Boyd was no source of stability for me; he never had been. I was foolishly upset because of my expectations that he would change but he was doing what he'd always done. I couldn't expect any more from him.

I saw Brett and Kayla one more time for lunch before our big day. It was a sweet time of dreaming for Alex's future and getting to know one another. Kayla and I even had a pleasant stroll as I did everything to get Alex to kick for her but to no avail. The next time we'd meet would be at the hospital on the date of my C-section. I hugged her good-bye and tried not to think of the monumental event coming in three short weeks.

My phone rang one afternoon as I was taking a nap. It was Boyd. I begrudgingly answered, apprehensive about what I might hear from his end. Boyd had demands he wanted to impress upon me. "Okay, I am going to go along with this, but we are not going through agencies. I want addresses, phone numbers, and last names."

"Excuse me?" Indignity rose as I sat up in bed, amazed at the audacity.

"Yeah, I'm not going through agencies. We can handle this ourselves."

For six months he had ignored me and the baby. Yet, here he was, calling and making demands. My rage was unleashed into the phone as I railed and vomited curse words into the phone.

"Who do you think you are, telling me how this is going to go?" I roared into the phone. "You could have done this with me, but you decided to walk away. You lost your right to tell me what to do about this a long time ago. You will come to the hospital, say good-bye to your daughter, sign those papers, and get out of our lives. End of the story. That is what you are going to do."

There would be no tears. I was thankful that he was not in front of me as I might have wanted bloodshed. I hung up, livid. There was no napping after that phone call.

Not long before the date of my C-section, my mother came back down from Boston to be with me, to care for Katie, and to see her granddaughter before Alex went with her new family. The morning of Alex's arrival came. Angel drove me to the hospital while my mother stayed with a sleeping Katie. They would come to the hospital later in the morning. I laughed to myself as I thought of the first time I gave birth. It was two excited, expecting parents desperately waiting to hold their daughter. Now, it was a single mom becoming a birthmother and having a baby only to give her to two joyous adoptive parents. It didn't have the same sheen.

I met Brett and Kayla in the lobby, and we embraced and headed for the maternity floor. I tried not to pay much attention to their beaming smiles. I got through the necessary paperwork and preparation in order to find a bed and await abdominal surgery. The thought of the upcoming recovery and the postpartum pain made me wish I was a kangaroo. I focused on getting settled once they found our room for us. My pleasant moment came when the nurses hooked my belly up to the fetal heart monitor. The swishing sound resonated in the speaker, and I told Kayla it was Alex's heartbeat. She made her way to the monitor, and her face softened as she focused on the rhythm. Soft tears formed as she let out a giggle and turned back to look at Brett. Finally, Kayla had something concrete to bond with Alex. In less than an hour, we'd be in the operating room with Kayla standing by, waiting for Alex's debut with the camera.

The surgery went smoothly. I watched the nurses rush Alex to the warming basket with Kayla close behind. A tear released as I saw her chunky newborn body and heard the familiar cry. It seemed anti-climactic to carry someone for nine months and not call her mine. Kayla, overcome with her own emotions, tearfully kissed my head and sobbed, "She's beautiful."

The next few days were spent with me in a hospital bed, looking on as everyone enjoyed my daughter. I was afraid to hold her for fear that I'd grow attached and change my mind. I felt gratitude and relief as I watched Brett and Kayla, and I saw how much they loved Alex. When my feelings threatened to overcome me with grief, I focused on Katie and Alex and how this decision was made in their best interests. I was emotionally unable to give them both what they needed. I was affirmed in that knowledge.

The last day came, and I spent breakfast finally holding Alex, sobbing and telling her how hard it was to let her go. I asked her to forgive me for sending her away, but I was doing the very best I could do for her. I chose life and adoption out of love for her, and she needed to know that. I told her about a journal I wrote for her during my pregnancy. In the journal, I wrote love letters to her, telling her about me, positive things about her Dad, funny stories about her sister, and the hopes I had for her future. If she had nothing else, she had my words penned in a beautiful butterfly-adorned journal.

Bethany arrived with the final paperwork. I was surprised to see Boyd make his appearance. I didn't think he had the guts or that he'd be sober enough to do so. He met everyone, presented me with a wilted yellow rose, and sat down across from Brett. They were meeting for the first time. My anxiety rose a little as I wondered how the next few minutes would play out. Boyd asked to hold Alex, and he bounced her in his arms, softly crying and telling me how beautiful she was. Someone suggested he sit on the bed with the baby to have his picture taken with her and me. I wanted to refuse. I didn't want to tolerate any depiction that would give the perception that I wanted to have anything to do with Boyd, but Bethany thought it would be good for Alex to have in the future so I relented. I did my best to form a decent smile.

The fateful time for the signing of paperwork arrived, and everyone was asked to leave the room, except Boyd and me. If others were present to sway our decision, it wouldn't be legal. Boyd went first, but not before he asked, "Are we really going through with this?"

I wanted to jab my pen in his eye. *Does he really have to make me feel worse*? I held my breath as Bethany explained each page to him, telling him where to sign and initial. I was relieved when he was done. Boyd was officially out of my life. I wanted to rejoice with loud praise and clapping, but it was my turn with the signatures. She explained each page to me. We arrived at the final page and she pointed to the line awaiting my signature. I tightened my grip on the pen as I moved my hand to the paper. There wasn't anything more final than that signature. I hadn't sensed that much conclusion since seeing Asher's death certificate. The signing was done. The adoption was finalized. I was ready to gather my things and go home.

The time had come to say good-bye. Brett walked Boyd downstairs, hugged him, and promised to love and care for his daughter. Only a true man could show so much love for someone he didn't know. This man would raise my Alex. I swelled at that realization. As we all made our way down the hallway with an orderly pushing me in a wheelchair and my mom right behind me, I felt a pang of grief. I was really leaving without Alex. My time with her was over.

I watched as Brett and Kayla loaded Alex and all of the baby things into their car. Kayla got into the back seat with Alex to ride home with her. We said our last good-byes and hugs, and I watched them drive away with my baby. I cannot verbally try to distinguish the intensity of the pain between letting go of my child and the death of my husband, although I can recognize their differences. Each was its own kind of loss, and I felt the grief in the core of my being.

Thirteen

"This is what it is to be loved and to know that the promise was when everything fell, we'd be held." Natalie Grant

The moving truck was ordered, car shipping confirmed, and Mom and Katie's plane tickets were purchased. I had checked everything off my list except a companion to drive back with.

Originally, I asked two potential road companions from the Boston area; however, as the moving date drew nearer, both needed to back out. I shared my dilemma with Angel over the phone one afternoon. The days were passing like minutes. I was getting edgy because I had no one to accompany me. I ran through all of the details, and the scant traveling companion possibilities when a little voice responded with, "I can."

I paused for a moment. I was ecstatic over the prospect of taking this journey with Angel! I loved spending time with her. What a great experience to have with one of the most incredibly loving people I know. However, I knew she had commitments in Siesta Key.

"Are you sure you can? What about the kids?" I asked, trying to sound diplomatic but I could hear the hope and excitement in my voice.

"I'll talk to the family about it, but it should be fine. I'll love the time away, to be honest," she replied.

Angel made the necessary arrangements on her end and officially became my traveling companion. I was thrilled. I could hear my mother's sigh of relief all the way down the East Coast. My mother adored Angel, too, so she felt confident that all would be well with us. The two of us knew enough people along the way to offer us beds and dinners for the nights we'd be traveling. I loved a good adventure, and I enjoyed meeting new people, so I was looking forward to our trip.

Since Mom was already there for Alex's birth, we spent the last few days before the move sorting through my stuff and processing the recent events. I was too overloaded emotionally to spend much time on it. She did her best to coach out some thread of how I felt, but I wasn't willing to give it up. I felt the desire to protect her from my true thoughts and feelings. I didn't want her to know how sad I was. I got angry with myself for being sad. I tried to look at things in a positive light, and I would "correct" my sad feelings and thoughts. I twisted my thoughts so they reflected the idea that Alex was a gift and how she was meant for her adoptive parents. I believed that I had no right to grieve. I wouldn't allow it. In my mind, the grieving was selfish and dishonored my part in God's plan. He had charged me with this responsibility, and allowing myself to grieve showed disrespect for His plan. Still, the pain was intense. I felt worse than I ever thought I could on some days, but I wouldn't show it. I wanted my mom to take Katie home so I could grieve in private, and without having to explain myself. I longed for Siesta Key to be in the past.

The day came when I said good-bye to Mom and put Katie on a plane with her. I experienced anxiety pangs as I thought about all the terrible things that could happen to Katie if she got away from my mom. What if she left her beloved Taggie blanket in the airport, never to be seen again? She'd had that little blanket since birth. That 12x12 square came home from the hospital with her. I'd be devastated. To me, it wouldn't be any more valuable if it had been made out of gold thread. I'd wind myself up with it and then breath out and think of Moses' mother putting Moses in the basket. If she could do it, so could I. I had to trust like Moses' mom.

Checking someone in for a flight in Siesta Key is about as fast as checking into a medium-size hotel. It didn't take much, so we headed to the airport's only restaurant to feed ourselves lunch and wait for their boarding time. It felt like the Last Supper. I didn't want them to go now. I wanted them to stay. As my daughter jumped up and down on the tile floor with exuberance over the prospect of a plane ride, I feigned excitement for her while I choked back tears. My mother must have noticed my strained face when she said, "No crying, Mama!" I grimaced back at her. Katie picked at her food, getting up and down to take a bite of grilled cheese and then go to the window to ask if that plane was her plane. I coached her as much as I could to stay at the table and eat, but she wouldn't relent. Finally, her plane arrived and it was time for them to load. We paid our check, and I walked them to the security line. I sat and waved and smiled at them as they wound around the ropes. They put their hands up with every turn around and said, "No crying, Mama!"

As soon as they were out of my sight, I cried. My breathing stuttered, and I huffed in and out as I tried to be quiet until I got to my car. The sorrow poured down like an island thunderstorm. I wouldn't see my little girl for 10 days. She'd only been separated from me for 10 minutes, and already I couldn't stand it. I heard my own pained whimper as I strained to gain composure. I wanted to leave the parking lot, but I couldn't see to drive.

I imagined some annoyed security guard tapping on my driver's side window with his baton to ask me if I was all right. I didn't want to have to explain anything to a perfect stranger or try to make excuses, so I had to make my retreat without any fanfare. I took a deep breath and held it for a few seconds. I felt a calm come over me and I exhaled. *Please, God. Just get me home* I prayed. *And please get my mother and Katie home safely.* I turned the key in the ignition and drove out of the airport parking lot.

I switched gears the next morning. There was so much to do. I needed to finish packing, throw out more stuff, arrange for someone to help me load everything into the U-Haul, and get the final details underway. I got everything finished in the time I had left. Angel's family helped me pack up the truck; my possessions filled every inch of the truck, down to the last box. Finally, my life in Siesta Key was now in the back of a U-Haul, and I felt great. I felt my shoulders relax from their tensed position under my earlobes for the first time in months. The lightness was almost gleeful. I have never been so excited to leave such a beautiful place. To me, it was painted with trial. I didn't see it as everyone else did. It was like trying to interact with a gorgeous woman who had an obnoxious personality.

My landlords invited me to partake in some of the town's festivities the weekend before I was to leave. Siesta Key had a festival every five minutes, so I didn't understand all the fuss. Partying was considered an everyday past-time there. I was supposed to meet them down on their stoop around 7 on Saturday evening, and we'd decide where to go from there. It would be nice to get out for a little fun. I didn't have Katie to worry about, so I could relax my sense of responsibility and focus on enjoying myself. Because I didn't have anything left in my condo, I was going to stay at Angel's house for the remainder of the weekend. That way, we could leave early on Monday. I got myself ready to meet up with them.

I was feeling pretty and ready to enjoy myself. I made my way down the stairs and rounded the corner toward my landlord's condo when I caught sight of Boyd making his way up the cobblestone drive, drink in hand. He had messaged me a couple days before about spending one last evening with him, but I didn't answer. Our history together taught me that he gets sentimental when he drinks. I figured he just wanted to reach out to me out of loneliness or drunken stupor. I couldn't understand why he thought I'd want to spend any time with him.

We stood face-to-face on that final Saturday night, and I stared up at him, waiting for him to speak. I could tell that he was already intoxicated, so anything could come out of his mouth. I braced, preparing to be either insulted or touched.

"I guess we aren't hanging out tonight," he stammered.

"No. I am meeting the landlords, and we have plans to go out tonight," I replied, curtly.

"Oh, okay, have fun."

"Yup, thanks." I started to walk away.

"You know, Sariah," he called after me, "a lot has happened between us, but I hope we can still stay in touch, for Alex's sake."

I couldn't figure out why I'd want to stay in touch with him, and bringing Alex into that equation didn't improve my stance toward him. He was exactly the type of person I was protecting her from. I had a little fantasy of him being dead before I'd have a chance to meet her again. That way, I could delicately explain that her father was no longer on this Earth, rather than the awful truth. *So, sorry, Alex, your Dad is, well, he was 'unwell.'* There would be no grand reunion where Boyd and I would be arm-in-arm as we walked up to meet her. How could he be so foolish? He'd be lucky if I'd even be in the same state when he met her, and that was if she'd ever want to.

"Ya, well…I don't know. We'll see." I waved him off. I wanted to lay him out in the lavender and rip him to shreds with my words. It wasn't like I didn't have it in me. However, something beyond my comprehension prevented the verbal assault. I was tired of the conflict. I didn't want one more duel with him. *Just go away already. God bless you, but be gone!* I thought.

I started to walk away, and Boyd followed behind me up to my landlord's walk. He thought it would be okay to say a quick "Hi" to them. If Lucifer himself had been standing behind me, I think he would have received a warmer reception than the glares they gave Boyd. He did his best to recover and make light conversation, but the response was like talking to a stone wall. There would be no friendly banter even out of politeness. Sooner or later, he got the hint and excused himself. I could now enjoy myself. I flashed a weak smile at them as he walked away. I exhaled and turned to make sure he was gone.

"He just wanted to say good-bye."

Bob grimaced and looked at me, nodded his head, and opened his mouth to speak. He looked down the sidewalk as if what he wanted to really say to me would be somewhere down the street.

"Sariah, do yourself and me a favor," he stated. "No more stray dogs."

I spent my last Saturday night having an amazing time with my landlords and the neighbor in the conch house behind the condo. I'd hardly said two words to her the whole time I was there. She was a neat person, as I came to find out, and I was disappointed in myself for not making more of an effort. When I moved into the condo, I assumed she was one of those weird animal hoarders. She had birds, dogs, cats, and who knows what else. I steered clear of her the whole time I lived in the condo. During that evening out, I discovered she trained animals for the film industry, which is why she had so many dogs. She also rescued dogs and retrained them for adoption. I was intrigued and spent much of our night walking around and asking her questions. I felt like I let myself down by ignoring her; I wished I'd made contact earlier because it's disappointing to discover fascinating people too late.

My last night in Siesta Key, Sunday, was spent at Angel's house. On that evening, a realization struck me - I was moving away from the state in which Alex was living. It was an odd feeling to know I would be so far away, not that she'd need me. I felt a little helpless. I couldn't be right there if she did need something. I kept thinking of Moses' mother placing her baby in the basket, and placing her trust fully in God. When I did, I felt better. Alex was in God's hands and in the arms of wonderful, loving parents whom I handpicked just for her. I knew it was all God's doing, but I liked to think that I had a little something to do with the selection process. It would be a good story to share with Alex one day.

The next morning, Angel and I woke early and collected ourselves. I'd drive the U-Haul, and Angel would drive my car to Miami, where we'd leave it at the place where it would be shipped up to Boston. I called my mom as we started out on the road up the Keys. It was a beautiful, sunny day, and the palms swayed like they were ushering us along and saying, "So long." Mom wished us a safe trip and told me to call her when we got to Orlando, where we were staying at the house of Angel's mother.

We drove several hours, following the directions on my GPS, and pulled into the address the gentleman had given me to deliver my car for shipping. It was a dingy two-floor office building in a less-than-desirable neighborhood. Not wanting to judge a book by the cover, I called the man who'd be greeting me to make sure I had the right place. Of course, I did. I hopped out of the truck and went upstairs to an office that looked either in the process of remodeling or had never been unpacked. I saw computer boxes on the floor and assumed they had moved in recently. The gentleman, er, I should say kid, stood there in a shirt that looked like he had worn it to a club the night before. He had ugly "I want to look like a movie star, but I am not" sunglasses atop his crunchy, gelled-in-place hair, luxury jeans, and huarache sandals. *What have I gotten myself into? Am I leaving my Benz with this guy?* I wondered.

"You guys just move in here?" I asked.

"No," he muttered.

My confidence in his ability to care for my car did not improve as we did the paperwork. I tried not to daydream about him laughing as I walked out the door, at which point, he would call up some mobster to victoriously inform him that he 'got another one' and he could pick up my beautiful new Mercedes to take to his chop-shop, never to be seen again. I felt uncomfortable alone in the office with him while Angel kept an eye on our stuff outside. He was taking too long to complete the paperwork, not to mention his overdose of cologne was making me nauseous. I was also eager to get on with my trip out of Florida. I left the building, paperwork in hand, convinced I'd never see my car again, but also laughing at myself over the worst-case-scenario I was putting myself through. Angel and I piled into the U-Haul and headed north to Orlando.

After the mobster chop-shop drop-off, the first travel day was relatively bland. We drove, ate lunch, and drove some more. We arrived at Miss Sally's palatial abode. It was an impressive contemporary home nestled at the bottom of a long driveway, abutting a large, tranquil lake. I felt like I was instantly on vacation as we made our way in the grand front entrance and straight out the glass-walled back to the pool, tiki bar, and boat slip. It was heaven. I tried to imagine where I'd want to take my morning coffee to watch the sunrise if I lived there. We walked around the property, with Angel showing me this and that, but my mind stayed with the hammock, strung up in the thatched roof canopy covering the boat slip. Oh, to rock and daydream away the hours. Such peace I could only imagine. *Who am I kidding?* I thought, laughing a little. *Even if I had such an inviting setup, I'd ignore it in favor of a thousand other things I needed to do. It would rot itself to the ground before I'd think of sitting in it.* We headed back through the house and retrieved our bags from the truck to settle in for the night.

The next morning I received a text message from my mother upon my waking "Is the TV on?" I felt the wind leave my lungs. Angel was in the middle of chatting about what time we'd go and how long it would be to South Carolina when I cut her off.

"Angel, put the news on."

"Why?" she asked.

"I don't know, but my mother is asking me if the TV is on, which means something awful has happened."

We scrambled to find the remote and set the TV to CNN. The most horrific pictures started flashing across the screen. The strength ran out of my legs, and my hearing doubled as I disappeared into the television. The tiny country of Japan had not only sustained a record-breaking earthquake but also was devastated by a tsunami. Tears rolled as my mind recalled the events and emotions of 9/11 and watching the towers crumble. The utter powerlessness and the disbelief rolled over me like a wave. We strained words to heaven as we held hands and prayed over Japan, standing right there in her mother's living room. We parted to find our cell phones and make calls to discuss the crippling news. Whenever I saw destruction of this magnitude, I acknowledged Armageddon, and the book of Revelations. I wondered if the end was really going to start this time.

Once we recovered from the staggering news, we showered and prepared to leave. On the second travel day we would be driving up to my cousin's home in South Carolina. Thankfully, our journey was about as exciting as cold oatmeal. I think we were overloaded by the trauma that Japan endured. We spent a lot of time discussing things of a heavenly realm, probably because we were reconciling our hearts to the idea that The End was impending, but no one has any idea when it will happen. There is something about an event that encompasses the frailties of life that sharpened my heart, helping me recognize what needs done in my spiritual life. I spent a lot of time in deep thought as I drove, contemplating whether or not God had actually, really, sincerely forgiven me for the past year and all the choices of which I was responsible. I was satisfied in my spirit that He had. The cleansing peace that His forgiveness brings, once experienced, was easy to tap into when I needed a reminder. I wanted everyone to feel that peace.

"But God demonstrates his own love for us in this: While we were still sinners, Christ died for us." Romans 5:7-9 NIV

I had heard that line so many times. I thought of Christ's death as a general "for us," not a "me" for us. When I reread this during my prayer time on that difficult morning, something stood out for the first time - the word "while." God loved me before I was even born. He knew exactly what my life would be like, and yet still, Christ died for me. God had clearly taken my own life into account before Christ died and He decided that I, Sariah, was worth the cost. It was a chance morning read on my trip that gripped my heart and pulled me down into the pages. I understood. It isn't that I had lost anything. The decision was already made before I could do anything. I just needed to accept it and there, on that morning, as if for the first time, I did. With a revelation like that, there was no stopping what comes next. I wanted everyone to understand; I wanted to make sure that they know His forgiveness is real. His forgiveness was - is still - for me and I don't have to earn anything to have it. I didn't need to clean up my life before seeking God because He already knows everything about me, and He didn't love me any less. He wanted me to know that.

"Therefore, if anyone is in Christ, the new creation has come: The old has gone, the new is here!" 2 Corinthians 5:16-18 NIV

So it was that I was a changed person. Was I really a Christian before all of this happened? Yes, I was, but I was clearly missing out on so much. I had only scratched the surface of understanding what being a Christian was about. My heart was full of devotion. Once I allowed myself to be rescued, cared for, and loved by Him, there wasn't anything I wanted more than to stay in that feeling. I wanted to run after Him, to remain at His feet, to sit on the hem of His robe and to listen to every word, just like Mary Magdalene. The desire to share this experience, to impart what I came to know, poured out of me like a faucet. I tickled all over, wanting to get it out.

On the third travel day, Angel spent much time glued to her cell phone. Her daughter had become ill with a massive hive reaction to an unknown allergen. Angel spent time exchanging information and trying to figure out how to help her. She'd been to the emergency room two times already, and no one could seem to get a handle on what it was or how to help her. Her daughter cried to her in anguish and frustration. I tried to focus on the drive as she talked on the phone. I looked out at the buildings as we rolled into Washington, DC, not wanting to eavesdrop, but unable to completely ignore the conversation happening right next to me. It was a crisp, sunny fall day. My ear caught a statement Angel said to her daughter that interrupted my drifting thoughts. Angel said something to the effect of her daughter being grateful that she had Christian friends. That statement stuck with me for a moment. My mind started spinning around and around, thinking about what a Christian friendship was supposed to be like.

Pictures of people whom I had the pleasure of getting to know at my beloved church in Siesta Key started to flip around like a slideshow. What Christian characteristics did they show? For one, they didn't shun me when they found out what I was facing in my life. There was no finger-wagging or brush-off. Secondly, they loved me every step of the way. They encouraged me, trusting that I was following God's heart and desire for my life and the decisions I needed to make for the immediate future regarding Alex.

They supported me in a roll-your-sleeves-up-and-prepare-to-get-dirty kind of way. Angel took care of Katie when I had doctor's appointments and when I was in the hospital. The women held a baby shower for Alex to give presents to her adoptive parents out of love for me and support for my decision. I never felt such an unabashed outpouring of Jesus' heart from any group of people as they shown me.

As I reminisced, I realized my best Christian friends had always shown up and got actively involved in my life. As a Christian, and as a friend, we're called to be there for others in a way that no one else could understand. It was with distress I realized how rarely this calling is fulfilled by the people in the Church.

I thought of my relationship with Angel. She had decided to share something very personal with me once, and the only thing I said to her afterward was, "I don't think of you any different than before you told me. Thank you for wanting to share that with me." Angel and I weren't afraid to exhort one another, but in a loving way and out of the mutual respect we both have for God's truth. It's a beautiful trust that comes when two people share in such an intimate and spiritual friendship.

Angel hung up the phone, and I was snapped out of my thoughts, back to the cab in the driver's seat next to her. She told me we'd arrive at her friend's house in DC in an hour or so. I decided not to share with her what I was thinking. I wanted to hang on to the gratitude for the sacrifices she made for me in honor of our relationship and out of reverence for God. We went over routes and GPS calculations for the next hour. Even as we talked logistics, I couldn't help but to see her from a totally different perspective after my enlightenment while she was on the phone. She was completely unaware of how an innocent phrase to her daughter had so significantly impacted me.

We made our way, now in the dark, to her friend's house in an affluent neighborhood in the suburbs of DC. We strained to see numbers on the sides of houses until we found the address for which we were looking. We were greeted warmly by her friend and seated immediately to a hot, home-cooked meal. I savored the hospitality with every bite. While they chatted about the trip and caught up with each other's lives, my eyes roamed around the over-sized colonial home. The layout was exactly like what I'd always wanted. A large open foyer with rooms that were enclosed by glass doors, complete with a half-bridle staircase to the upstairs. The ceilings were too high for me to guess, and the crown moldings were splendid throughout. I tried to imagine how I'd decorate this house as I gazed. No one was trying to get my attention, and I was appreciative, being worn out from the hours of driving. I was content with entertaining myself in the daydream of living here.

The night's sleep was too short. We woke early because we had a long drive to Boston. We had gone back and forth over whether or not we'd make it or should we try, but I longed for Katie. I wanted to hold my baby. I longed for her gigantic smile and sparkly steel blue eyes. *Please, Lord,* I prayed, *don't let anything keep me from getting to her tonight.*

It would be a 13 hour day to get to our destination, and only if we were blessed by clear highways through New York City. I knew I was asking for a lot, but I was willing to be optimistic in God answering my prayer to see Katie. Anyone who has ever driven through New York City would say, "When isn't it congested through there?" No such time exists, but we were pleasantly graced by not getting stuck in rush hour mania. I was grateful.

The drive went on and on. As the dark drew near, I wondered if Angel would ask me to give up on making it to Boston. My mother was texting me, regularly asking for updates on my arrival. I knew she was anxious for me to arrive, and I was worried that she'd been gearing Katie up for my arrival, too. I didn't want to disappoint my sweet baby girl. To my relief, Angel didn't ask, and we pressed on.

At long last, we made it to the city of Boston. As we drove through the city, I narrated interesting things about the impressive buildings in the skyline. We agreed to come into the city by train the next day and let her check things out as we passed through the tunnel. My stomach was tight and my heart quickened as I got closer to my parents' exit. What would it be like to hold her again? Would she be excited and yelling, "Mama!" with her arms outstretched for me, running to the door? Would she be mad at me for being gone so long and shun me upon my arrival? My anxiety over the reunion built with every mile closer we came to my parents' house.

Finally, we arrived on my parents' street. I slowed and pulled the orange and white box truck into my parents' half-circular driveway. They have a quaint English farmhouse-style house, with a farmer's porch and real fieldstone fireplace. The home was my father's pride and joy. He bought his parents' four-room ranch from his brother and sister after his Dad passed from cancer. He remodeled and molded the home into the stunning masterpiece in front of Angel and me. I am always proud to show it to visitors. I know my father's face practically cracks off from smiling when people compliment him on it. We hopped out of the truck as soon as I parked, and I strode up the walk to the door with Angel close behind me.

We were quietly welcomed as Katie had fallen asleep on the couch, waiting for me to come home. My mother didn't want me to be let down by coming back to Katie already being put to bed for the night, so she left her there waiting for me. I couldn't stop myself; I bent down next to her sleeping face, gave her a kiss gently on the cheek, and stroked her soft, tender little head.

"Mama's home now, Baby." Upon hearing my voice, her eyes blinked quickly and then opened. She looked up at me with her head still on the couch cushion.

"Hi, Mama!" she croaked as she batted her eyes awake, and lazily smiled up at me. She rolled up to a seated position and maneuvered herself onto my lap. I inhaled the smell of her freshly washed hair and tenderly kissed the top of her head as I cradled her in my arms. I hugged her tightly, completely consumed by the act of losing myself in her and in my love for her. I wanted her to be as close to me as I could without causing her discomfort. She didn't mind. We both felt safe. Home was where Katie was.

The next day we took the train into town to show Angel as much of downtown Boston as we could show her in a few hours. It was a chilly, overcast November day, a big contrast to the sunny, hot Florida weather to which I'd become accustomed. I wondered how Angel would handle the difference.

We toured Faneuil Hall and the Boston Gardens. We walked around quickly to stay warm but had to stop once in Starbucks for coffees and hot chocolate for my little princess. I was not surprised when soon after Angel let me know that she'd be okay to go back to my parents' home. People from warm climates are better off to visit Boston in the late summer.

Angel left the next morning. I drove her to the airport with a reluctant spirit. My heart grieved that I had to say goodbye to her. I tried not to cry when I got her luggage out of the back of my mother's SUV and threw my arms around her before stepping back to watch her go through the airport doors. What would I do without my Angel to guide me on the rest of my journey? She was hard to let go.

I felt like Dorothy from the Wizard of Oz. Siesta Key was a memory, a place where I both lost and found myself and God. Now I had to rebuild my life. The prospect seemed like an avalanche ready to fall, but I was prepared for spiritual heli-skiing, so I looked forward to navigating the churning mass of my future down the mountain with me riding on top.

ACKNOWLEDGEMENTS

Where would this book be without the people who propped me up, listened to me cry, and cheered me along while I tried to tell my story? These select few got the raw version of me as I unraveled these experiences. I will be forever grateful that they saw merit in rolling up their sleeves and getting dirty for me. I am so grateful to God for you all. Know that your piece of this was significant, no matter how small you thought it was. I am here typing this because of you. Thank you.

The LORD, thank you for not killing me when I said I didn't need you anymore.

My Beloved, you are my darling daughter and my greatest cheerleader. You are the Qi that helped me press on.

Mom, I don't know how you made it through this, but you did. I needed you. Thanks for being there.

Mom #2, my life might have turned out terrible, if not for you. Thanks for loving me unconditionally, birthing my bestest friend, reading along, and sharing it with your pool ladies.

Angel, thank you. I don't even know how to tell you that you saved my life.

Pastor Harry, thank you for being the most authentic godly man I could have had in my corner. I still think your Christian Suffering Series was 9 weeks. Maybe it just felt that way, but it was amazing!

The ladies of my favorite southern church, I love you all. I brag on you every chance I get! Thank you for loving me, regardless.

Red, you told me to figure out what I love doing and find a way to get paid for it. Best advice ever! Also, thank you for reading this and walking with me down this challenging road.

Husband, Thank you for loving me. Thank you for encouraging me.

Thank you for reading this book with such enthusiasm and for loving me anyway. Loving you until the wheels fall off.

To the guy on the Smather's beach who told me I'd never be an author because his brother never got a book deal, thank you for the motivation.

To my adopted daughter and her beloved family, you are in my heart and in my thoughts every day. I love you more than you'll ever know. My gratitude for your love and support are beyond words.

About The Author

Sariah James is a proud wife to her second husband and loving mom to her beloved daughter. She is a professional writer and Pro-Life speaker, with many speaking events and women's retreats to her credit. Sariah has penned hundreds of blogs and bodies of work to help women struggling with widowhood, adoption, and life in general. Most of all, she enjoys using her gift to serve God. She never tires of sharing God's truth with other women. Sariah has been interviewed on Christian radio shows and podcasts a dozen times on the subject of Pro-Life issues, namely Adoption.

To those that know her best, Sariah is a passionate student of God's Word. She is seldom at a loss for words, sometimes gets so excited talking that she interrupts people (a shortcoming she is working on), loves to send cards to people she loves for no reason, is a fearless cheerleader for all things related to Katie, and is a trusted friend. She also loves cooking for her husband, who especially enjoys her homemade meat sauce and amazing meatballs.